W9-CEB-023

THE MARKETING PLAN

A Handbook

Marian Burk Wood, M.B.A.

Prentice
Hall

Upper Saddle River, New Jersey 07458

Library of Congress Cataloging-in-Publication Data

Wood, Marian Burk.
  The marketing plan : a handbook / Marian Burk Wood.
    p. cm.
  Includes bibliographical references and index.
  ISBN 0-13-061317-7
      1. Marketing — Management — Handbooks, manuals, etc.   I. Title.

HF5415.13.W66 2002
658.8'02 — dc21

2002022914

Editor-in-Chief: Jeff Shelstad
Senior Editor (Editorial): Bruce Kaplan
Assistant Editor: Melissa Pellerano
Editorial Assistant: Danielle Serra
Media Project Manager:
  Anthony Palmiotto
Senior Marketing Manager:
  Michelle O'Brien
Marketing Assistant: Christine Genneken
Managing Editor (Production):
  John Roberts
Production Editor: Maureen Wilson
Production Assistant: Dianne Falcone
Permissions Coordinator:
  Suzanne Grappi

Associate Director, Manufacturing:
  Vincent Scelta
Production Manager: Arnold Vila
Manufacturing Buyer: Michelle Klein
Cover Design: Bruce Kenselaar
Cover Illustration/Photo: Picture Perfect
  USA, Inc.
Cover Printer: Lehigh
**Full-Service Project Management and
  Composition:** Compset, Inc.
Production Manager: Janet Domingo
Printer/Binder: Von Hoffman

Credits and acknowledgments borrowed from other sources and reproduced, with permission, in this textbook appear on pages 192–193.

Pearson Education LTD.
Pearson Education Australia PTY, Limited
Pearson Education Singapore, Pte. Ltd
Pearson Education North Asia Ltd
Pearson Education, Canada, Ltd
Pearson Educación de Mexico, S.A. de C.V.
Pearson Education–Japan
Pearson Education Malaysia, Pte. Ltd

10 9 8 7 6 5 4 3
ISBN 0-13-061317-7

Brief Contents

Contents

Preface

Behind every successful product is a good marketing plan. Marketing textbooks often contain marketing plan outlines or discuss the general use of marketing plans, but don't explain exactly *how* to develop a marketing plan—yet that's what student marketers really need. This book fills the gap, supplementing the material in marketing principles texts, marketing management texts, and marketing strategy texts with step-by-step coverage of the structured process that leads to a complete and actionable marketing plan. Only with such a detailed map can marketers explore the most promising marketing opportunities in today's highly volatile global environment. Marketers are therefore pathfinders, charting paths to profitability and identifying potential trouble spots to avoid during the journey. The pathfinder theme runs subtly throughout the book, supported by Marketing Pathfinder's Quotes (at the start of every chapter) and Pathfinder's Tips (in the margin).

Plan of the Book

The Marketing Plan: A Handbook provides "how to" coverage of the marketing planning process in logical order, supported by three appendixes and a glossary. This table shows the contents chapter by chapter:

Chapter	*Contents*
Chapter 1: Introduction to Marketing Planning	Overview of the marketing planning process, the contents of a marketing plan, and key tools and principles for marketers.
Chapter 2: Analyzing the Current Situation	How to examine the internal and external environment in preparation for a SWOT (strengths, weaknesses, opportunities, threats) analysis.
Chapter 3: Understanding Markets and Customers	How to investigate consumer/business markets and customers by analyzing needs, demand, growth, share, attitudes, buying behavior, satisfaction, and other characteristics.
Chapter 4: Planning Segmentation, Targeting, and Positioning	How to apply knowledge of markets and customers to identify, evaluate, and target specific customer segments and formulate a positioning strategy for competitive advantage.
Chapter 5: Determining Objectives and Strategic Direction	How to set marketing and financial objectives to support overall organizational goals and strategic direction.

Chapter	Contents
continued	
Chapter 6: Developing Marketing Strategies and Programs	How to design external and internal marketing strategies and tactics, consistent with positioning, to achieve marketing and financial objectives.
Chapter 7: Budgeting, Forecasting, and Tracking Progress	How to use budgets, forecasts, schedules, and selected metrics to set standards and measure progress toward objectives and goals.
Chapter 8: Controlling Plan Implementation	How to analyze marketing plan results and apply standards to track performance, identify problems, and take corrective action if needed.
Appendix 1: Marketing Plan Resources	Convenient listing, by category, of valuable printed and online resources for marketing planning.
Appendix 2: Sample Marketing Plan	Detailed sample plan for Sonic personal digital assistant, as a model for developing and documenting the marketing plan.
Appendix 3: Documenting a Marketing Plan with *Marketing Plan Pro* Software	Detailed instructions for using the bundled software to study sample plans and prepare new marketing plans.
Glossary	Alphabetical listing of key terms and definitions, showing the chapter where each is first defined.

Marketing Plan Pro Simplifies Planning

Bundled with the book, the highly rated *Marketing Plan Pro* software is an easy-to-use program for documenting marketing plans. The software also includes sample marketing plans from a variety of for-profit and nonprofit organizations, including manufacturers, retailers, consulting firms, service businesses, and a community theater group. Preparing the financials to support a marketing plan can be tedious and time-consuming; this software package streamlines the process with built-in spreadsheet and charting capabilities. Turn to Appendix 3 for full details about using *Marketing Plan Pro* to study the sample plans and document a marketing plan following the chapter-by-chapter steps in this handbook. And check the special Web site at www.paloalto.com/prenticehall for technical support, FAQs, and more.

Special Features Support Planning

The Marketing Plan: A Handbook supports the hands-on development of creative yet realistic marketing plans through a series of special features:

- *Valuable resource lists.* Where do marketers find the facts, figures, and background data they need? Chapter-by-chapter lists of online and printed resources show where information and background data can be found. These resources are summarized by category in Appendix 1.
- *Detailed checklists.* What questions should marketers be asking? Fourteen checklists, strategically positioned in chapters 2–8, summarize the key points that marketers need to investigate.

- *Current examples.* How are companies actually putting their marketing plans to work? Every chapter showcases at least 10 recent, real-world examples of businesses and nonprofit organizations applying marketing principles—including many international examples.
- *Key term definitions.* What is the proper terminology? Key terms are carefully defined in the text and highlighted in the margin. All key terms are collected in a back-of-book glossary for quick reference.
- *Sample marketing plan.* What does a marketing plan look like? Appendix 2 presents a sample marketing plan for the hypothetical Sonic personal digital assistant. This sample plan coordinates with the marketing plan and exercises in Philip Kotler's *Marketing Management* text.

More Features on Dedicated Web Site

Visit www.prenhall.com/wood where more features to support the use of this book are available. For convenience, the Web site includes hotlinks to all the online resources shown in Appendix 1, arranged by category. The site also has a hotlink to Palo Alto Software's special Web page for Prentice Hall users (www.paloalto.com/prenticehall) where answers to technical questions about *Marketing Plan Pro* software and other useful tools can be found. Because the marketing textbooks that this book can supplement are periodically updated, the Web site will have the latest topic-by-topic coordination with all the books' tables of contents. Finally, the Web site presents two discussion questions per chapter, with instructor's manual information in a password-protected area for faculty.

Value Packages and Integration with Marketing Texts

For convenience, several correlation guides are provided that show how *The Marketing Plan: A Handbook* can be used to supplement seven leading Prentice Hall marketing textbooks. The ISBN listed with each textbook below makes it easy to order a *Prentice Hall Value Package*, which includes the textbook packaged with *The Marketing Plan: A Handbook* at a deeply discounted price.

- *Marketing Management, 11e* by Philip Kotler
  ISBN 0130782866
- *A Framework for Marketing Management* by Philip Kotler
  ISBN 0130782505
- *Marketing Management* by Noel Capon and James M. Hulbert
  ISBN 0130782599
- *Marketing Management* by Russell S. Winer
  ISBN 0130782580
- *Market-Based Management, 2e* by Roger J. Best
  ISBN 0130145467
- *Marketing: An Introduction, 6e* by Gary Armstrong and Philip Kotler
  ISBN 0130782564
- *Principles of Marketing, 9e* by Philip Kotler and Gary Armstrong
  ISBN 0130782572

Here is how each chapter in *The Marketing Plan: A Handbook* corresponds to the material covered in specific chapters of these texts.

Marketing Plan **Chapter**	Kotler, *Marketing Management*	Kotler, *Framework for Marketing Management*
Chapter 1, Introduction to Marketing Planning	Chapter 3, Building Customer Satisfaction, Value, and Retention; Chapter 4, Winning Markets: Market-Oriented Strategic Planning	Chapter 3, Winning Markets Through Strategic Planning
Chapter 2, Analyzing the Current Situation	Chapter 6, Scanning the Marketing Environment; Chapter 9, Dealing with Competition	Chapter 4, Understanding Markets, Demand, and the Environment; Chapter 7, Dealing with Competition
Chapter 3, Understanding Markets and Customers	Chapter 5, Gathering Information and Measuring Demand; Chapter 7, Analyzing Consumer Markets; Chapter 8, Analyzing Business Markets	Chapter 4, Understanding Markets, Demand, and the Environment; Chapter 5, Analyzing Consumer Markets; Chapter 6, Analyzing Business Markets
Chapter 4, Segmentation, Targeting, and Positioning	Chapter 10, Identifying Market Segments and Target Markets; Chapter 11, Positioning and Differentiating the Market Offering	Chapter 8, Identifying Market Segments, Selecting Target Markets
Chapter 5, Objectives and Strategic Direction	Chapter 4, Winning Markets: Market-Oriented Strategic Planning	Chapter 3, Winning Markets Through Strategic Planning
Chapter 6, Marketing Strategies and Programs	Chapter 12, Developing New Market Offerings; Chapter 14, Product and Branding Strategy; Chapter 15, Designing/Managing Services; Chapter 16, Designing Price Strategies and Programs; Chapter 17, Designing and Managing Marketing Channels; Chapter 18, Managing Retailing, Wholesaling, Market Logistics; Chapter 19, Managing IMC; Chapter 20, Managing Advertising, Sales Promotion, Direct Marketing and PR; Chapter 21, Managing the Sales Force	Chapter 9, Developing Products; Chapter 10, Managing Products; Chapter 11, Designing/Managing Services; Chapter 12, Designing Pricing; Chapter 13, Selecting Channels; Chapter 14, Managing Retailing, Wholesaling; Chapter 15, Managing IMC; Chapter 16, Managing Sales Force; Chapter 17, Managing Direct Marketing
Chapter 7, Budgeting, Forecasting, Tracking Progress	Chapter 5, Gathering Information and Measuring Demand; Chapter 22, Managing the Total Marketing Effort	Chapter 3, Winning Markets Through Strategic Planning; Chapter 4, Understanding Markets and Demand
Chapter 8, Controlling Plan Implementation	Chapter 22, Managing the Total Marketing Effort	Chapter 3, Winning Markets Through Strategic Planning

Marketing Plan Chapter	Kotler/Armstrong, *Principles of Marketing*	Armstrong/Kotler, *Marketing: an Introduction*
Chapter 1, Introduction to Marketing Planning	Chapter 1, Marketing in a Changing World; Chapter 2, Strategic Planning	Chapter 1, Marketing in a Changing World; Chapter 2, Strategic Planning
Chapter 2, Analyzing the Current Situation	Chapter 3, Marketing Environment; Chapter 4, Marketing Research; Chapter 18, Competitive Strategies	Chapter 3, Marketing in the Internet Age; Chapter 4, Marketing Environment; Chapter 5, Managing Marketing Information
Chapter 3, Understanding Markets and Customers	Chapter 5, Consumer Markets; Chapter 6, Business Markets	Chapter 6, Consumer and Business Buyer Behavior
Chapter 4, Segmentation, Targeting, and Positioning	Chapter 7, Segmentation, Targeting, Positioning	Chapter 7, Market Segmentation, Targeting, Positioning
Chapter 5, Objectives and Strategic Direction	Chapter 2, Strategic Planning	Chapter 2, Strategic Planning
Chapter 6, Marketing Strategies and Programs	Chapter 8, Product and Services Strategy; Chapter 9, New-Product Development; Chapter 10, Pricing Considerations; Chapter 11, Pricing Strategies; Chapter 12, Distribution Channels; Chapter 13, Retailing/Wholesaling; Chapter 14, IMC; Chapter 15, Advertising/Promotion; Chapter 16, Personal Selling; Chapter 17, Direct/Online Marketing	Chapter 8, Products/Services Strategy; Chapter 9, New-Product Development; Chapter 10, Pricing; Chapter 11, Distribution Channels; Chapter 12, Retailing/Wholesaling; Chapter 13, IMC: Advertising, Sales Promotion, PR; Chapter 14, IMC: Personal Selling, Direct Marketing
Chapter 7, Budgeting, Forecasting, Tracking Progress	Appendix 1, Measuring/Forecasting Demand	Chapter 2, Strategic Planning
Chapter 8, Controlling Plan Implementation	Chapter 2, Strategic Planning	Chapter 2, Strategic Planning

Marketing Plan Chapter	Capon/Hulbert, *Marketing Management*	Winer, *Marketing Management*	Best, *Market-Based Management*
Chapter 1, Introduction to Marketing Planning	Chapter 1, Marketing and Management; Chapter 2, Environmental Imperative; Chapter 3, The Externally Oriented Firm	Chapter 1, Concept of Marketing; Chapter 2, Marketing Manager's Job; Chapter 13, Customer Relationship Management	Chapter 1, Market Orientation; Chapter 14, Building a Marketing Plan
Chapter 2, Analyzing the Current Situation	Chapter 2, Environmental Imperative; Chapter 5: Competitors and Complementers	Chapter 4, Marketing Research; Chapter 7, Market Structure and Competitor Analysis	Chapter 3, Market Definition; Chapter 6, Competitor Analysis; Chapter 11, Portfolio Analysis, Strategic Market Plans
Chapter 3, Understanding Markets and Customers	Chapter 4: Customers	Chapter 5, Consumer Behavior; Chapter 6, Organizational Behavior; Chapter 15, Technology-Based Markets	Chapter 4, Customer Analysis
Chapter 4, Segmentation, Targeting, and Positioning	Chapter 7, Market Segmentation/Targeting	Chapter 5, Consumer Behavior; Chapter 6, Organizational Behavior	Chapter 5, Market Segmentation
Chapter 5, Objectives and Strategic Direction	Chapter 8, Market Strategy; Chapter 9, Introduction and Growth Strategies; Chapter 10, Maturity and Decline Strategies	Chapter 3, Strategic Framework	Chapter 2, Market-Based Performance; Chapter 16, Profit Impact; Chapter 12, Offensive Marketing Plans; Chapter 13, Defensive Market Plans
Chapter 6, Marketing Strategies and Programs	Chapter 11, Managing Brands; Chapter 12, Managing the Product Line; Chapter 13, Developing New Products; Chapter 14, IMC; Chapter 15, Directing Sales; Chapter 16, Distribution; Chapter 17, Services and Customer Service; Chapter 18, Managing Price and Value; Chapter 21, Marketing and the Internet	Chapter 8, Communications; Chapter 9, Distribution; Chapter 10, Personal Selling; Chapter 11, Pricing; Chapter 12, Sales Promotion; Chapter 14, Service Markets; Chapter 17, New Product Development	Chapter 7, Product Strategies; Chapter 8, Pricing Strategies; Chapter 9, Channels and Sales; Chapter 10, Marketing Communications

Marketing Plan Chapter	Capon/Hulbert, _Marketing Management_	Winer, _Marketing Management_	Best, _Market-Based Management_
continued			
Chapter 7, Budgeting, Forecasting, Tracking Progress	Chapter 3, Externally Oriented Firm		Chapter 2, Market-Based Performance; Chapter 15, Strategy Implementation; Chapter 16, Profit Impact of Market-Based Management
Chapter 8, Controlling Plan Implementation	Chapter 2, Environmental Imperative; Chapter 20, Monitor/ Control Execution		Chapter 15, Strategy Implementation

Acknowledgments

In the course of planning, writing, rewriting, and again rewriting this book, I was extremely fortunate to have the help of many good people. My sincere thanks to the following faculty reviewers for their keen insights and important suggestions, which contributed immeasurably to the quality of the finished product:

Brent Cunningham, Jacksonville State University
Ralph M. Gaedeke, California State University, Sacramento
Dennis E. Garrett, Marquette University
Kathleen Krentler, San Diego State University
Ron Lennon, Barry University
Byron Menides, Worcester Polytechnic Institute
Henry O. Pruden, Golden Gate University
Scott D. Roberts, Northern Arizona University
Gary R. Schornack, University of Colorado, Denver
Michael J. Swenson, Brigham Young University

In addition, I wish to thank the knowledgeable experts who so kindly provided the inspiring Marketing Pathfinder's Quotes that open every chapter:

Joseph Blackburn, author of *Time-Based Competition*
Kevin Clancy, coauthor of *Counterintuitive Marketing: Achieve Great Results Using Uncommon Sense*
Philip Kotler, author of *Kotler on Marketing: How to Create, Win, and Dominate Markets*
Gary L. Lilien, coauthor of *Marketing Engineering*
A. Parasuraman, coauthor of *Techno-Ready Marketing: How and Why Your Customers Adopt Technology*
Arvind Rangaswamy, coauthor of *Marketing Engineering*
Mohan Sawhney, coauthor of *The Seven Steps to Nirvana: Strategic Insights into eBusiness Transformation*
Judy Strauss, coauthor of *E-Marketing*

Let me offer a rousing round of applause for Tim Berry, Doug Wilson, and the entire team at Palo Alto Software, who provided the *Marketing Plan Pro* software that accompanies this book as well as the detailed screen shots illustrating the software's usage. Their ingenuity and marketing savvy were invaluable.

A heart-felt salute to the very talented professionals at Prentice Hall who worked with me every step of the way, starting with the expert guidance and supervision of editor-in-chief Jeff Shelstad. Special thanks to Whitney Blake for getting this project off the ground; to Bruce Kaplan, Melissa Pellerano, and Danielle Rose Serra, who cheerfully and skillfully shepherded my manuscript through the development process; and to Anthony Palmiotto for putting his special touch on the screen shots. I also appreciate the hard work of Suzanne Grappi, Maureen Wilson, John Roberts, Arnold Vila, and Michelle Klein, plus Janet Domingo of Compset, in transforming my manuscript into an actual book. And many thanks to Michelle O'Brien for adding her exceptional marketing prowess to this project. What a pleasure it has been to work with everyone on this team!

This book is dedicated to my beloved husband, Wally Wood, who offers love, friendship, and wise counsel at every twist and turn along life's journey.

—Marian Burk Wood
MarianBWW@netscape.net

ABOUT THE AUTHOR

Marian Burk Wood has held vice-presidential level positions in corporate and non-profit marketing with Citibank, Chase Manhattan Bank, and the National Retail Federation, as well as management positions with national retail chains. Working with well-known academic experts, she has co-authored undergraduate college textbooks on principles of marketing (with Dr. Bill Nickels of University of Maryland), principles of advertising (Courtland Bovée of Grossmont College), and principles of management (Courtland Bovée of Grossmont College). Wood has developed dozens of marketing plans over the years for a wide range of goods and services. She has also created detailed, realistic chapters, cases, features, exercises, and print and electronic supplements for numerous college texts in marketing and related disciplines. Wood holds an M.B.A. in marketing from Long Island University in New York and a B.A. from the City University of New York.

1

Introduction to Marketing Planning

Chapter Contents

MARKETING PATHFINDER'S QUOTE

"Marketers, by profession, are the best equipped to help their companies cut through the market thickets in search of the hidden gold."
— DR. PHILIP KOTLER, AUTHOR OF *KOTLER ON MARKETING: HOW TO CREATE, WIN, AND DOMINATE MARKETS*[1]

Overview of Marketing Planning

In this age of global commerce, sophisticated technology, and markets that change at the click of a mouse, companies need marketing as a vital path-finding function. The increasingly complex marketing environment is being shaped by technological advances that provide a wider spectrum of tools and techniques for marketing and improve companies' internal efficiencies while simultaneously boosting customer power and knowledge, expanding channel and communication possibilities, and expediting marketing transactions. Ever-accelerating change is thus the only constant that marketers can depend on when planning the most profitable path to introducing a new product or devising an effective marketing strategy to capitalize on an emerging opportunity.

Consider the situations of Reflect.com and Achieva, two start-ups planning for profitable paths to very different opportunities:

Reflect.com. Reflect.com (www.reflect.com) is an online cosmetics start-up in which Procter & Gamble (P&G) holds a majority stake. Nathan Estruth, P&G's marketing director for beauty care, and Andrew Swinand, Reflect.com's director of marketing, have broken new marketing ground by offering online customers the ability to order custom-blended beauty products such as shampoos and makeup. Customers log onto the Web site and answer questions about personal preferences so the company can create products tailored to their needs—quite a departure from P&G's typical standardized product line. "The key point for us is we have built the Reflect brand and marketing plan in a completely new way," explains Estruth. "We're starting a service business, which means thinking in a new way." Although Eve.com and other competing beauty sites have failed, Reflect.com is continuing on the path laid out by its marketing plan, Estruth says: "We're focused on developing the concept. If we develop the concept, we're going to change the world."[2]

Achieva. Jeff Livingston and siblings Carolyn and Carlos Watson cofounded Achieva, a business that helps students prepare for college. In developing a marketing plan, chief executive officer (CEO) Carlos Watson remembers telling his partners to "start from scratch with the individual customers we want to attract, then we'll figure out what to charge and how we're going to make it profitable." They initially decided to target high school seniors and juniors; then, searching for a path to "deeper, longer, much more productive relationships with our clients," the CEO realized Achieva's services would be even more valuable if the company began working with college-bound students in the ninth grade. After opening their first college-prep center, the trio was surprised to learn that customers expected to pay more for services of Achieva's quality. So they raised prices—and enrollment skyrocketed.[3]

Clearly, new ventures like Reflect.com and Achieva face special challenges in defining their initial objectives, identifying appropriate markets, researching and analyzing the marketing environment, and developing effective marketing strategies for success. Although established businesses have more experience with their customers, markets, and competitors, these organizations are subject to the same environmental dynamics as start-ups. E-businesses have the added complications of designing and running a Web site, handling customer service, and managing order fulfillment challenges as they work on all the other elements of marketing strategy. Still, marketers for start-ups, like their counterparts in established businesses and e-businesses, are most effective when they follow a structured series of steps for marketing planning.

The purpose of this handbook is to provide an overview of the structured marketing planning process that contributes to the development of a viable marketing plan. This process is one that marketing pathfinders in every company, regardless of industry or product, must use as they perform analyses to make informed decisions about choosing the most profitable marketing paths. Marketing principles and techniques are discussed in the context of each step in the process, along with extended examples showing their effective use in a wide range of businesses and e-businesses. Despite organization-by-organization variations in the formality and timing of the process, the aim is to emerge with a plan that maps out the most effective strategies and actions for the chosen markets.

Bundled with this handbook is *Marketing Plan Pro* software, a package that simplifies the process of documenting a new marketing plan. The software also incorporates sample plans showing the results of the marketing planning process undertaken by 10 different for-profit and nonprofit organizations, including manufacturers, retailers, consulting firms, service businesses, and a community theater group. Appendix 3 provides full details about how to use *Marketing Plan Pro* to document a marketing plan following the chapter-by-chapter steps in this handbook.

MARKETING PLANNING DEFINED

Marketing planning can be defined as the structured process of researching and analyzing the marketing situation; developing and documenting marketing objectives, strategies, and programs; and implementing, evaluating, and controlling activities to achieve the objectives. This systematic process enables companies to identify and evaluate any number of marketing opportunities that can serve as paths to the organization's goals, as well as potential threats that might block these paths (see Exhibit 1.1). In practice, the marketing environment is so changeable that paths to new opportunities can open in an instant, even as others become obscured or completely blocked. Thus, marketing planning must be approached as an adaptable, ongoing process rather than a rigid, annual event designed only to produce a written report.

The outcome of this structured process is the **marketing plan,** a document that summarizes what the marketer has learned about the marketplace and indicates how the firm plans to reach its marketing objectives. The marketing plan not only documents the organization's marketing strategies and shows the activities that employees will implement to reach the marketing objectives, but it shows the mechanisms that will

 PATHFINDER'S TIP

Following a structured planning process helps the marketer pathfinder identify, evaluate, and select paths toward the most promising opportunities for the organization to pursue.

MARKETING PLANNING The process of researching and analyzing the market and situation and then developing marketing objectives, strategies, and plans that are appropriate for the organization's resources, competencies, mission, and objectives, followed by implementation, evaluation, and adjustments as needed to achieve the objectives.

MARKETING PLAN A document that summarizes marketplace knowledge and the marketing strategies and specific plans to be used in achieving marketing objectives and financial objectives.

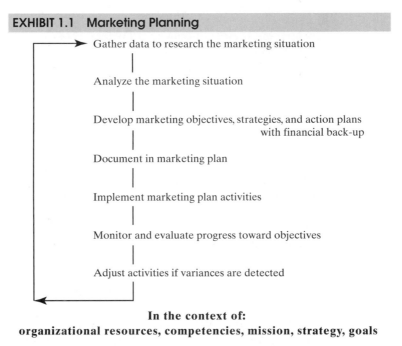

EXHIBIT 1.1 Marketing Planning

Gather data to research the marketing situation

Analyze the marketing situation

Develop marketing objectives, strategies, and action plans
with financial back-up

Document in marketing plan

Implement marketing plan activities

Monitor and evaluate progress toward objectives

Adjust activities if variances are detected

In the context of:
organizational resources, competencies, mission, strategy, goals

measure progress toward the objectives and allows for adjustments if actual results take the organization off course.

A marketing plan is one of several official planning documents created by a company: These include the business plan, which outlines the organization's overall financial and operational objectives and strategies, and the strategic plan, which discusses the organization's general long-term strategic direction. Sir George Bull, chairman of the British supermarket chain Sainsbury, stresses that the marketing plan is distinguished from the business plan by its focus. "The business plan takes as both its starting point and its objective the business itself," he explains. In contrast, "the marketing plan starts with the customer and works its way round to the business."[4] The company's strategic plan fits in between, laying out the broad strategies that will guide the strategic management of all divisions and functions over a 3- to 5-year planning horizon. The marketing plan is created at a lower level than either the business or strategic plans, and it is intended to provide shorter term, specific operational direction for how the organization will implement its strategies and move toward achieving its overall financial targets.

In the past, marketing planning was often sequestered in the marketing department until the marketing plan was reviewed by management, revised, and then printed for distribution to sales and other departments. These days, however, marketing planning encompasses more bottom-up, organization-wide input and collaboration. At Nokia, for example, managers and employees all over the organization contribute ideas that are incorporated into the plan that, with tweaking to allow for endless environmental shifts, guides the company's marketing strategies in telecommunications and other industries. Such collaboration is a necessity when, like Nokia, a company is introducing dozens of new products every year.[5] It also can be an excellent way to build the internal consensus, support, and cooperation that any business or e-business—of any size—needs for smooth implementation.

Larger organizations frequently require a marketing plan for each unit (e.g., individual stores or divisions) as well as for each product. Before Ferrari reintroduced the Maserati sports car to U.S. markets after a 10-year absence, management worked out a detailed marketing plan for selling 1,200 of the $80,000 Spider two-seater models within the first year. This marketing plan was part of a broader strategic plan to boost Ferrari's global revenues and profits.[6] Technology giant IBM has even developed marketing plans for individual Web sites:

IBM. A marketing plan helped shaped the development and implementation of IBM's Global Services E-Business Resources Web site (www.ibm.com/e-business), which supports the company's e-business initiative by providing businesses with practical information about e-commerce technology. "In order for us to implement the marketing objectives that the company wanted to achieve, we started the plan by researching the audience," explains Aimee Dean, the site's content strategist. "After identifying what the visitor needed, we could focus on providing the information and drive them to inquire about solutions for implementations of the practices learned through the information they received from us." As a result of the focus provided by a detailed marketing plan, the site has produced conversion rates nearly double that of IBM's expected rate, helping the corporation reach its short-term customer acquisition and sales objectives.[7]

CONTENTS OF A MARKETING PLAN

PATHFINDER'S TIP

Rather than using a previous marketing plan as a guide, marketers can get a fresh perspective on their situation by starting from scratch each year to create an entirely new marketing plan.

Although the exact contents, length, and format may vary from organization to organization, most marketing plans contain the sections shown in Exhibit 1.2. (See the sample plans in *Marketing Plan Pro* for a closer look at the way marketing plan contents and length can vary depending on the type of organization and its purpose.) The executive summary, which appears at the beginning of the plan, must logically be the final section to be written, because it serves as a brief overview of the main points. Marketers generally work on the other sections in the order in which they appear in the plan, because each successive section builds on the content in the previous one. Company managers are unable to prepare budgets and other financial plans, for example, until the marketing objectives, strategies, and action programs have been set. It is important to note that when the company makes a change in one part of the marketing plan, it also may have to make a change in other parts of the plan, due to the interrelated nature of the sections.

Although the marketing plan generally becomes a printed document once it has been approved, it must be continually revised in accordance with changes in the company's products, performance, and marketing environment. Consider what happened to the marketing plan Sony used to coordinate the worldwide launch of its PlayStation 2 entertainment module, which has the capability to play video games as well as DVD videos and music CDs:

Sony. Sony originally planned to sell 10 million PlayStation 2 units worldwide within the first year of introduction. The marketing plan called for an aggressive presale promotional campaign to build demand and overshadow competitive game units from Nintendo and other rivals. Sony initially launched the new product in Japan, where the planned hype caused a buying frenzy in which almost

EXHIBIT 1.2 Main Sections of a Marketing Plan

Section	Description
Executive summary	Briefly reviews the plan's highlights and objectives.
Current marketing situation	Summarizes environmental trends: • Internal and external situational analysis (products, markets, previous results, competitors, other environmental forces) • SWOT analysis (internal strengths and weaknesses, external opportunities and threats)
Objectives and issues	Outlines the specific marketing objectives to be achieved and identifies issues that may affect the organization's attainment of these objectives.
Target market	Explains the segmentation, targeting, and positioning decisions and analyzes the market and segments to be targeted through marketing strategy.
Marketing strategy	Shows the strategy to be used in achieving the marketing objectives.
Marketing programs	Lays out the programs supporting the marketing strategy, including specific activities, schedules, and responsibilities for: • Product • Price • Place (channel) • Promotion • Service
Financial plans	Details expected revenues, expenses, and profits based on the marketing programs in the plan.
Implementation controls	Indicates how progress toward objectives will be measured and how adjustments will be made to keep programs on track.

1 million units were sold within the first 3 days. However, unexpected components shortages kept the company from building enough units to stay on schedule. As a result, Sony was forced to revise its marketing plan by delaying the European launch and reducing the number of PlayStation 2 units shipped to stores in Europe and the United States; this delay, in turn, prevented Sony from reaching its corporate sales and profit objectives for the year.[8]

Sony's marketing experts are keenly aware that the success of their marketing plan depends on a complex web of internal and external relationships as well as on numerous environmental factors that are out of their control; when suppliers are unable to ship their components to Sony on time, for example, Sony is unable to get its products to market on time. On the other hand, Sony's marketing plan also affects the marketing plans of closely related products. Because the PlayStation 2 plays DVD movies, DVD sales in Japan are rapidly increasing, whereas VHS video sales are steadily decreasing. As another byproduct, PlayStation 2's popularity is putting downward pressure on the prices of conventional DVD players.[9]

Tragic events such as the terrorist attacks on New York and Washington can alter the marketing environment in a matter of minutes and make even the best contingency plans obsolete. With consumers and business personnel shocked and saddened by the terrorist attacks, economic activity plummeted following the attacks, even as the temporary suspension of flights into and around the United States prevented many companies from delivering products as planned. Yet admiration for the rescuers created an unexpected opportunity for Mattel, the largest U.S. toy manufacturer, to publicly show its support for New York City firefighters. The company's Fisher-Price unit makes a line of action figures called Rescue Heroes, featuring Billy Blazes, who wears a New York City Fire Department uniform. Higher demand for such products encouraged Mattel to increase production and donate all proceeds from sales of the fire-fighting figures to the Fire Safety Education Fund in New York.[10]

As these examples indicate, marketing management ultimately must realize that no marketing plan is ever in final form. Rather, the marketing plan has to be updated and adapted as the organization's situation, priorities, and results change.

Developing a Marketing Plan

Marketing plans generally cover a 1-year period, although some (especially those covering new product introductions) may project activities and financial performance farther into the future. Marketers must start the marketing planning process at least several months before the marketing plan is scheduled to go into operation; this allows sufficient time for thorough research and analysis, management review and revision, and coordination of resources among departments and business units.

The Phoenix Suns basketball team, for instance, starts its planning cycle for the following season even before the current year's playoffs are over. During the early stages of working on the marketing plan, team management reviews the current season's ticket and merchandise sales performance, analyzes game-by-game attendance, weighs fan feedback and market research, and swaps best-practices ideas with other National Basketball Association teams. With months of lead time, management is able to properly examine the team's current situation, identify market segments for special attention, set appropriate objectives, and prepare forecasts of future results.[11]

The seven broad steps in developing a marketing plan are:

1. Analyze the current situation.
2. Understand markets and customers.
3. Establish segmentation, targeting, and positioning.
4. Determine objectives and direction.
5. Develop marketing strategies and programs.
6. Track progress and activities.
7. Implement and control the plan.

The following sections examine each of these seven steps in turn, providing an overview for the remainder of this handbook.

ANALYZE THE CURRENT SITUATION

PATHFINDER'S TIP
This analysis helps marketers identify opportunities, threats, strengths, and weaknesses—all of which affect the firm's marketing objectives, strategies, tactics, and performance.

The first step in developing a marketing plan is to study the current location and the surrounding terrain before charting the organization's marketing course. Management must start by looking at the overall situation outside the organization to detect trends and changes in the broad demographic, economic, technological, political-legal, ecological, and social-cultural forces that can affect marketing, performance, and profits. This step also requires management to analyze how customers, competitors, suppliers, distributors, partners, and other key stakeholders might influence the firm's ability to effectively implement the marketing plan and achieve the desired results.

In this early stage of the marketing planning process, marketing managers are trying to assess the company's internal capabilities and the strategies of competitors so they can build on internal strengths while finding ways of exploiting rivals' weaknesses. They are also trying to identify and evaluate potential opportunities and threats created by emerging shifts in the external environment to find profitable new possibilities and avoid unpleasant surprises. Ignoring or misinterpreting the warning signs of change can be extremely damaging to a company's ability to smoothly implement its marketing plan, as one top executive found out:

> **Romac.** David Dunkel, CEO of the staffing company Romac International, first heard comments about how the Internet would change recruiting in 1995. Although he paid little attention, believing that the personal touch was needed to match the right applicant with the right job, he found by 1998 that e-businesses such as Monster.com were attracting thousands of employers and job candidates. Dunkel and his managers quickly worked out plans to cut costs and streamline recruiting by moving the firm's operations onto the Web. After 35 years as Romac, the company reinvented itself online as kforce.com (www.kforce.com), emphasizing its strength in personal relationships to become an advocate for job seekers, not just another job board. Kforce.com faces considerable online competition, but Dunkel is now monitoring the environment much more closely and keeping his marketing plan flexible enough to change overnight.[12]

Chapter 2 contains more detail on the process of gathering and analyzing data to examine the current situation. The chapter also includes numerous sources of information about the internal and external environments.

UNDERSTAND MARKETS AND CUSTOMERS

PATHFINDER'S TIP

Market and customer analysis gives management the background needed to determine who is to be targeted and how to meet the target market's needs.

In addition to analyzing the overall environment, marketers need to analyze their markets and their customers, whether consumers or businesses. This means looking closely at market share trends, changing customer demographics, product demand and future projections, buying habits, needs and wants, customer attitudes, and customer satisfaction. Among the many questions that must be researched are: Who is doing the buying—and why? How are buying habits changing—and why? What products and categories are in demand?

Cutting-edge technology now enables marketing managers to examine detailed customer buying behavior based on Internet and store sales. The Limited retail chain, for instance, is using a software package that allows it to track and analyze Web and store customer purchases hour by hour, providing critical data that can help the chain make timely decisions about distributing merchandise and starting or changing promotions.[13]

However, marketers must be careful not to overdo customer research. Until recently, different groups within IBM were conducting 48 or more surveys to measure customer satisfaction with products, sales, and service; one survey involved 40,000 interviews spread over 58 countries. Some IBM customers complained about being surveyed up to five times a year. "When you're the CEO of one of our major customers, and you hear from IBM three times in a month on a survey that sounds identical to the last one you answered, you get a little annoyed," notes IBM's director of worldwide customer satisfaction management, who is consolidating the surveys and the responses to make research data available across the corporation.[14]

More information about the analyses that companies should perform to understand markets and customers can be found in Chapter 3.

ESTABLISH SEGMENTATION, TARGETING, AND POSITIONING

PATHFINDER'S TIP

Segmentation and targeting are used to focus attention on promising groups within the overall market; positioning is used to stake out an advantageous competitive position.

SEGMENTS Groups within a market having distinct needs or characteristics that can be effectively addressed by specific marketing offers and programs.

Knowing that organizations can never be all things to all people, marketers have to apply their knowledge of the market and customers—acquired through research—to determine which parts of the market, known as **segments**, should be targeted for marketing activities. In the past, this meant dividing the overall market into separate groupings of customers, based on characteristics such as age, gender, geography, needs, behavior, or other variables. With today's technology, however, some companies can now build segments one customer at a time, based on what they know (or can find out) about each one, consumer or business.

The purpose of segmentation is to group customers with similar needs, wants, behavior, or other characteristics that affect their demand for or usage of the good or service being marketed. For example:

Green City Designs. Kate Corwin, owner of Green City Designs, which makes high-end gardening sheds and gates, is focusing on a segment she has defined by gender (women), annual income ($80,000+), and buying behavior (previously purchased expensive products by mail). To reach this profitable segment, Corwin buys the names of customers who recently ordered from upscale mail-order firms such as Smith & Hawken, then mails her full-color catalog to the list. These people are more likely to buy the company's products, compared with people who lack the interest, income, or experience of buying by mail, so this segmentation approach is more cost-effective than some other tactics she has tried, such as paying to be listed in general gardening directories.[15]

TARGETING
Decisions about which market segments to enter and in what order, and how to use marketing in each.

POSITIONING
Using marketing to create a distinctive place or image for a brand or product in the mind of customers.

Once the market has been segmented, the next set of decisions centers on **targeting,** including whether to market to one segment, to several segments, or to the entire market, and how to cover these segments. The company also needs to formulate a suitable **positioning,** which means using marketing to create a competitively distinctive place (position) for the brand or product in the mind of targeted customers. This positioning must effectively set the product apart from competing products in a way that is meaningful to customers.

For example, Hefty differentiates its trash bags using a positioning that can be summed up in one word: strength. Similarly, Volvo differentiates its cars using a safety positioning. And Kohl's has successfully communicated its positioning as a "family-focused, value-oriented specialty department store offering moderately priced national brand apparel, shoes, accessories, and home products."[16] To be effective in creating a particular image among targeted customers, companies must convey their positioning through every aspect of their marketing programs.

Chapter 4 discusses the use of segmentation, targeting, and positioning in further detail.

DETERMINE OBJECTIVES AND DIRECTION

PATHFINDER'S TIP

The marketing and financial objectives set by marketing managers must be in support of the organization's overall goals and mission.

GOALS Longer-term performance targets for the organization or a particular unit.

OBJECTIVES Shorter-term performance targets that support the achievement of an organization's or unit's goals.

Marketing pathfinders are responsible for setting the direction of the organization's marketing activities, based on goals and objectives. **Goals** are longer-term performance targets, whereas **objectives** are shorter-term targets that support the achievement of goals. Before charting any path, therefore, marketers must review the organization's overall mission and goals, then set marketing objectives that will steer the organization closer to its ultimate destination. The marketing and financial objectives that are set (and eventually achieved) will give the organization more momentum on the journey toward its overall goals, whatever they may be and however they may be expressed (in terms of sales, profits, market share, or other measures).

Starting in the 1970s, for example, executives at Target Stores established a mission strategy to guide the company's growth. Although the mission has been revised periodically, basic tenets that have not changed for 30 years include the idea that Target is a "trend merchant" and sells "higher quality merchandise." This mission provides ongoing direction for the retailer's top management to set specific long-term growth goals and short-term marketing and financial objectives to be achieved through the development and implementation of a detailed marketing plan.[17]

Like Target, most businesses and e-businesses use their marketing plans to support growth strategies (see Exhibit 1.3). One option is to increase sales of existing products in current markets; a second is to sell existing products in new markets; a third is to develop new products for current markets; and a fourth is to diversify by creating new products for new markets.[18] For example, the pioneering Web portal Yahoo! (www.yahoo.com) is pursuing the growth strategy of diversification by creating new products for new markets. Offering to build corporate portals and operate Internet conferences (new products) for business customers (new market), the e-business plans on increasing annual sales by $200 million.[19] Unilever, by contrast, is going for growth by creating new products for current markets. The company is looking to its new Wisk Dual Action laundry detergent tablets (sold under the Persil brand in Europe) to boost sales and grab market share from rival Procter & Gamble's Tide detergent products.[20]

More detail about establishing marketing plan objectives can be found in Chapter 5.

DEVELOP MARKETING STRATEGIES AND PROGRAMS

PATHFINDER'S TIP

Marketing strategies and programs are the heart of the marketing plan, based on the information presented about market analysis, objectives, segmentation, targeting, and positioning.

At this point in the marketing planning process, the company has examined its current situation, looked at markets and customers, set objectives, and identified targeted segments and an appropriate positioning. Now management can create the marketing strategies and tactics that will take the firm down the path toward its destination, working with the basic marketing mix tools of product, place, price, and promotion, enhanced by service strategies to build stronger customer relationships.

Marketing strategies and programs must be consistent with the organization's overall direction, goals, and strategies, as Amazon.com's experience suggests.

EXHIBIT 1.3 Growth Strategies Grid

Sell more of existing products in current markets *(market penetration)*	Sell existing products in new markets *(market development)*
Sell new products in current markets *(product development)*	Sell new products in new markets *(diversification)*

> **Amazon.com.** Online retailer Amazon.com (www.amazon.com) has long stressed rapid sales growth. Over the years, its marketing plans have supported this overriding growth goal by moving the online retailer into an increasingly diverse product assortment, from books, music, and videos, to toys, hardware, and electronics. But as pressure mounted for the company to become profitable, CEO Jeff Bezos laid off employees, closed facilities, and critically evaluated each product category, scouting for new profit possibilities. Now Amazon's marketing plans are more geared toward the corporate goal of reporting profitable sales results.[21]

External marketing strategies also should be established for the supply chain and distribution channel to build relationships with suppliers, partners, and channel partners. In addition, companies need an internal marketing strategy to build support among employees and managers, ensure proper staffing to carry out marketing programs, and motivate customer care consistent with the established strategy and positioning.

Chapter 6 covers marketing strategies and programs, including application of the marketing mix, in greater depth.

TRACK PROGRESS AND ACTIVITIES

PATHFINDER'S TIP

Marketers must establish realistic forecasts, budgets, and schedules to measure progress toward objectives and pinpoint problems to be corrected.

Once strategies and programs are in place, the company needs to plan for ways to determine effectiveness by identifying mechanisms and metrics to be used to measure progress toward objectives. Most companies use sales forecasts, budgets, schedules, and other tools to set and record standards against which progress can be measured. By comparing actual results against daily, weekly, monthly, quarterly, and yearly projections, management can see where the firm is ahead, where it is behind, and where it needs to make adjustments to get back on the right path.

In the course of reviewing progress, marketers also should look at what competitors are doing and what the markets are doing so they can put their own results into context. For example, after setting and achieving triple-digit growth objectives for several years, Amazon.com's growth recently slowed to double-digit levels. Although the company's projections had called for higher growth, its actual results were in line with lower growth levels among online retailers—and still respectable for any retailer, with or without bricks.[22]

More information about standards, measurement, and documenting progress can be found in Chapter 7.

CONTROL IMPLEMENTATION

PATHFINDER'S TIP

How a company plans for implementation is as important as how it plans for creative marketing strategies and programs.

The best marketing plan is useless without effective implementation, as numerous businesses and e-businesses have learned the hard way. Living.com, for example, was an online furniture retailer determined to revolutionize the way consumers buy furniture. Its marketing plan centered on the sale of upscale sofas and other home furnishings; too late, the company realized that few top-end furniture manufacturers were willing to sell through Internet retailers. The company also assumed that consumers would visit local furniture stores to browse, then buy online. In reality, Web surfers looked at Living.com's site, then went to local stores to buy. Moreover, the company failed to plan for returned merchandise, so items that customers sent back were simply thrown away. Living.com burned through millions of dollars before closing down.[23]

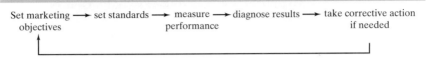

EXHIBIT 1.4 Marketing Control

Set marketing objectives ⟶ set standards ⟶ measure performance ⟶ diagnose results ⟶ take corrective action if needed

MARKETING CONTROL The process of setting objectives and standards, measuring and diagnosing results, and taking corrective action when needed to keep marketing plan performance on track.

To control implementation, marketers should start with the objectives they have set, establish standards for measuring progress toward those targets, measure the performance of the marketing programs, diagnose the results, and then take corrective action if results fail to measure up. This is the **marketing control** process. As Exhibit 1.4 shows, the control process is iterative; managers should expect to retrace their steps as they systematically implement strategies, assess the results, and take action to bring performance in line with expectations. Companies use this control process to analyze their marketing implementation on the basis of such measures as market share, sales, profitability, and productivity.

Chapter 8 provides more information about how marketers can plan to effectively control the implementation of the marketing plan.

Preparing for Marketing Planning

The volatility and complexity of the marketing environment, as well as the consolidation that has led to intense competitive rivalry in many industries, makes the marketing planning process even more challenging for many organizations. In approaching this process, marketing pathfinders should be prepared with a number of professional and organizational strengths, some of which are listed below. They also should be prepared to use all of the primary marketing tools and to apply the five guiding principles for marketing in the twenty-first century.

- *Knowledge of markets and customers.* Marketers need current, in-depth knowledge of what their customers want, how and why they buy, how they perceive competing products, and so on. It is now possible for marketers to harness the power of technology to collect and analyze detailed data about specific customers instead of relying on a more general, composite picture of the average customer. In practical terms, this means companies can carefully fine-tune their marketing efforts to build one-to-one customer relationships, rather than basing their planning efforts entirely on general data such as knowing that the average U.S. household consists of 2.63 people.[24]

CORE COMPETENCIES The set of skills, technologies, and processes that allow a company to effectively and efficiently satisfy its customers.

- *Core competencies.* **Core competencies** are the set of skills, technologies, and processes that gives the company competitive superiority in effectively and efficiently satisfying customers. Marketers identify these by looking inward at employees' talents and expertise as well as at the technologies and operational processes the firm employs. How can the company most effectively build on these core competencies to satisfy customers and achieve marketing objectives? Just as important, how can management find ways to work around areas outside the firm's core competencies by outsourcing, forging strategic alliances, and other methods?

VALUE The difference between total benefits and total costs, as perceived by customers.

- *Relationships.* Links with suppliers, wholesalers and retailers, marketing agencies, and other companies form the network through which the organization creates and delivers **value**—the difference between the perceived benefits that customers receive and the perceived price (plus other costs) they pay. The higher the perceived benefits, the higher the value to customers. But creating and delivering value requires strong relationships with suppliers, distributors, and other organizations. Through supply chain management, for example, a business can coordinate its suppliers' activities and the physical logistics needed to support production or service operations, all of which contribute to value creation and delivery. And because the marketing function must work with every other company function in satisfying customers, good relationships within the organization are also critical for success.

PRIMARY MARKETING TOOLS

PATHFINDER'S TIP

Every marketing plan must indicate how the company will use the marketing mix, supplemented by customer service enhancements, to do a competitively superior job of satisfying customers.

In addition to relying on these three main strengths, the primary set of tools used by marketing pathfinders are the components of the four-part marketing mix (product offering, pricing, channel, and promotion) plus the organization's customer service strategy. Some of the key elements in each component of the marketing mix are shown in Exhibit 1.5. These tools are discussed in more detail in Chapter 6 in the context of the development of marketing strategies and programs.

Product Offering

Although the product being offered can be either a tangible good or an intangible service, many offerings are actually a combination of tangibles and intangibles. Verizon, a major provider of cell phone services, for example, frequently offers a free or discounted cell phone (tangible) to customers who enroll in certain service plans (intangible) over a given period. Similarly, some dealerships provide free maintenance service (intangible) when customers buy a new car, truck, or van (tangible). In planning product strategy, therefore, marketers must think about the components and the customer perceptions of the entire offering, not just the basic product.

Pricing

What should the organization charge for its product offering? Internet technology is bringing new practices and new flexibility to pricing, as eBay (www.ebay.com), Hotwire (www.hotwire.com), and other Web-based businesses have demonstrated. To plan an effective pricing strategy, marketers need to consider a number of factors, including: how customers perceive the value of the offering; how the organization positions the product; what the product's development, production, and distribution costs

EXHIBIT 1.5   The Marketing Mix

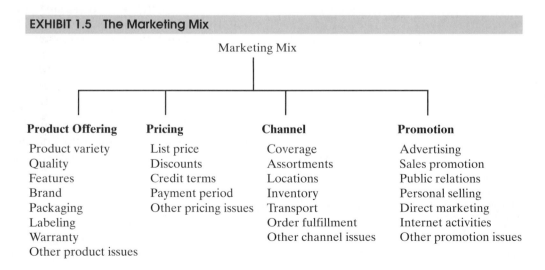

Product Offering	Pricing	Channel	Promotion
Product variety	List price	Coverage	Advertising
Quality	Discounts	Assortments	Sales promotion
Features	Credit terms	Locations	Public relations
Brand	Payment period	Inventory	Personal selling
Packaging	Other pricing issues	Transport	Direct marketing
Labeling		Order fulfillment	Internet activities
Warranty		Other channel issues	Other promotion issues
Other product issues			

are; and the competitive structure of the market. As noted earlier, Achieva's customers saw the price of its college preparation services as indicative of its quality. The company substantially increased its sales by raising its prices in line with customer perceptions. Too-aggressive pricing, on the other hand, can erode profits, which is why pricing is such an intricate but important part of the marketing planning process.

Channel

How will customers obtain the organization's products? Channel strategy lays out the distribution methods and partners the firm will use to reach customers in its target market. Reflect.com, for example, uses a direct channel to sell beauty products directly to customers, an unusual strategy for Procter & Gamble. This consumer products giant has traditionally used indirect channels to get products such as Pampers disposable diapers and Crest toothpaste into local stores where consumers can buy them. The Internet is changing channel strategies as all kinds of businesses go online to expand distribution and reach new markets.

Promotion

Also known as the marketing communications mix, promotion covers all the tools used to communicate with the target market, including: advertising; public relations; sales promotion; personal selling; and direct marketing techniques such as e-mail, wireless, and direct mail messages. Alloy Online, for example, is a Web and catalog retailer that uses contests and other promotions to bring teen customers to its site (www.alloy.com).[25] When using a variety of messages and media, marketers must carefully manage the overall content and impact through the use of integrated marketing communications.

Customer Service

Enhancing the marketing mix, many businesses and e-businesses add value by incorporating some form of customer service with their products. The label of nearly every food product in the supermarket contains an invitation to call toll free with questions or comments, only one form of customer service. Other forms of customer service are installation (e.g., for floor coverings or giant turbines), technical support (e.g., for computer products), and training (e.g., for software products). In many cases, customer service can make or break the offering. It gives customers first-hand experience with the organization, and helps them get the most benefit from the product. Clearly, customer service strategy is a critical part of any marketing plan, especially for Web-based businesses, which are unable to offer in-person customer service and therefore must rely on some mix of e-mail, live text chat, live online telephony, or toll-free telephone contact to deliver service.

GUIDING PRINCIPLES

Supplementing the marketing strengths and tools discussed above, today's marketing pathfinders need to follow five broad guiding principles to contribute to customer value and stay competitive as they proceed through the marketing planning process: (1) maintain vigilance; (2) focus on relationships; (3) involve everyone; (4) seek alliances; and (5) be innovative. These guiding principles, summarized in Exhibit 1.6, are explored below.

Maintain Vigilance

The global networked economy is a fact of business life, with technologies such as the Internet and wireless communications enabling buyers and sellers to conduct cross-border business anywhere in the world. In practical terms, this means marketers can

PATHFINDER'S TIP
By being vigilant, the company can locate suitable supply-chain partners, spot new rivals, and identify emerging opportunities and threats.

EXHIBIT 1.6 Guiding Principles

Defend against competitors ←———— Maintain vigilance ————→ Contribute to customer value
Focus on relationships
Involve everyone
Seek alliances
Be innovative

more easily scan the environment for the best suppliers, partners, resellers, and deals, because geographical distance is not nearly the obstacle it used to be. At the same time, competitors can more easily explore the territory of their rivals, so marketers must be especially vigilant and ready to fend off rivals from different areas at any time.

Another reason to remain vigilant is to stay abreast of the latest industry and market trends that can affect the business and its customers, as the European retailer Zara does:

> **Zara.** Throughout the 937 stores in the global Zara clothing chain, salespeople talk with customers and then use wireless devices to transmit a steady stream of comments and orders to the head office in Spain. This constant feedback system helps Zara spot trends early and keep its factories churning out just the styles that sell well. Zara offers 12,000 different pieces of clothing during the course of a year, adding and dropping items and even changing colors based on customer comments. Staying alert to new opportunities has allowed Zara to minimize its inventory costs and grow both sales and profits.[26]

Constant vigilance also helps marketers stay on top of the competitive changes that can occur at any point. For example, Garden.com was a high-flying retailer of online garden supplies when, with little warning, it ran out of money to fuel expansion and shut down before the peak of the holiday shopping season in 2000. This sudden shift—not an isolated incident among Web-based businesses—opened the door for niche competitors to strengthen their position. It also provided a new opportunity for old-line seedmaker W. Atlee Burpee and e-tailer Walmart.com (www.walmart.com) to buy some of Garden.com's online content and brand assets.[27]

FOCUS ON RELATIONSHIPS

Thanks to technology, consumers, businesses, and nonprofit customers have more information, more control, and more choices these days. Although this gives customers more power—which may lead them to choose other products and companies—it also opens the way for marketers to forge closer relationships with customers (as well as suppliers, channel partners, and other key **stakeholders**, people and organizations that are influenced by or can influence your company's performance).

Traditionally, companies communicated by monologue, sending information to their markets through advertisements and other techniques. With a dialogue, however, the communication goes two ways—from the firm to its customer, and from the customer to the firm. Such two-way connections can provide clues to what customers need, want, and expect, allowing marketers to fine-tune marketing programs in progress and find new ways of delivering value to earn customer loyalty for the long term. Unless a customer initiates the conversation, a firm might start with a question

PATHFINDER'S TIP
Focusing on relationships enables the marketer to forge closer customer and stakeholder relationships, glean clues to customer needs, and fine-tune marketing programs.

STAKEHOLDERS
People and organizations that are influenced by or that can influence an organization's performance.

about satisfaction, a special product offer, or a request for feedback on something new; once customers respond, a dialogue is started. Then smart marketers keep it going by judiciously asking additional questions or soliciting comments from time to time. Lands' End and Neiman Marcus, for example, are two of a growing list of online retailers that use instant messaging to provide immediate answers to customers' questions and concerns—part of a coordinated customer relationship management effort designed to attract new customers and retain existing customers.

Some marketing pathfinders are taking the dialogue a step further, building a sense of community by connecting customers with each other. Sumerset Custom Houseboats, for example, hosts six houseboating regattas every year to allow customers to get together, see each other's houseboats, and find out what's new from Sumerset. The company even posts photos and daily updates on its Web site (www.sumerset.com) so customers who can't attend can still share the excitement online. Thanks to its close connections with customers, Sumerset was able to triple its sales in just 3 years—now ringing up more than $30 million in boat sales every year.[28]

Motorcycle manufacturer Harley-Davidson has been helping its customers connect in a similar fashion since 1983:

> **Harley Owners Group.** The Harley Owners Group (HOG) is an organization of Harley-Davidson owners who attend special motorcyling events and help raise money for the Muscular Dystrophy Foundation and other charities. HOG members buy more than a motorcycle from Harley-Davidson: they also buy the company's logo apparel, cycling gear, and lifestyle. Contrary to the now-outdated image of a leather-clad outlaw, the typical Harley owner is a middle-aged married man with a household income of over $70,000. HOG has been an effective vehicle for building the company's relationship with customers as well as for allowing customers to connect with each other, helping Harley boost global demand and sales.[29]

INVOLVE EVERYONE

PATHFINDER'S TIP

By involving everyone, the company can build stronger internal and external relationships to more effectively create and deliver value to customers.

At one time, marketing and sales personnel were the only people within the company responsible for marketing functions. Now every employee must be involved in the marketing effort, and every contact point must be seen as another opportunity to strengthen customer connections. Everything about the company sends a signal, so companies must be sure to project the right impression whenever customers visit the Web site, contact the company, receive an invoice, or open a shipment.

To keep employees involved, companies also have to keep them informed about new products, special promotions, and any other details they need to have informed interactions with customers. Many firms post the latest news on internal Web sites (*intranets*) or send updates via e-mail to keep employees informed. Charles Schwab, the giant investment brokerage firm, posts meeting reports on its intranet for employees to read; it also publishes a daily online newsletter to keep employees informed about breaking news in the industry as well as the company. In addition, Schwab's top executives respond to any and all employee questions during four annual online sessions.[30]

SEEK ALLIANCES

PATHFINDER'S TIP

Seeking alliances with suppliers, distributors, partners, and customers provides the marketer with insights and resources to reach the company's objectives and best the competition.

The most successful pathfinders rely on a network of alliances with carefully chosen suppliers, channel members, partners, and even customers—networks that often cover hundreds or thousands of miles (see Exhibit 1.7). The purpose is to strengthen the

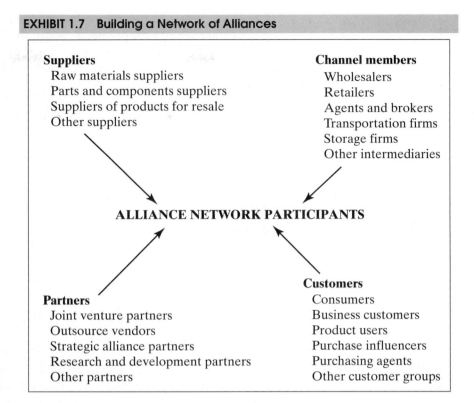

EXHIBIT 1.7   Building a Network of Alliances

Suppliers
Raw materials suppliers
Parts and components suppliers
Suppliers of products for resale
Other suppliers

Channel members
Wholesalers
Retailers
Agents and brokers
Transportation firms
Storage firms
Other intermediaries

ALLIANCE NETWORK PARTICIPANTS

Partners
Joint venture partners
Outsource vendors
Strategic alliance partners
Research and development partners
Other partners

Customers
Consumers
Business customers
Product users
Purchase influencers
Purchasing agents
Other customer groups

mutual support, capabilities, and innovations that all of the network participants need to satisfy their customers, achieve their goals, and effectively compete against their rivals.

- *Suppliers* not only provide raw materials, components, and other supplies, they also offer valuable insights regarding the industry, the market, future trends, and other key data. Increasingly, companies are strengthening connections with suppliers to lower costs while exchanging data to support mutually profitable exchanges over the long term. These alliances are critical because the quality of a company's product depends, in large part, on the quality of the suppliers' materials.
- *Channel members* such as wholesalers and retailers have daily contact with customers, making them another source of vital information that can help marketers refine their strategies. Companies gain valuable benefits when resellers provide feedback about customer buying patterns and preferences, just as channel partners benefit when producers share data about their products and plans. Again, the choice of channel partners is a critical one because customers associate the firm's brand with the quality and convenience of their shopping experience.
- *Partners* such as companies that share in joint ventures or outsourcing arrangements contribute their core competencies as well as their market knowledge. When a company links up with a partner possessing complementary capabilities and strengths, both have the potential to gain more power in the marketplace. Consider the alliance between Juniper and Nortel:

Juniper and Nortel. Juniper Networks makes superfast network routers, a high-tech product that Nortel Networks doesn't currently offer to its telecommunications equipment customers. So the two formed an alliance in which Nortel's salespeople sell Juniper's routers along with Juniper's regular product line. This arrangement allows Nortel to offer a complete product line, and it gives Juniper another sales channel.[31]

- *Customers* can be excellent partners because they are intensely interested in new and improved products that solve their problems or—in the case of businesses—give them the ability to better serve their own customers. 3M, for example, often brings in selected customers to discuss unusual problems or atypical uses of adhesives, wound treatment products, and other items. In addition, some research scientists take field trips to customer sites to see how 3M's products are actually being used. Within the company, groups that forge such partnerships with customers generate four times the number of new product ideas compared with groups that don't; just as important, the products developed from these partnerships are expected to boost 3M's revenues by $1.2 billion annually over a 5-year period.[32]

BE INNOVATIVE

PATHFINDER'S TIP

Setting the pace means delighting customers and fending off competitors by finding ways to innovate in all areas of the business.

To succeed in today's pressured marketing environment, companies must seize every opportunity to be innovative. Even research into customer attitudes can be energized by creativity. Sears, for example, has started printing mini-customer surveys on the back of cash-register receipts. Customers who call the listed toll-free number to respond to the survey receive a discount coupon or another small reward in appreciation. The results help the retail chain monitor customer satisfaction and identify potential problems at the individual store level, keeping the companies on track toward their objectives. "What we've discovered is customer service connects very closely with our bottom line," explains a Sears spokesperson.[33]

Some of the most ingenious innovations are occurring in the Internet world, where companies are applying technology to more effectively satisfy customer needs and provide better customer service:

Lands' End. At the Lands' End Web site (www.landsend.com), shoppers can create a "virtual model" by inputting their measurements so they can get an idea of how different clothing items will look on them. The company also invites shoppers to visit participating malls where full-body scanners are available to electronically take and submit measurements for the virtual model program, a process that takes about one minute. In addition, Lands' End allows visitors to its Web site to talk with a customer service representative at the click of a mouse. These innovations have helped push online sales sharply higher, and have made the Lands' End site profitable since it went live in 1995.[34]

E-businesses have built on the basic set of marketing mix tools by devising a wide variety of innovations, such as online auction pricing (offered by eBay, among others) and online product personalization (Reflect.com and others). Yet Internet technology is not the only way to innovate. Continental Airlines, for example, created a comprehensive database to allow its reservation and gate personnel to access customer history files so they can reward the airline's frequent fliers with upgrades and other perks. First Union Bank, as another example, uses special coding to help customer service representatives identify the best customers for preferential treatment when they call with questions or problems.[35]

Chapter Summary

Marketing planning is the structured process companies use to research and analyze their marketing situation; develop and document marketing objectives, strategies, and programs; and then implement, evaluate, and control marketing activities to achieve their marketing objectives. The marketing plan, which documents the results of the marketing planning process, serves an important coordination function by helping to develop internal consensus, providing internal direction, encouraging internal collaboration, coordinating resource allocation, and outlining the tasks, timetable, and responsibilities needed to reach the marketing objectives.

The seven broad steps in developing a marketing plan are (1) analyze the current situation; (2) understand markets and customers; (3) establish segmentation, targeting, and positioning; (4) determine objectives and direction; (5) develop marketing strategies and programs; (6) track progress and activities; and (7) implement and control the plan. In preparation for marketing planning, companies need to depend on a number of professional and organizational strengths as well as the four-part marketing mix supplemented by a customer service strategy. There are five broad guiding principles to follow through the marketing planning process in order to contribute to customer value and keep the organization competitive: (1) maintain vigilance; (2) focus on relationships; (3) involve everyone; (4) seek alliances; and (5) be innovative.

2

Analyzing the Current Situation

Chapter Contents

MARKETING PATHFINDER'S QUOTE

"Since marketing plans are executed in uncertain environments, they are incomplete without a procedure for monitoring and adapting to change."

—DR. JOSEPH BLACKBURN, AUTHOR OF *TIME-BASED COMPETITION*[1]

Environmental Scanning and Analysis

MACROENVIRON-MENT Largely uncontrollable elements outside the organization that can potentially influence its ability to reach set goals and objectives: demographic, economic, ecological, technological, political-legal, and social-cultural forces.

MICROENVIRON-MENT Groups that have a more direct effect on the organization's ability to reach its goals and objectives: customers, competitors, channel members, partners, suppliers, and employees.

To map an effective marketing plan, the marketer needs to stay abreast of key factors in the **macroenvironment** that can affect organizational performance, including broad demographic, economic, ecological, technological, political-legal, and social-cultural forces. In addition, the marketer must look at specific groups in the **microenvironment** that have a more direct influence on performance, including customers, competitors, channel members, partners, suppliers, and employees (Exhibit 2.1).

Through *environmental scanning and analysis,* marketers collect data about these aspects of the environment and then analyze their findings to better understand the company's strengths, weaknesses, opportunities, and threats:

- *Strengths* are internal capabilities that can help the firm achieve its goals and objectives; for a toy manufacturer, strengths might include a well-known brand name and creative toy designers.
- *Weaknesses* are internal factors that can prevent the firm from achieving its goals and objectives; high management turnover and out-dated equipment might be two weaknesses for a computer chip manufacturer.
- *Opportunities* are external circumstances that the organization might be able to exploit for higher performance; renewed public interest in 1950s music might be an opportunity for a doo-wop music publisher.
- *Threats* are external circumstances that can potentially hurt the organization's performance, now or in the future; for a high-end restaurant, threats might include a weak economy or more stringent IRS guidelines for deducting business meals.

EXHIBIT 2.1   The Macroenvironment and Microenvironment for Marketing

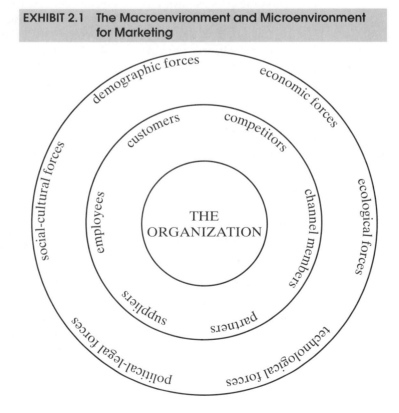

As shown in Exhibit 2.2, marketing pathfinders can tap a wide variety of internal and external sources for environmental scanning and analysis. In addition, Appendix 1 presents a variety of printed and online sources of information to support the marketing planning process.

Consider how the founder of PC maker Gateway used environmental scanning and analysis to monitor his company's performance and support marketing planning decisions:

> **Gateway.** Ted Waitt, who founded Gateway on his parents' farm in South Dakota, stepped out of day-to-day operations when he hired Jeff Weitzen away from AT&T to become CEO. As chairman, Waitt continued to scan the internal and external environments for clues to the company's performance. He noticed turnover in the management ranks, lower customer satisfaction ratings, lower revenues, and higher costs. Evaluating the impact of this information, the founder realized his company was not going to achieve its high-growth goals and objectives, so he and the board of directors confronted Weitzen, who left under pressure. Once Waitt returned as CEO and made changes such as allowing customer service representatives to take sufficient time with customer questions, customer satisfaction levels began to rise again. Now the CEO and his top managers are formulating a new marketing plan to deal with a slump in PC sales brought on by global economic difficulties.[2]

As Ted Waitt's experience at Gateway demonstrates, environmental scanning must be an ongoing process, not a once-a-year exercise, to prevent the company from following an outdated marketing plan. "A marketing plan is not a static document but must be constantly updated to reflect current developments and emerging threats and opportunities," observes branding expert Kevin Lane Keller.[3]

Savvy companies therefore take steps to follow environmental developments by systematically gathering data using two main systems: *a marketing information system,*

EXHIBIT 2.2 Internal and External Sources for Environmental Scanning

Internal Sources	*External Sources*
• Company files and databases (covering sales; financial indicators; market share; customer acquisition, retention, churn; product lines; etc.)	Microenvironmental trends: • Customer advisory panels • Marketing research suppliers • Industry groups, publications, Web sites, databases, and meetings • Competitor products, Web sites, literature
• Workforce (feedback and suggestions from sales personnel and other employees)	
• Customer service records (covering complaints and comments from customers)	Macroenvironmental trends: • Government agencies and officials • Academic and professional publications, Web sites, and studies • Consumer and business media • Distributors, suppliers, partners, other stakeholders
• Marketing research reports (covering previous studies of the market, customer satisfaction surveys, etc.)	

which is used to track internal results and reports and provide the supporting data that management needs to make informed decisions, and a *marketing intelligence system,* which is used to track and analyze external happenings. Together, these two systems can provide a wealth of data about the internal and external environments to support marketing planning and decision-making.

See Appendix 3 for detailed information on how to document the results of this analysis in a marketing plan using *Marketing Plan Pro* software.

Scanning and Analyzing the Internal Environment

PATHFINDER'S TIP

This analysis provides vital background information for setting marketing plan objectives, making targeting decisions, and developing marketing-mix strategies appropriate for the organization's strengths and weaknesses.

MISSION Statement of the company's fundamental purpose, its focus, and how it will add value for customers and other stakeholders.

In the course of internal environmental scanning, marketers start by looking to the organization's overall mission for direction in their marketing planning efforts. They also examine the organization's resources, offerings, previous results, business relationships, keys to success, and warning signs; Checklist 2.1 summarizes these internal areas for exploration.

MISSION

Knowing their organization's mission helps marketers make decisions about appropriate strategies and programs. The **mission** states the company's fundamental purpose—its core ideology, in the terminology of Collins and Porras—and defines its focus, indicates how it will add value for customers and other stakeholders, and outlines what Collins and Porras call the envisioned future. This definition provides decision makers with direction about aligning strategy and organizational resources to stimulate progress toward the envisioned future.[4]

For example, IBM's mission statement clearly defines the company's focus and future: "At IBM, we strive to lead in the creation, development, and manufacture of the industry's most advanced information technologies, including computer systems, software, networking systems, storage devices, and microelectronics. We translate these advanced technologies into value for our customers through our professional solutions and services businesses worldwide."[5] This mission directs IBM's marketers to concentrate on goods and services based on practical advanced technologies that can help customers solve problems or serve their own customers. It also points the organization toward a future leadership position in its chosen areas of focus.

As another example, consider the mission of Morgan Stanley: "Our goal is to be the first choice of clients, shareholders, and people choosing careers in financial services. To be first choice, we work every day around the world to forge closer relationships with our clients . . . to develop innovative products, services, and platforms . . . to shape new markets . . . to foster teamwork . . . to reward initiative and ideas . . . and to build new business models in a rapidly changing global economy."[6] This concise yet specific mission directs Morgan Stanley's marketers to concentrate on innovations that move the company toward its envisioned future of enhancing relationships with clients and, in the process, attracting talented employees and returning solid value for shareholders.

PATHFINDER'S TIP

Check that resources are adequate to support successful completion of current marketing programs and lay the foundation for future marketing strategies.

RESOURCES

Next, marketers look at the resources their organizations possess or can obtain, including human, financial, informational, and supply resources. No company has unlimited resources; it is therefore imperative that management carefully balance the resource allocation to ensure successful performance and the achievement of all objectives and

CHECKLIST 2.1   Areas of Focus Within the Internal Environment

Mission
❑ What is the organization's fundamental purpose?
❑ What is the organization's main focus?
❑ How does the organization add value for customers and other stakeholders?
❑ What are the implications for marketing planning?

Resources
❑ What are the skills, talents, training, and morale of employees and managers?
❑ What is the organization's financial situation and strength?
❑ What information does the organization have or need to address marketing?
❑ What supplies and suppliers can the organization tap to support marketing programs?
❑ How will resources affect marketing programs, implementation, and control?

Offerings
❑ What is the composition of the product mix?
❑ What product lines are offered to which customers at which price points?
❑ What are product age, sales, and profit trends and contributions?
❑ How do offerings relate to the organization's mission and resources?
❑ What are the implications for marketing planning?

Previous Results
❑ How do last year's sales and profit results compare with results of previous years?
❑ Which previous marketing programs were effective?
❑ What are the trends in customer relationship management?
❑ What are the implications for the current cycle of marketing planning?

Business Relationships
❑ Are costs of dealing with suppliers, distributors, and partners in line?
❑ Do suppliers, distributors, and partners have adequate capacity and quality?
❑ How have business relationships changed over time?
❑ Is the organization overly dependent on one supplier, distributor, or partner?
❑ What are the implications for marketing planning?

Keys to Success, Warning Signs
❑ What special factors make the difference between good and poor performance?
❑ What critical warning signs indicate potential problems leveraging keys to success?
❑ How can these keys to success and warning signs be factored into the marketing plan?

goals. Here are some of the questions marketers must ask as they examine their internal resources:

- *Human resources:* Does the workforce have the needed skills and talents? Do managers have the initiative and entrepreneurial spirit to support the mission? Is the company using recruitment and training to prepare itself for the future? Is morale high or low? Is turnover high?
- *Financial resources:* Does the company have the capital (or access to capital) to underwrite marketing activities? What funding issues must be addressed over the period covered by the marketing plan?

- *Informational resources:* Does the company have the data needed to address its markets and challenges? What informational sources can it tap to support marketing planning, implementation, and control?
- *Supply resources:* Does the company have (or can it obtain) steady supplies of parts, components, materials, and services needed for operations and production at manageable costs? Are suppliers committed to the organization and its mission?

In many cases, organizations can arrange external sources of needed resources or supplement existing resource arrangements through new strategic alliances, outsourcing deals, and new supply chain relationships. But only by analyzing internal resources will marketers learn about gaps and strengths that can affect marketing planning, implementation, and control.

OFFERINGS

In this part of the analysis, marketers look at what the organization is currently offering in the way of goods and services. At a minimum, it is necessary to look at the product mix and the lines within that mix, asking questions such as: What products are being offered, at what price points, and for what customer segments? What is the age of each product and its sales and profit trend over the years? How are newer products faring in relation to older products? What is the market share of each product or line? How does each product support sales of the line—are some sold only as supplements or add-ons to others? How does each product contribute to the company's overall performance? Does one product account for a large portion of sales and profits? Where is each product in its life cycle, and how can marketing further extend or enhance the life cycle?

Just as important, marketers must determine how the organization's offerings relate to its mission and to its resources. Do the current offerings use the firm's resources most effectively and efficiently while following the core ideology stated in the mission? Are other offerings needed to restore the focus or fulfill the long-term purpose described in the mission? Answering these questions will give management a better sense of internal strengths and weaknesses in preparation for planning future marketing activities.

PREVIOUS RESULTS

PATHFINDER'S TIP

Put recent results into context by systematically analyzing the effects that environmental factors may have had on the organization's performance.

The company's previous results also offer important clues to internal strengths and weaknesses that can affect current and future results. By analyzing last year's unit and dollar sales, profits, and other financial results—and comparing these results with trends over several years—marketers can get a big picture of overall performance. Marketers also need to analyze the results of previous years' marketing programs to see what worked and what didn't.

In addition, trends in customer acquisition and retention can reveal problems or successes in forging strong customer relationships. Marketing pathfinders should look carefully at costs related to customer acquisition and retention, because excessive costs can outweigh the value of the relationship. Traditional catalog retailers spend about $38 to acquire a new customer, but the price can be considerably higher for new e-businesses trying to establish a customer base.[7] The point of all this analysis is to separate effective from ineffective activities and understand related costs as a prelude to planning the coming year's marketing programs.

For example, FTD.com, the online arm of the FTD floral delivery firm, recently made major changes after monitoring the initial results of its first marketing plan:

FTD.com. Floral retail site FTD.com originally budgeted $43 million for marketing to introduce its site using splashy television commercials and print advertising. Disappointing results showed the campaign wasn't paying off, so management quickly pruned the marketing budget to $20 million and returned to the previous strategy of mailing catalogs before major holidays like Mother's Day and Valentine's Day. Because the parent company continued its national advertising, FTD.com was also able to build on that campaign and a legacy of high awareness for the FTD brand to attract online customers. FTD.com reported a profit soon thereafter.[8]

BUSINESS RELATIONSHIPS

A closer look at relationships with suppliers, distributors, and partners will help marketers determine whether changes are needed to support the coming year's marketing plan. Although cost is always a critical factor, companies also must ask whether their suppliers and distributors have the capacity to increase volume if needed; whether their suppliers maintain a suitable quality level; and whether their suppliers and distributors can be true partners in adding value and satisfying customers. How has the roster of suppliers and dealers changed over time? Is the company overly dependent on one supplier or channel partner? Does the company expect its partners to provide special expertise or unusual services? All these questions are geared toward getting a well-rounded picture of strengths and identifying weaknesses that can affect the organization's offerings and marketing plans.

Food producers, for example, must work with a national broker if they want to get their products onto supermarket shelves across the United States. Yet smaller producers are having difficulty arranging for nationwide distribution because consolidation among food brokers has affected relationships throughout the industry:

Food brokers. The number of national brokers handling food products has decreased significantly through industry-wide consolidation, leaving just three brokers who cover the entire United States: Acosta, Advantage Sales and Marketing, and Crossmark. Smaller producers such as Chocolate Chix and the Krema Peanut Butter Company are largely unable to obtain national distribution without building a relationship with one of these three brokers. However, to persuade a broker to carry their products, these producers must show that their products do not directly compete with any products already on the broker's list; they also must demonstrate sizable sales results and be prepared to pay fees ranging up to 5 percent of the product's wholesale price. "It doesn't matter how good the product may be," comments a food broker, "we can only take on manufacturers that have a proven national sales record." Once a broker relationship has been established, producers feel locked in: "It's not like you can drop your broker if you don't like the service," says one producer. "The other two are working for your competitor."[9]

KEYS TO SUCCESS AND WARNING SIGNS

Not everything in a marketing plan is equally important. Marketers must therefore identify, in just a few sentences, the special factors that will have the most effect in moving the firm toward fulfilling its mission and achieving superior performance.

Pinpointing these keys to success can help a marketer focus on the right priorities in planning the year's marketing strategies and programs. For example, Wal-Mart has built its retail empire on the promise of low prices and strategic location. Thus, its two major keys to success are (1) maintaining policies and practices that keep selling prices low and (2) selecting promising locations that are underserved by competing retailers.

Likewise, every organization should scan for the major warning signs that indicate potential problems with leveraging the keys to success and performing as planned. For Wal-Mart, one such issue might be rising costs for merchandise and transportation: unless the chain can find ways of containing or lowering the costs, it may be forced to hike prices—a big problem when low selling prices are a key to success. Other possible warning sign issues for Wal-Mart: lack of available real estate in areas where the chain wants to expand and a guaranteed-lowest-price policy enacted by a key rival. Paying close attention to these issues will help Wal-Mart's marketing pathfinders chart a more effective plan to reach profitable, customer-satisfying objectives.

Scanning and Analyzing the External Environment

 **PATHFINDER'S TIP**

This comprehensive analysis helps marketers identify opportunities and threats to be factored into segmentation, targeting, and positioning activities as well as decisions about goals, objectives, strategies, and implementation.

Within the external environment, marketers need to examine broad demographic, economic, ecological, technological, political-legal, and social-cultural trends. They also must pay special attention to strategies and movements of competitors. (Customer and market analysis are discussed in more detail in Chapter 3.) Whereas scans of the internal environment are designed to uncover strengths and weaknesses, scans of the external environment are designed to uncover opportunities and threats that can be effectively addressed in the marketing plan. Checklist 2.2 summarizes these external areas for exploration, and Exhibit 2.3 shows specific printed and electronic resources for scanning each of these environmental areas.

DEMOGRAPHIC TRENDS

Consumer and business markets are moving targets—never static, always changing. For marketers of consumer products, population trends and characteristics suggest the size of the market and strength of demand. For marketers of business products, indicators of market size and strength can be found within trends in business formation, profitability indicators, and related organizational characteristics. However, these point-in-time examinations of demographic trends must be routinely updated to track the changes that can occur at any time.

Consumer Demographics

Continuing population growth is creating and expanding markets around the world—sometimes through higher birth rates, sometimes through lower death rates, sometimes through immigration. At the same time, the population is actually shrinking in some areas, such as in Connecticut. For this reason, marketers need to follow the population trends in the markets where they currently do business or are considering doing business, using U.S. Census data and other research (see Exhibit 2.4).

Delving below the surface, management also should look at the composition of the consumer population: age, gender, ethnic and religious makeup, education, occupation, household size, and income—and at trends in these characteristics. Specific products may demand a closer look at particular characteristics, such as the population's acceptance or use of technology. The following example shows how Starwood Hotels & Resorts spotted an opportunity to target a particular group of techno-savvy customers:

EXHIBIT 2.3 Selected Environmental Scanning Resources

Area of Focus	Resources
Demographic trends	• *Statistical Abstract of the United States* (www.census.gov/prod/www/statistical-abstract-us.html) • *American Demographics* (www.americandemographics.com) • U.S. Bureau of Economic Analysis (www.bea.gov) • *CIA World Factbook* (www.cia.gov/cia/publications/factbook) • United Nations Population Fund (www.unfpa.org)
Economic trends	• U.S. Department of Commerce statistics (www.stat-usa.gov) • Financial news coverage (such as www.bloomberg.com, money.cnn.com) • Business Information Solutions (www.infods.com) • *The Economist* (www.economist.com)
Ecological trends	• U.S. Environmental Protection Agency (www.epa.gov) • U.S. Department of Energy Office of Environmental Management (apps.em.doe.gov/ost) • Management Institute for Environment and Business (www.wri.org/meb) • Global Network of Environment and Technology (www.gnet.org)
Technological trends	• U.S. Patent and Trademark Office (www.uspto.gov) • Smart Business (www.smartbusinessmag.com) • CyberAtlas (cyberatlas.internet.com) • TechNews World (www.technewsworld.com)
Political-legal trends	• U.S. Congress (thomas.loc.gov) • Taxsites.com (www.taxsites.com/state.html) • U.S. Federal Trade Commission (www.ftc.gov) • *CIA World Factbook* (www.cia.gov/cia/publications/factbook) • Stateline.org (www.stateline.org)
Social-cultural trends	• Information Please (www.infoplease.com) • Social Science Information Gateway (sosig.ac.uk) • *PopMatters* magazine (popmatters.com) • General Social Survey (www.norc.org)
Competitive analysis	• *Gale's Encyclopedia of Associations* (print) or Internet Public Library Associations on the Net (www.ipl.org/ref/AON/) • Hoover's Online (www.hoovers.com) • U.S. Securities and Exchange Commission filings (www.sec.gov) • ProductScan (www.productscan.com) • Marketing Click (www.marketingclick.com)

CHECKLIST 2.2   Areas of Focus Within the External Environment

Demographic Trends

❑   What is the size and change of consumer population in selected markets?

❑   What is the composition of the consumer population in terms of age, gender, ethnic and religious makeup, education, occupation, household size, and income?

❑   What changes in specific consumer characteristics are directly related to product purchase or use?

❑   What is the size and change in number of businesses, number of locations, number of employees, sales volume, and capacity for selected business markets?

❑   What are the trends in new business formation for the targeted industry or market?

❑   Which cities and states host the most new start-ups?

❑   How will these trends affect the organization and its marketing plans?

Economic Trends

❑   What is the state and direction of the local, regional, national, and global economy?

❑   What are the current and expected trends in the target market's buying power, as evidenced by income, debt, credit usage, and other indicators?

❑   How will these trends affect the organization and its marketing plans?

Ecological Trends

❑   What are the trends in availability of raw materials and energy?

❑   How do pollution problems affect the organization?

❑   What is the effect of environmental issues that attract government regulation or influence social attitudes?

❑   How will these trends affect the organization and its marketing plans?

Technological Trends

❑   How are innovations affecting customers, suppliers, distributors, marketing, and processes?

❑   How are technologies affected by or affecting standards and regulations?

❑   How much is being invested in research and development by the industry and by competitors?

❑   How will these trends affect the organization and its marketing plans?

Political-legal Trends

❑   What legal and regulatory mandates (or proposals) apply to the company's business and marketing practices?

❑   What do political developments signal for changes in legal and regulatory priorities?

❑   How will these trends affect the organization and its marketing plans?

Social-cultural Trends

❑   What is the makeup of specific geographic markets in terms of nationality, religion, language, and other details?

❑   What is the effect of popular culture?

❑   What is the effect of core beliefs and values?

❑   How will these trends affect the organization and its marketing plans?

CHECKLIST 2.2   (cont.)

Competitor Analysis

❏   Who are current and possible future competitors?

❏   What are the trends in market share among competitors?

❏   What are the barriers to entry and exit in the industry?

❏   What are each rival's unique competitive advantages, and are they sustainable?

❏   What are the strengths, weaknesses, opportunities, and threats of each rival?

❏   How are pressures such as the balance of power between suppliers and buyers affecting competition within the industry?

❏   Do competitors have the resources to exploit opportunities and strengths?

❏   What substitutes or new products are likely to affect the competitive situation?

❏   How have competitors mounted challenges in the past—and with what results?

❏   What other competitive issues are critical in your industry or markets?

❏   How is the competition likely to affect the organization and its marketing plans?

Starwood Hotels & Resorts. Management at this hotel chain, which includes properties under the St. Regis, Sheraton, and Westin brands, noticed that more travelers were using wireless devices such as Palm Pilots to access e-mail and Web sites. Although this was a relatively small segment of the overall population, Starwood recognized significant growth among the ranks of wireless users. As a result, it formed a partnership with Classwave Wireless to appeal to this part of the population by offering wireless services to its hotel guests (and its employees).[10]

Business Demographics

Companies that operate in business markets need to scan the environment for information about the size and growth of the industries that they sell to, as measured

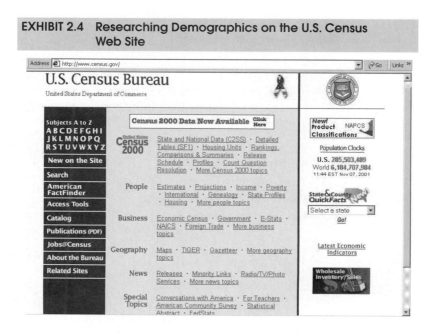

EXHIBIT 2.4   Researching Demographics on the U.S. Census Web Site

by number of companies, number of locations or branches, number of employees, and sales revenues. They also should pay close attention to trends in new business formation, which can signal emerging opportunities to market products such as office furniture, computer equipment, accounting services, telecommunications services, and cleaning supplies. Palo Alto Software, which makes the Marketing Plan Pro software packaged with this text, is particularly interested in new business formation as an indicator of demand for its marketing planning software as well as its Business Plan Pro business planning software.

Just as consumer marketers examine population trends in different geographic markets where they are selling or want to sell, business marketers must look at business population trends for the same reason. *Inc.* and other magazines regularly publish studies of the cities and states hosting the most new start-ups, among other business population analyses that can point the way toward good markets for certain business goods and services.

PATHFINDER'S TIP

Even companies that limit their geographic reach to local areas must be aware of the influence of regional, national, and international economic trends on customer buying power, supplier strength, and competitive trends.

ECONOMIC TRENDS

Economic trends clearly exert a great deal of influence over consumer and business buying. In today's interconnected global economy, deepening recession in one part of the world can affect consumer and business buying patterns thousands of miles away. Thus, marketing pathfinders have to keep a close eye on local, regional, national, and even global economic trends and watch for signals of coming change.

Marketers also need to analyze income, debt, and credit usage to better understand the buying power of consumers (or business customers). When personal income is rising, consumers have more buying power; lower debt and more available credit also fuel consumer buying. Similarly, businesses with higher debt may not buy as much or as often as businesses with lower debt and more available credit. In examining local, regional, national, and global economic trends, marketers should consider how specific trends may affect their own industries, products, and geographic markets.

ECOLOGICAL TRENDS

The natural environment can influence businesses and nonprofits in a variety of ways. One of the most obvious is the availability of raw materials such as water, timber, oil, minerals, and other essentials for production; shortages, as one example, can cause major headaches for companies that depend on these materials. A related problem is the availability of energy resources. Internet giant Yahoo! recently ran into problems when severe energy shortages in California caused intermittent outages of its Web portal and instant messaging services. "This could be a difficult time for the high-tech industry," warned the Stanford Institute of Economic Policy Research.[11]

In addition, marketers have to examine the various environmental issues that affect their organizations because of government regulation or social attitudes. What pollution or environmental problems directly and indirectly affect the business? How can the organization build on growing interest in environmentally safe goods and services? WorldWise, for example, responded to this trend by creating a series of "green" products such as rain-forest snack foods sold through Costco, Target, and other retail chains. As another example, New Leaf Paper sells a line of top-quality recycled paper products.[12] Even businesses that don't position their products as ecologically sound must watch trends in the natural environment and anticipate movements or regulations that can help or hurt performance.

TECHNOLOGICAL TRENDS

Changes in technology have created both opportunities and threats for a wide range of businesses and e-businesses. These key trends include the ongoing global penetration of Internet and PC usage; the convergence of computer and media technology; and incorporation of electronic capabilities into a wider range of products. The Internet alone has spawned countless opportunities, from online retailing (targeting consumers) to infrastructure equipment (targeting businesses), as well as threats such as security problems from viruses, stolen data, and other sources. Yet the influence of technology reaches into every aspect of the marketing mix, from digitally enhanced advertisements to new packaging materials and methods and beyond, making this an increasingly vital part of the macroenvironment.

Broad questions marketers should ask about technological trends include: What cutting-edge innovations are being introduced, and how do they affect the organization's customers, suppliers, distributors, marketing, and processes? How are these technologies affected by—or generating—industrywide standards and government regulations? What substitutes or innovations are becoming available due to new technology, and how are these changes likely to affect suppliers, customers, and competitors? How much is being invested in research and development by the industry and by selected competitors? Answering these questions will point marketers toward threats (such as discovering that the firm's research and development budget is much smaller than that of competing firms) and opportunities (such as becoming one of the first to use a brand new technological standard).

POLITICAL-LEGAL TRENDS

As part of the external scanning process, marketers need to examine the legal and regulatory guidelines that govern diverse business and marketing practices. Numerous state and federal laws cover competitive behavior, pricing, taxation, promotion, distribution, product liability, labeling, and product purity, among other elements, in the United States (see Exhibit 2.5). In addition, government agencies such as the Federal Trade Commission (FTC) keep a careful eye on emerging business practices in uncharted territory. Covisint, the online automotive parts market operated by Ford, General Motors, and Daimler-Chrysler, attracted regulatory scrutiny even before it opened because of the FTC's concerns about the potential effect on pricing and competitive behavior in the automotive industry.[13] General Electric was forced to call off its acquisition of Honeywell after European Union regulators tried to impose antitrust measures that the companies could not accept.

Political developments also can signal changes in legal and regulatory priorities—posing new threats or opening new opportunities. Political pressure to deregulate industries in the United States has resulted in both, for instance. For electricity distribution firms in California, for example, the first years of energy deregulation led to sharply higher energy costs without a legal mechanism for raising prices to customers. On the other hand, state-by-state deregulation cleared the way for Green Mountain Energy to begin offering electricity from environmentally friendly sources to consumers and businesses in California, Pennsylvania, Connecticut, and New Jersey.

Companies that operate globally need to pay close attention to the concerns of regulators in all the countries and regions where they operate, because regulatory obstacles can derail even the most carefully planned strategies. General Electric learned this the hard way, when it was forced to drop its planned takeover of Honeywell after European Commission regulators vetoed the $43 billion deal over antitrust issues—despite approval from U.S. regulators.[14]

EXHIBIT 2.5   Tracking Legislative Action on the U.S. Congress Thomas Web Site

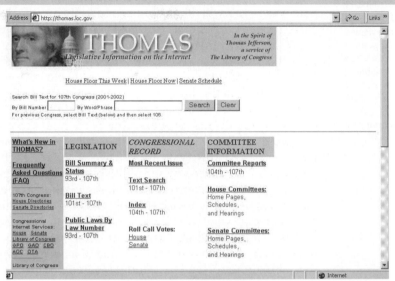

SOCIAL-CULTURAL TRENDS

Increased diversity in markets—and in the workforce—is a key social-cultural trend affecting today's marketing. Using U.S. Census data and other sources, marketers can learn more about the cultural diversity of specific geographic markets—including nation of origin, primary language, and other details that can help in tailoring the offer and the message to specific groups. Diversity opened several promising opportunities for online grocer EthnicGrocer.com, which operates three United States–based Web sites selling products preferred by immigrants and expatriates of specific nationalities. Namaste.com (www.namaste.com) features Indian products, Gongshee.com (www.gongshee.com) features Chinese products, and Querico.com (www.querico.com) features Hispanic products.[15]

Marketers constantly remain alert to the unexpected opportunities and threats created by popular culture; makers of fad products such as the singing fish are quite familiar with the pattern of meteoric sales increases followed by sharp sales declines. Yet the core beliefs and values that pervade a society or subculture, which change only slowly over time, also create opportunities and threats. Attitudes toward ethical and social responsibility issues, influenced by core beliefs and values, can affect marketing plans and programs, as cigarette marketers have learned.

On a more general level, consumer interest in healthier lifestyles, for example, has led to marketing opportunities for selling sports drinks, work-out clothing and equipment, vitamin and herbal supplements, personal training services, and many other goods and services. The same social trend has put pressure on marketers of cigarettes and other products perceived as unhealthy, leading to the use of different marketing messages and media. Beef producers also have developed multifaceted marketing plans to reverse the decline in consumption of their products by consumers who worry about cholesterol and other food-related issues. Now producers are using advertising, sales promotion, and public relations to address these public concerns by explaining the high nutritional value of beef products.[16]

COMPETITOR ANALYSIS

PATHFINDER'S TIP

Rather than focusing mainly on competitors' weaknesses, marketers can garner valuable ideas for new strategies and programs by thoroughly probing customer reaction to competitors' strengths.

Analyzing competitors can help marketers better understand market dynamics, anticipate what rivals will do, and create more practical marketing plans. Start by identifying current competitors and—just as important—possible sources of competition in the near future, to avoid being blindsided by a new entrant. For instance, the online auction site eBay sprang up as a new and unexpected competitive threat to traditional auction firms. Also look at trends in market share held by competitors to get a sense of which are becoming more powerful. Exhibit 2.6 depicts Michael Porter's model of the competitive forces affecting industry profitability and attractiveness. As this model suggests, it is important for marketing pathfinders to examine competitive barriers to entry and exit, which can affect the number of new entrants and the number of firms that leave the industry, as well as the power of both suppliers and buyers and the potential threat caused by substitute products.

As part of this competitive analysis, marketers must learn about the unique competitive advantages of each rival. FTD.com's competitive advantages, for example, are its 95 percent brand awareness and its coast-to-coast network of 17,000 local florists—two advantages that are difficult for competitors to match, let alone surpass. Yet customers ultimately determine the value of a firm's competitive advantage, which means that any organization can build advantage by discovering what customers need or desire and delivering it more effectively and efficiently (and perhaps more distinctively) than competitors. That's how Starbucks was able to turn a run-of-the-mill product, coffee, into an everyday luxury and an experience for which millions of customers pay handsomely. Now any new entrants to the upscale coffee market must contend with Starbucks' established brand and market leadership position.

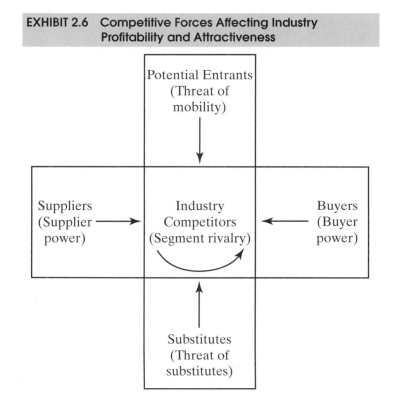

EXHIBIT 2.6   Competitive Forces Affecting Industry Profitability and Attractiveness

COST LEADERSHIP STRATEGY Generic competitive strategy in which the company seeks to become the lowest-cost producer in its industry.

DIFFERENTIATION STRATEGY Generic competitive strategy in which the company creates a unique differentiation for itself or its product based on some factor prized by the target market.

FOCUS STRATEGY Generic competitive strategy in which the company narrows its competitive scope to achieve a competitive advantage in its chosen segments.

SWOT ANALYSIS Summary of an organization's strengths, weaknesses, opportunities, and threats.

Competitive analysis helps marketers determine which of Porter's generic competitive strategies is most appropriate for the company's unique situation.[17] With a **cost leadership strategy,** the company seeks to become the lowest-cost producer in its industry. With a **differentiation strategy,** the company creates a unique differentiation for itself or its product based on some factor prized by the target market. With a **focus strategy,** the company narrows its competitive scope to achieve a competitive advantage in its chosen segments. Which specific strategy a particular company chooses depends, in part, on its analysis of internal strengths and weaknesses and external opportunities and threats.

SWOT ANALYSIS

All the data gathered through scanning and analysis comes into play during this part of the marketing planning process, as marketers take the data they have gathered and distill it into a **SWOT analysis** showing the *s*trengths, *w*eaknesses, *o*pportunities, and *t*hreats of their organizations. They also conduct a SWOT analysis of each competitor and consider the possible influence on each firm's marketing, on the overall industry, and on the market as a whole.

Exhibit 2.7 shows part of a SWOT analysis for Sonic's personal digital assistant (PDA), the subject of the sample marketing plan in Appendix 2. In competing with Palm, Handspring, and other PDA manufacturers, Sonic can build on a number of strengths that are meaningful to customers, including voice recognition of user commands, integrated wireless access, MP3 capabilities, and lower price. On the other hand, it must overcome daunting weaknesses such as lack of brand awareness. In the external environment, increasing demand for PDAs is opening a path toward opportunity—but increasing competition may pose a serious threat to the new product's ability to break into the market.

Armed with this SWOT analysis—and a similar analysis for key competitors—Sonic's marketers can create a marketing plan that incorporates the firm's strengths and defends against its weaknesses. For example, the product's unique voice recognition capabilities can be leveraged as a key success factor in building differentiation to combat competition within a crowded marketplace. Sonic's marketers also can parlay the product's value-added features offered at a low price as a second key success factor. In addition, they can use their knowledge of the competition to design marketing-

---

EXHIBIT 2.7 Sample SWOT Analysis for Sonic PDA

Strengths (internal capabilities that can support the firm in achieving its goals):
- Voice recognition capabilities
- Built-in wireless Web access
- Built-in MP3 capabilities
- Can use Palm-compatible peripherals
- Priced lower than competing models

Weaknesses (internal factors that can prevent the firm from achieving its goals):
- Lack of brand awareness and image
- Monochrome display
- Heavier than most competing models

Opportunities (external circumstances that may be exploited for higher performance):
- Increasing demand
- Availability of diverse add-on peripherals
- Availability of diverse applications for home and business use

Threats (external circumstances that may potentially hurt performance):
- Increasing competition
- Downward pressure on pricing
- Growing popularity of multifunction cell phones

mix programs that take advantage of rivals' weak points (such as higher price points) and defend against rivals' strengths (such as high brand awareness). The sample plan in Appendix 2 provides more detail about Sonic's application of its SWOT analysis.

Refer to Appendix 3 for instructions on how to use *Marketing Plan Pro* software to document the data you have gathered and your analysis of markets and customers in the appropriate sections of a written marketing plan.

Chapter Summary

The macroenvironment consists of key environmental factors that can affect organizational performance, including broad demographic, economic, ecological, technological, political-legal, and social-cultural forces. The microenvironment consists of groups that have a more direct influence on performance, including customers, competitors, channel members, partners, suppliers, and employees. Environmental scanning and analysis is the process of gathering data about these aspects of the environment and then analyzing the findings to gain a more thorough understanding of the company's strengths, weaknesses, opportunities, and threats.

In scanning the internal environment, marketers examine the organization's mission, resources, offerings, previous results, business relationships, keys to success, and warning signs. In scanning the external environment, they examine demographic, economic, ecological, technological, political-legal, and social-cultural trends, as well as analyzing the competitive landscape. All the data gathered during these environmental scanning steps is used to develop a SWOT analysis that helps marketers formulate a marketing plan that will take advantage of strengths and opportunities while defending against weaknesses and threats.

Understanding Markets and Customers

Chapter Contents

MARKETING PATHFINDER'S QUOTE

"The secret to marketing success lies in truly, deeply, and passionately understanding your customers."

—DR. KEVIN CLANCY, COAUTHOR OF *COUNTERINTUITIVE MARKETING: ACHIEVE GREAT RESULTS USING UNCOMMON SENSE*[1]

Analyzing Markets

MARKET   All the potential buyers for a particular product.

All the world's a market—but clearly, no company can afford to sell to or satisfy everyone. A **market** is defined as all the potential buyers for a particular product. Even well-heeled giants like Sony, Intel, and Nestlé must make informed decisions about which local, regional, national, and international markets to serve and, within each, which potential buyers they can most profitably satisfy. Likewise, smaller businesses and e-businesses need to take particular care in defining their markets so they can apply their limited resources in the most efficient and effective manner.

This chapter discusses how marketers research and analyze markets and customers to support decision making during the marketing planning process. Marketers first identify the broad market and research overall characteristics and needs, a prelude to selecting markets and segments to target. Next, they take a closer look at current and potential sales in that market, knowing that today's market will probably look quite different from tomorrow's market—an important consideration for planning future marketing activities. Finally, they more closely investigate needs and market share for their product and competing products, as a baseline for understanding market dynamics and setting marketing goals.

As Exhibit 3.1 indicates, market analysis is only part of the equation, a backdrop for understanding customer needs and buying behavior—because people, not statistics or projections, constitute markets. Whether buying for themselves (or their families) as part of the consumer market, or buying for their companies as part of the business

EXHIBIT 3.1   Market and Customer Analysis

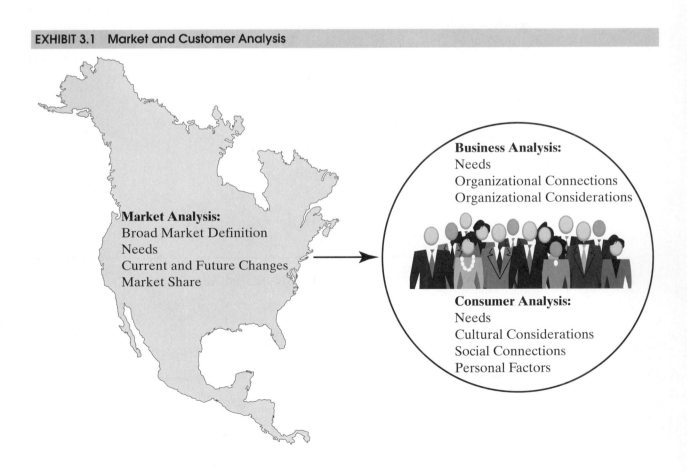

Market Analysis:
Broad Market Definition
Needs
Current and Future Changes
Market Share

Business Analysis:
Needs
Organizational Connections
Organizational Considerations

Consumer Analysis:
Needs
Cultural Considerations
Social Connections
Personal Factors

market, customers are ultimately the primary focus of every company's marketing plan. Knowing this, marketers must perform a comprehensive market analysis so they have a context within which to understand the requirements, behavior, and attitudes of customers in the marketplace.

BROAD DEFINITION OF MARKET AND NEEDS

PATHFINDER'S TIP

Before companies can target specific market segments and design a marketing mix to fit customers' needs, behavior, and attitudes, they need a basic understanding of the broad market for their product.

The first step in understanding the market is to identify it in fairly broad terms. It is helpful to think about five basic levels of market definition: potential market, available market, qualified available market, served or target market, and penetrated market.[2] These are explained in Exhibit 3.2. Ultimately, the pathfinder wants to narrow the company's focus to the target market—by gaining a thorough understanding of the potential, available, and qualified available markets.

For planning purposes, marketers describe their markets in terms of geography as well as by product or customer definition. "The U.S. personal digital assistant market" is a broad description of the target market that Sonic (the company represented in the sample marketing plan in Appendix 2) seeks to serve. If Sonic wanted to expand beyond U.S. borders, it would define each new market geographically: "The Canadian personal digital assistant market" or "The Eastern Canadian personal digital assistant market."

The geographic description must be more precise when the company is focusing on a specific region. The online auction firm eBay, for instance, offers global auction listings as well as local auction listings in certain areas. Thus, eBay can define a series of markets for its services: "The Orange County, California market for online auction services," "The San Francisco market for online auction services," and "The Vancouver, Canada market for online auction services" are descriptions of three specific eBay

EXHIBIT 3.2 Defining the Market		
Type of Market	*Definition*	*Rental Car Example*
Potential market	All customers who may be interested in a particular offering	Any driver who needs temporary transportation
Available market	A subset of the potential market: customers who are interested, possess adequate income, and have access to the offering	Any driver who can afford the rental fees and is in the area served by rental-car services
Qualified available market	A subset of the available market: customers who are qualified to buy based on age (for products that cannot be sold to underage consumers) or other criteria	Drivers in the available market who have licenses and meet minimum (or maximum) age restrictions
Target (served) market	A subset of the qualified available market: customers that the company intends to target for a particular offer	Drivers in the qualified available market who need to travel from airports to final destinations in the area
Penetrated market	A subset of the target market: customers who are already buying the type of good or service sold by the company	Drivers in the target market who have previously used rental car services

geographic markets. This helps eBay's marketers focus on the needs and preferences of a particular set of buyers in specific locations.

Next, the company must conduct research to obtain an overview of the needs of the available market. Here, the emphasis is on identifying general needs prior to a more in-depth investigation of the specific needs of each segment. This research also helps the company identify what customers value and how its image, products, services, channels, and other attributes can be positioned for competitive differentiation. For example:

> **Omron and Tokio Marine & Fire Insurance.** Noting a 63 percent increase in car theft over a 3-year period and the resulting need for more effective antitheft devices in Japan, Tokio Marine & Fire partnered with Omron to develop a new high-tech product. The system monitors the car's battery, engine, trunk, door, and ignition for unauthorized access. It sounds an alarm if the car is stolen—but does not trigger a false alarm if the car is accidentally jostled, a unique feature that customers appreciate. And, in response to customer needs, the system also alerts the owner via cell phone and tracks the stolen car's location for recovery purposes.[3]

Along with a broad understanding of needs, marketers need to look at general demographics, such as the number and characteristics of the consumer or business population, to get a sense of what each market is like—in the aggregate. In the business market, marketers use the North American Industry Classification System (NAICS) to classify industries and investigate industry size in the United States; the main source for such data is the U.S. Census Bureau (see Exhibit 3.3). Additional research about different industries, products, and geographic markets is available from a wide variety of printed and offline sources, such as international trade organizations, global banks, foreign consulates, universities, and publications that cover international markets.

EXHIBIT 3.3 NAICS on the Web

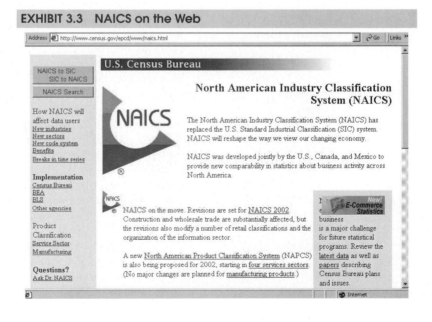

Consumer marketers also can consult U.S. Census sources to find out how many people and households are located in specific areas of the United States, then get more of a close-up of the market by examining gender, age, education, marital status, or other characteristics that relate to their particular products. Hanes and other manufacturers of men's underwear would look at the number of men in the market; AARP and other organizations that offer services for seniors would look at the number of consumers aged 50 and older.

Marketers researching other national markets also can find printed and online sources of demographic data. For instance, the Istituto Nazionale di Statistica (demo.istat.it/e/) provides updated demographics and projections for the Italian market. Another good source is the CIA *World Fact Book* (www.cia.gov/cia/publications/factbook/geos/it.html).

In addition, marketers must research income levels or use proxies to see whether the available market can afford their products. Marjorie Schaffner, CEO of Success-Lab Learning Centers, does this in a unique way:

> **SuccessLab Learning Centers.** This Chicago-based $4 million company focuses on inner-city markets, offering tutoring services to children in grades 1 through 12. The market for supplemental education services in urban areas is $6 billion and growing, based largely on government funding. Schaffner notes that Title I school funding—pegged to the size of the low-income student population—has gone up steadily for more than 35 years. Most of SuccessLab's revenues come from government funding, although parents who bring their children for tutoring in community centers pay privately. Still, the company's tutoring costs much less than traditional tutoring, because it obtains free space from school and community center partners.[4]

On the business side, marketers can use Census data and other sources to find out about the number and type of businesses in a geographic area, then examine meaningful characteristics that relate to the product being marketed, such as annual sales, number of employees, or industries served. Sun Microsystems, for example, sells computer servers and software to businesses in the United States and other countries. Not every business is a potential buyer, however. So the online division, eSun, describes its U.S. market as *Fortune 500* companies, meaning the largest businesses as ranked by annual sales volume.[5]

With this overview as a foundation, the marketer is ready to look at each market in more detail.

MARKETS AS MOVING TARGETS

PATHFINDER'S TIP

Targeting and segmentation, goals, strategies, programs, and implementation plans must take into consideration the market of tomorrow, not just today.

Planning marketing strategy is a challenging process because markets are always changing: Consumers move in or out, are born or die, start or stop buying a good or service. The same is true for business customers, who may change location, go into or out of business, or start or stop buying a product. Thus, at this stage of the market analysis, marketers need to locate projections of demographic changes in the markets and forecast future demand for (or sales of) their type of product, as a way of sizing the overall market over time. Common methods of forecasting market demand are discussed in Chapter 7.

Is the population expected to grow or shrink—and by how much? How many new businesses are projected to enter or leave the market? What are the projections for total industry sales of the product over the coming years? Do these projections suggest a healthy and attractive market, a stagnant market, or a shrinking market? The answers to these questions will influence decisions about which markets and segments to target and what goals to set.

Much research is publicly available for major markets and for products; consult government agencies, trade associations, and other sources. However, marketers of ground-breaking products that are brand new to the world—such as the first MP3 music player and the first personal digital assistant (PDA)—often have to conduct their own research studies as background for constructing projections of future demand and sales.

This part of the marketing planning process also feeds into the SWOT analysis discussed in Chapter 2, because it can reveal new opportunities or threats that must be addressed. Consider the rapidly-expanding global market for PDAs, including Palm Pilot and Handspring Visor:

> **Palm and Handspring.** The research firm International Data Corp. estimates that 12.5 million PDA units were sold worldwide in 2000. According to its projections, 40 million units will be sold in 2004. In dollar terms, the total global market in 2000 accounted for $2.3 billion in sales; future sales projections are correspondingly rosy. Palm Computing—which popularized the PDA, following well-publicized failures by Apple and other early players—is responsible for the vast majority of sales in this market. Handspring is a distant second, but far ahead of smaller competitors. Projections of future sales are only rough estimates, yet the combination of strong sales in recent years and future growth forecasts has attracted many new market entrants, including Compaq and Hewlett-Packard.[6]

PATHFINDER'S TIP

Data on market share can help a company develop competitive marketing strategies and construct realistic goals and standards against which to evaluate implementation.

MARKET SHARE
The percentage of sales in a given market held by a particular company, brand, or product; can be calculated in dollars or units.

MARKET SHARE AS A VITAL SIGN

As the PDA example suggests, marketers need to go beyond their research into current and projected market size to investigate the market share they hold and the share held by competitors. This usually changes over time as the market grows or shrinks and competitors enter or exit. Market share information is important because it serves as a baseline for understanding historical market dynamics and a standard for setting and measuring goals to be achieved through implementation of the programs laid out in the marketing plan.

Market share is the percentage of sales in a given market held by a particular company, brand, or product, calculated in dollars or units (ideally, both). In simple terms, a company's share can be determined by dividing its product unit or dollar sales by the entire unit or dollar sales of that type of product in that market. Thus, if a firm sells 2 million units and overall market sales for all competitors selling that kind of product are 10 million units, the firm holds a 20 percent share. Calculated in dollars, the same firm's share would be 15 percent if its product sales totaled $15 million and overall market sales totaled $100 million.

Remember that a market share calculation is only a point-in-time snapshot showing relative positions of the competitors over a particular period—positions that can and do constantly change. For example, in the year before Handspring introduced its Visor PDA, Palm Computing held 77.5 percent of the worldwide market of PDA units sold. By the end of the following year, Palm's share had dropped to 72.1 percent of the market, while Handspring had grabbed 13.9 percent market share through its highly successful introduction of the Visor. Despite losing some market share, Palm remained a strong contender because the overall market was larger and expected to continue growing, as noted above. At the same time, Handspring's strong market entry intensified the competitive pressure felt by Palm and all the smaller competitors offering PDA products.[7]

Clearly, market share is one of the vital signs of a business, to be monitored over time as a way of spotting potential problems as well as potential opportunities in the marketplace. Companies should develop share information for each of their products in each of their markets—and regularly update these to stay on top of shifts such as Handspring's sudden and dramatic impact on the PDA market. For marketing planning purposes, major changes in share should be investigated and serve as triggers for control measures (discussed in detail in Chapter 8).

In addition, market share directly affects segmentation and targeting, because a company that creates marketing strategies to capture a larger and larger share of a shrinking market segment could end up with nearly 100 percent of a market too small to be profitable. On the other hand, most companies take special notice of markets in which product demand is projected to skyrocket—using share over time to identify opportunities, understand competitive dynamics, and then set and measure progress toward goals.

Checklist 3.1 summarizes some of the key questions to ask during the market analysis stage of marketing planning.

Analyzing Customer Needs and Behavior

With the market analysis as backdrop, marketing pathfinders can now use research to analyze the needs, buying behavior, and attitudes of the consumers or business customers in their general markets. This research forms the foundation for decisions about which markets and segments within markets to target; the most effective way to position the product in the market; and what marketing strategies and tactics are most appropriate for profitably satisfying customers. The chapter-ending section on marketing research briefly reviews the tools that marketers can use to investigate consumer and business needs and behavior.

Forces in the external environment play a key role in influencing the who, what, when, where, why, and how of consumer and business buying behavior. This is one of the reasons for studying the current situation, as discussed in Chapter 2. For example, when the economy is not doing well, many consumers and business customers change their buying habits—sometimes purchasing less or less often, sometimes seeking out less expensive alternatives. Here's how Knight Ridder coped with a change in business buying patterns:

Knight Ridder. During a recent recession, Knight Ridder newspapers and many other papers found that business customers were buying fewer help-wanted ads because they were not hiring as many employees. The economic downturn therefore cut into the newspapers' advertising revenues and profits, but technological forces were involved, as well: a growing number of companies were recruiting online rather than buying newspaper ads. In response, Knight Ridder teamed up with the Tribune Company to acquire CareerBuilder.com, an online recruitment site that is expanding participation among company recruiters and job-seekers.[8]

CHECKLIST 3.1 Analyzing Markets

Broad Market Definition

☐ What is the geographic description of the market? Is a more precise definition possible or necessary?

☐ What is the product description of the market?

☐ What are the broad needs and preferences of customers in the market as they pertain to this product and category?

☐ What are the general demographics of the market as they pertain to the product?

☐ In a consumer market, how many people or households are present, and what are the gender, age, education, marital status, and other characteristics (depending on product)?

☐ In a business market, how many and what type of businesses are present, and what are their annual sales, workforce size, industries served, and other characteristics (depending on product)?

☐ What are the implications for marketing planning?

Market as Moving Target

☐ What specific needs do people in the market exhibit for the product and category? How are these needs changing over time, and how quickly?

☐ What are the current and projected demographics of the market as they pertain to the product?

☐ What are the current and projected sales of or demand for the product?

☐ What do projected demographic and demand changes suggest for the health and profitability of the market?

☐ What are the implications for segmentation, targeting, goals, and SWOT analysis?

Market Share

☐ What is the market share of the company, product, or brand, as measured in units or dollars?

☐ What market share is held by each competitor?

☐ How are the market shares of the company and its rivals changing over time?

☐ What are the implications for goal setting, SWOT analysis, and control measures?

At the same time, the attitudes and habits of consumers and business customers are clearly affected by the marketing-mix programs implemented by different companies competing for their attention, loyalty, and buying dollars. From the customer's perspective, no tactic in the company's marketing plan stands in isolation: it is one of many stimuli in the market, some of which are noticed and acted upon, and most of which are not. As a result, marketers must not only understand their markets and the environmental forces shaping customer actions, but also learn to see the marketing activities of their firms and of competing firms through their customers' eyes.

Luckily, technology now exists to help marketers identify, research, and analyze the behavior of individual customers in particular markets, instead of relying solely on averages or aggregate data. Then, as companies establish relationships with individuals in their consumer or business markets, they can gather even more data about each customer's behavior and track customer changes over time, allowing the creation of even more effective marketing plans.

In addition, marketers must be responsive to growing consumer concerns about privacy, not just about online transactions but also in the financial services industry, among others. For years, America Online resisted storing cookies on users' hard drives to track consumer reaction to its online ads. Finally, the company changed its privacy policy to specifically permit the use of cookies for collecting anonymous data about which of its 30 million members have viewed a particular ad. The Privacy Foundation, a privacy group, notes that America Online remains opposed to monitoring users' online activities and profiling individual users for marketing purposes.[9]

In general, the needs, wants, attitudes, behavior, and decision-making processes of customers in the consumer market differ from those of customers in the business market. The next three sections highlight important attributes that marketers need to understand when preparing marketing plans for the consumer or business market. Checklist 3.2 summarizes the main issues to be examined through customer analysis.

PATHFINDER'S
TIP

The process of meeting underlying customer needs is at the heart of the marketing concept; therefore, needs must be carefully researched and analyzed as the basis of marketing strategy decisions.

CUSTOMER NEEDS

At the most basic level, understanding markets requires that companies study and analyze customer needs. By determining the underlying needs and wants that customers are seeking to fulfill through the purchase of a particular good or service, marketers can search out one or more paths that will lead to more effective marketing strategies in their chosen markets. Whirlpool's experience in India serves as a good example of the importance of understanding customer needs in each market:

CHECKLIST 3.2   Analyzing Customers

Customers in the Consumer Market

❑   What are the needs of the market as they pertain to the product and category?

❑   Who are our customers in each market (in terms of gender, geography, etc.)?

❑   How do users and others influence this consumer purchase?

❑   How do culture, subculture, and class affect the customer?

❑   How do social connections such as family and social groups influence the customer?

❑   How do personal factors such as life cycle, lifestyle, and psychological makeup influence the customer?

❑   Which main customer needs, wants, attitudes, behavior, and purchasing patterns are shaped by these influences?

❑   When, where, how, and how often do customers buy—and why?

❑   How can these influences be woven into marketing strategy and tactics to build competitive advantage while initiating or strengthening customer relationships?

Customers in the Business Market

❑   Who is involved in the buying decision, and what is each person's function and influence?

❑   What does each player need to know—and when—during the buying process?

❑   What is the company's size and industry, share and growth, competitive situation, buying policies and procedures, financial constraints, and timing of purchases?

❑   What long-standing relationships exist with competing suppliers?

❑   What supplier evaluations and quality and performance standards apply?

❑   Which main customer needs, wants, attitudes, behavior, and purchasing patterns are shaped by these influences?

❑   How can these influences be woven into marketing strategy and tactics to build competitive advantage while initiating or strengthening customer relationships?

Whirlpool. Although Whirlpool has its headquarters in Michigan and markets appliances all over the world, the company is keenly aware that markets differ in their needs as well as their demographics. Projecting no growth in U.S. demand for major appliances such as washing machines, Whirlpool wants to grab a good portion of the growing demand in overseas markets. Through research, its marketers learned that consumers in India were concerned about the eventual discoloration of white clothes washed in local water. Then the company created a washing machine that is especially effective in maintaining the color of white clothing. Thanks to a thorough understanding of consumer needs—and savvy marketing keyed to the market's unique characteristics—Whirlpool was able to increase its sales in India by 80 percent in just 5 years.[10]

Marketers must delve below the surface when researching what it is that customers need and want. Stated needs are generally the tip of the iceberg; customers also have unstated needs (e.g., good service) and even secret needs (e.g., relating to their self-concept or other internal needs). Thus, the company has to come to an understanding of the problem a customer wants to solve and what the customer is really seeking from the solution.[11]

CONSUMER MARKETS

PATHFINDER'S TIP

This comprehensive analysis will help the company determine which segment(s) of the consumer market to target, what strategy to use, and what combination of marketing mix elements would be most effective.

What makes consumers buy? Who is doing the buying—and what, when, where, and how do they buy? Although the exact level of influence varies from individual to individual, cultural considerations, social connections, and personal factors are important in shaping consumer needs, wants, and behavior patterns.

Cultural Considerations

As buyers, consumers feel the influence of the culture of the nation or region in which they were raised as well as the culture where they currently live. This means that consumers in different countries often approach buying situations from different perspectives because of differing values, beliefs, and preferences. Without research, marketers can't know exactly what those differences are or how to address them in the marketing plan. Consider Hering's experience selling harmonicas in different countries:

Hering. Alberto Bertolazzi, head of Brazilian harmonica maker Hering, competes with Hohner, Suzuki, and Tomba for a share of the $130 million global harmonica market. He is concentrating on two main markets: Japan, where consumers annually buy $10 million worth of harmonicas, and the United States, where consumers annually buy $7.5 billion worth of all musical instruments. Analyzing these markets, Bertolazzi learned that each culture had different expectations about his product. "In the [United] States, people said Hering harmonicas were great but looked cheap, so we upgraded the plates from brass to bronze," he says. For products being exported to Japan, Bertolazzi applied markers to indicate the three octaves on each harmonica, because "the Japanese prefer them that way." By modifying Hering's products based on consumer research, Bertolazzi is aiming to boost annual sales beyond $4 million.[12]

SUBCULTURES
Distinct groups within a larger culture that exhibit and preserve distinct cultural identities through a common religion, nationality, ethnic background, or lifestyle.

Subcultures are distinct groups within a larger culture that exhibit and preserve distinct cultural identities through a common religion, nationality, ethnic background, or lifestyle. Within the United States, for example, a variety of subcultures drive consumer decisions and behavior. Cuban Americans frequently have different food preferences than, say, Chinese Americans. Teenagers—an age subculture—have different food preferences than seniors. To create an effective marketing plan for reaching consumers in a specific subculture, marketers must research that group's behavior and analyze its effect on buying decisions.

Class distinctions, even when subtle, also influence consumer behavior. The members of each class generally buy and use products in a similar way; in addition, people who aspire to a different class may emulate the buying or usage patterns of that class. Savvy marketers delve under the surface to learn how such distinctions operate and then apply this knowledge to make decisions about products, marketing communications, distribution arrangements, price levels, and service strategies.

Social Connections

Consumers have a web of social connections that influence how they buy—connections such as family ties, friendships, work groups, and civic organizations. Family members, for example, directly or indirectly control household spending for a multitude of goods and services. Children ask parents to buy products advertised on television; parents buy things to keep their children healthy or safe; families make group decisions about vacation plans.

Understanding how these connections affect buying decisions is critical for marketers creating marketing plans for products intended for specific family members, usage, or occasions. Heinz, as one example, designed its EZ Squirt green ketchup to be appealing to children yet acceptable to parents. In the same vein, children ask parents to buy Quaker Treasure Hunt Oatmeal so they can see how the brown and yellow morsels change to gem-like colors.[13] In both instances, parents take their children's preferences into consideration when buying food for the family, social connections that Heinz and Quaker clearly factored into their marketing plans.

As with class distinctions, aspirations to different social connections can be a powerful influence on buying behavior. In apparel, for example, preteens want to look as grown up as possible, so they emulate teenage fashions; teenagers dress like the movie stars they admire; and managers seeking to move up follow the clothing cues of higher-level managers. Within each social group, consumers look to certain opinion leaders for advice or guidance about buying decisions. Thus, supermodel Claudia Schiffer's deal to sell specially outfitted Palm PDAs on her Web site gives Palm a boost in reaching out to Schiffer fans and fashion-conscious consumers.[14]

Personal Factors

Personal factors are another major category of influences on consumer buying, covering life cycle, lifestyle, and psychological makeup, among other factors. *Life cycle* refers to the individual's changing family situation over time—whether single, cohabitating, engaged, married, married with children, divorced, remarried, and so on. Each of these life cycle phases entails different buying needs, attitudes, and preferences that, in turn, can be identified through research and addressed through appropriate marketing strategies and tactics. Engaged couples, for instance, are targeted by marketers selling formal wear, wedding services, and related goods and services; new parents are targeted by a different set of marketers selling entirely different products (such as Pampers disposable diapers and Johnson & Johnson Baby Shampoo).

LIFESTYLE The pattern of living that an individual exhibits through activities and interests.

Lifestyle is the pattern of living that a person exhibits through activities and interests—how the individual spends his or her time. To understand the complexities of lifestyle and its influence on consumer buying, marketers use sophisticated techniques to examine variables known as **psychographic characteristics,** which together form a picture of the consumer's lifestyle. Some markets can be better approached primarily through psychographics. For example, the Royal Caribbean cruise line would be particularly interested in marketing to consumers who love to take cruises, although age, gender, and other demographic elements are helpful secondary descriptors of this market.

PSYCHOGRAPHIC CHARACTERISTICS Variables used to analyze consumer lifestyle patterns.

Internal elements such as motivation, perception, and attitudes—all part of the consumer's psychological makeup—are important influences on consumer buying. **Motivation** stems from the consumer's drive to satisfy needs and wants. JCPenney.com's description of its market emphasizes motivation, not just demographic elements: "self-directed women, aged 20 to 54, with moderate incomes."[15] Perception is how the individual organizes environmental inputs (such as ads, conversation, and media) and derives meaning from them. When marketers talk about "cutting through clutter," they are discussing how to make their marketing message stand out among the many messages bombarding consumers throughout the day—not just to capture attention but to motivate consumers to respond.

MOTIVATION What drives the consumer to satisfy needs and wants.

ATTITUDES An individual's lasting evaluations of and feelings toward something.

Attitudes are the individual's lasting evaluations of and feelings toward something, such as a product or a person. Web-based marketers are particularly interested in consumer attitudes toward technology, looking for clues that will enable them to design more appealing marketing strategies and programs. Tech-savvy amateur photographers, for instance, are the market for Snapfish.com, Zing.com, and other e-businesses that provide digital photo image storage and printing.[16] Only through careful research can marketing pathfinders become knowledgeable about the personal factors that influence their customers.

Consumer Buying Decisions and Behavior

No analysis of a consumer market is complete without research into consumer buying decisions and behavior. Who in the household is doing the buying, when, where, and why? How do consumers decide what and how often to buy? What are consumers buying, and how are their purchasing patterns changing? Checklist 3.2 shows just some of the main questions to be researched in preparation for developing marketing strategies and tactics. Companies need to customize their customer-analysis questions to fit the characteristics of their products and markets.

When considering more complex purchases, such as a truck or a home, consumers generally take more time, gather more information about alternatives, weigh the decision more carefully, and have strong feelings in the aftermath of the purchase. Inexpensive items bought on impulse, such as candy, are not usually subjected to as much analysis and scrutiny before or after the purchase. By investigating the entire process consumers use to buy their products, marketing pathfinders can determine how, when, and where to initiate suitable marketing activities.

Early in the buying process, for example, marketers may need to emphasize benefits that solve consumer problems; later in the process, marketers may need to help consumers locate dealers where the product can be purchased; still later, marketers may want to stress the security of the product's warranty. The exact nature and timing of the marketing activities will depend on what the marketer learns about consumer decision making (as well as on the marketer's strategy and resources, of course).

BUSINESS MARKETS

PATHFINDER'S TIP

Through this analysis, marketers can dig deeper into the needs, standards, and internal concerns of business customers while learning how to get on the approved supplier list.

Like consumer markets, business markets are made up of people—individuals who buy on behalf of their company, government agency, or nonprofit organization. In the context of business buying, however, these people are generally influenced by a different set of factors. Marketers therefore need to examine both organizational considerations and organizational connections when analyzing business buying decisions and behavior.

Organizational Connections

Exactly who does the buying differs from company to company. But officially designated purchasing agents are not the only people who get involved with the buying decision. Buyers are usually connected with other internal players. For instance, another employee or manager may initiate the buying process by suggesting a purchase; those who actually use the product may play a role, by providing specifications, testing alternatives, or evaluating purchases; and buyers may need connections to the managers who are authorized to approve a purchase.

In addition, depending on the organization and its structure, other internal players may become involved by wielding some type of influence (such as insisting on compatibility with existing goods or services) or controlling access to buyers. Not every player will participate in every purchase, so marketers must understand the decision process that takes place inside key customer organizations so they can plan appropriate marketing activities to reach the right players at the right time with the right information.

Finally, it's important to learn about the organization's current relations with competing suppliers, including long-term contracts, evaluations, requirements, and other elements. Campbell's and many other major companies have long-term buying relationships with suppliers who meet preset quality and performance standards. A marketer who has researched the business customer's supplier connections and requirements has taken the first step toward getting on the short list of approved suppliers and making the sale.

Organizational Considerations

Organizational considerations include the company's size and industry, share and growth, competitive situation, buying policies and procedures, financial constraints, and the timing of purchases. In researching these factors, marketers need to find out, for example, whether a corporation buys centrally or allows units to buy on their own; whether companies participate in online marketplaces; and what funding and scheduling issues affect the purchase. Analyzing these considerations reveals clues to needs that marketers can satisfy through their marketing efforts.

For instance, Nabisco, the $8 billion marketer of Oreos and other branded foods, had internal timing needs and financial concerns that supplier Digital River was able to understand and satisfy:

Nabisco and Digital River. When Nabisco wanted to expand its gift marketing catalog to the Web, it needed to move quickly, but would have had to spend heavily to develop the e-commerce expertise to handle the project internally.

Deciding it was more cost effective to outsource, the company talked with more than a dozen e-commerce service providers before signing with Digital River, which also handles e-commerce sites for 3M and Siemens. "The major driver for me," says Sharon Fordham, president of the global e-business unit, "was their front-end expertise—the large amount of e-commerce experience they had, their ability to link seamlessly with our fulfillment partner, and their ability to partner with us in developing online marketing programs." Perry Steiner, Digital River's president, sums up his marketing message as: "Don't spend a penny on e-commerce. Outsource it all to us."[17]

Planning Marketing Research

PATHFINDER'S TIP

Summarize marketing research findings and identify additional needs in the marketing plan, then include new research projects when planning budgets and schedules.

SECONDARY RESEARCH
Research data already gathered for another purpose.

PRIMARY RESEARCH
Research conducted specifically to address a certain situation or answer a particular question.

This chapter has covered a wide variety of issues that marketers should research to get a better understanding of their markets and their customers. Generally the best way to start is with **secondary research**—information already collected for another purpose, such as data that the U.S. government is legally required to gather during the census. Secondary research is faster and less expensive to use than **primary research,** research conducted to address a specific situation. Exhibit 2.3, "Selected Environmental Scanning Resources," in the previous chapter, includes online and printed sources of secondary research covering different aspects of markets and customer behavior. Exhibit 3.4 shows some sources of secondary research for business and consumer markets and customers, as starting points for more extensive research.

Before relying on any secondary research, marketers must check the dates and sources. Some sources offer new or updated statistics and profiles on a regular basis; others provide a snapshot covering a specific period, which can be useful but may be quickly outdated. Also consider the source's credibility to be sure the information is from an unbiased and reputable source. If a source reports data but did not actually conduct the research, it is important to find out where the information was drawn from and how or if it was changed from the original. Marketers should also attempt to verify the information with a second source as a double-check on accuracy.

Secondary research can help marketers construct a good overview of the market, but it's usually too general to answer specific questions about particular markets and types of customers. That's where primary marketing research comes in. Marketers who are qualified to do so can conduct primary research on their own, work with internal research specialists, or hire outside specialists to collect and interpret data through surveys and other methods. In planning primary research to support marketing planning, be specific about what the company needs to know and how that knowledge will be put to use in developing and implementing a more practical or effective marketing plan. If marketing research is not available or must be carried out, indicate this in the marketing plan and include the research as part of the plan's budgets and schedules.

Marketers also need to plan ongoing marketing research that will help measure results during the implementation phase of their marketing plans. Research studies of customer satisfaction, market share changes, and customer attitudes and buying patterns can be valuable for spotting and analyzing clues to the company's effect on the market and on customers as well as how competitors are doing. The Internet is helping more companies conduct marketing research more quickly. Consider Procter & Gamble's (P&G) experience testing a new product prior to its retail introduction:

EXHIBIT 3.4   Selected Sources of Secondary Research

Market	Source
Consumer	The Conference Board Consumer Research Center: data on market patterns, consumer spending (www.crc-conquest.org)
	Journal of Consumer Research: studies of consumer behavior (www.journals.uchicago.edu/JCR/home.html)
	Academy of Marketing Science Review: studies of market issues and consumer behavior (www.amsreview.org)
	Gartner Group: research on technology-related consumer products and markets (www.gartnergroup.com)
	Media Metrix: data on Internet user behavior (www.jmm.com)
	Global Statistics: international and regional demographics (www.geohive.com)
Business	*Inc.* magazine: "State of Small Business" survey and other research and news about smaller firms (www.inc.com)
	Fortune magazine: "Fortune 500" listing of largest businesses and business news (www.fortune.com)
	U.S. Census Bureau: NAICS industry classification data (www.census.gov/epcd/www/naics.html)
	American City Business Journals: listings of largest U.S. regional businesses and industry statistics; business news (www.bizjournals.com)
	CEO Express: links to industry, national, and regional sources of research and news (www.ceoexpress.com)
	Brint.com: links to sources of market and customer data (www.brint.com/interest.html)

Procter & Gamble. P&G believes so strongly in Web-based research that it test-markets nearly half of its 6,000 new products online. Before launching Crest Whitestrips, which helps consumers whiten their teeth at home, the company posted an offer for the new product on www.whitestrips.com, drumming up traffic through online and media advertising. In just 8 months, the company sold 144,000 kits through this special Web site. Just as impressive, the company found that 12 percent of the online visitors who requested product information went on to place an order. This research convinced P&G that the product would be highly successful when introduced in stores—and it was, ringing up $50 million in total U.S. sales within 3 months.[18]

Finally, be aware that marketers are often forced to make decisions based on incomplete data; given the fast pace of the global marketplace, marketers rarely have enough time or money to conduct exhaustive research. Each company therefore must assess the risk of waiting for more research compared with the risks entailed in seizing an appealing opportunity before it slips away or making a move to combat competitive pressure.

Refer to Appendix 3 for instructions on how to use *Marketing Plan Pro* software to document the data you have gathered and your analysis of markets and customers in the appropriate sections of a written marketing plan.

Chapter Summary

In analyzing markets, companies start by broadly defining the general market and its customer needs. Markets are always changing, as consumers or business customers enter or leave, start or stop buying a product. For this reason, marketing pathfinders need to project market changes and forecast future demand for or sales of their product, prior to selecting a specific market segment to target. Many companies track their own market share and compare it with that of competitors over time to better understand market dynamics and to establish a standard for measuring results of marketing efforts.

Research is important for analyzing consumers and business customers. In consumer markets, cultural considerations, social connections, and personal factors are important in shaping needs, wants, and behavior patterns. Marketers also must research how consumers think and act in each stage of the buying decision process. Business buyers are influenced by both organizational considerations and organizational connections as they make buying decisions. Companies can use secondary research and primary research to gain a better understanding of their markets and customers. However, marketers may be forced to plan marketing activities based on incomplete data in order to keep up with fast-moving market opportunities or parry competitive initiatives.

Planning Segmentation, Targeting, and Positioning

Chapter Contents

MARKETING PATHFINDER'S QUOTE

"Every customer is different, and every customer has a different value for your firm; to succeed at marketing, you must understand and exploit these differences by matching offerings to customer needs, and by focusing resources on your most valuable customers."

—DR. MOHAN SAWHNEY, COAUTHOR OF *THE SEVEN STEPS TO NIRVANA: STRATEGIC INSIGHTS INTO EBUSINESS TRANSFORMATION*[1]

Overview of Segmentation, Targeting, and Positioning

PATHFINDER'S TIP

No company or product can be all things to all customers, so use segmentation, targeting, and positioning to narrow the focus of the marketing plan.

For a long time, marketing pathfinders could successfully follow one path to satisfy the entire market—think of dairy producers and the milk market, for instance. These days, however, markets are increasingly fragmented and diverse, with customers exhibiting a much wider variety of needs, attitudes, and behavior. At the same time, companies have been feeling more intense competitive pressure and have therefore started searching for ways to effectively differentiate themselves in the markets where they choose to compete.

The combination of these two trends has resulted in a move away from *mass marketing*—using one marketing mix to reach the entire market—and toward *segment marketing,* adapting the marketing mix for specifically identified groups (segments) within the market. Consider milk: a huge variety of milk products are now available, including whole milk, skim milk, low-fat milk, no-fat milk, soy milks, shelf-stable milks, flavored milks, and numerous other milk products.

MARKET SEGMENTATION Grouping customers within a market according to similar needs, habits, or attitudes that can be addressed through marketing.

Thus, **market segmentation** is the process of grouping customers within a market according to similar needs, habits, or attitudes that can be addressed through marketing. The point is to identify distinct segments, defined in Chapter 1 as sizable groupings of consumers or business customers with similarities (such as similar needs or buying preferences) that respond to marketing efforts. In the milk market, for instance, one segment consists of people who want to limit their fat intake and therefore want low-fat varieties; another consists of people who prefer flavored varieties; and a third consists of people who buy larger sizes for family consumption. Within each segment, customers have similar needs or are seeking the same benefits. Yet each segment can be considered distinct because the people will react differently to marketing-mix stimuli, compared with people in other segments. If all the people in all the segments react the same way to the same marketing mix, there would be no need for segmentation.

NICHE Smaller segment within a market that exhibits distinct needs or benefit requirements.

Even within a large segment, marketers can often identify **niches**—smaller segments with distinct needs or benefit requirements, such as people who buy low-fat milk in individual serving sizes at meal time. Over time, tiny niches can grow into larger segments, as Small Planet Foods found out:

Small Planet Foods. Small Planet Foods, recently acquired by General Mills, markets a variety of organic food products for the niche of "health seekers," people who want to eat healthier. Originally, this niche was quite tiny but has grown into a $7.7 billion business—and grows by 20 percent each year. Small Planet initially focused on organic produce but changed as the market changed. Now the company markets a diverse line of processed foods, including TV dinners, all geared to the habits and preferences of consumers in the "health seeker" niche.[2]

With technology and an in-depth knowledge of markets and customers, some marketing pathfinders can now identify segmentation paths leading to individual customers and tailor their marketing attention for each one. One example is the General Mills My Cereal Web site (mycereal.com/store), where consumers can log on to order custom mixes of breakfast cereal, based on taste, health, and nutrition preferences. More than 1 million different combinations of ingredients are possible, allowing General Mills to create a customized cereal mix to satisfy the specific needs of every individual customer. By creating a dynamic database of customer needs and preferences, the company can easily strengthen customer relationships by quickly filling repeat orders and offering compatible products to individual customers.[3]

Segmentation is an important part of marketing planning because it allows marketers to focus their resources on the most promising opportunities. This means better efficiency and effectiveness, because marketers get to know their segment customers very well and therefore understand exactly what they want and need—and what they don't want or need. Such customer intimacy also enables the company to notice changes in the segment and move quickly in response. Finally, it helps companies manage their competitive situation by entering segments where only a limited number of competitors are active or where their most powerful rivals are not competing.

TARGET MARKET
Segment of the overall market that a company chooses to pursue.

As shown in Exhibit 4.1, segmentation lays the foundation for targeting, decisions about which market segments to enter and the segment coverage strategy to use. The **target market** is the segment of the overall market that a company chooses to pursue. With these decisions, marketers are ready for positioning, using marketing to give the brand or product a distinctive and meaningful place (position) in the minds of targeted customers. The next section discusses how marketers segment the market; targeting and positioning are discussed later in this chapter.

EXHIBIT 4.1   Segmentation, Targeting, and Positioning

Segmentation
- Select the market
- Select the segmentation approach
- Assess and select segments for targeting

Targeting
- Select number and priority of segments for entry
- Select segment coverage strategy

Positioning
- Select meaningful attributes for differentiation
- Apply positioning through marketing strategy and tactics

Segmenting the Market

The market segmentation process, as outlined in Exhibit 4.1, consists of three main steps: (1) select the market, (2) select the segmentation approach, and (3) assess and select segments for targeting. Here's a closer look at how marketing pathfinders can apply this process in the course of developing a marketing plan.

SELECT THE MARKET

PATHFINDER'S TIP

Start with the broad market definition based on the market and customer analysis, then sharpen the precision by eliminating inappropriate markets or segments.

The first step in segmentation is to select the general market(s) in which the company will target customers, based on the market definition, situational analysis, and SWOT analysis previously completed (see Chapter 3). Sharpen the focus by eliminating markets or segments that have no need for the product or are inappropriate for other reasons, such as geographic distance, lack of purchasing power, ethical issues, or troubling environmental threats. Consider Coca-Cola's experience in eliminating Angola as a market and then reversing that decision decades later:

> **Coca-Cola.** Coca-Cola operates in many markets around the world, but it withdrew from Angola more than 25 years ago during the country's protracted civil war. When Coke made the decision to reenter Angola not long ago, despite continued fighting within the country, it felt that the opportunities finally outweighed the risks. Still, the company has had to work around numerous obstacles, such as a curfew that curtails employees' working hours and snarls delivery schedules for supplies as well as bottled beverages. By pricing Coke at affordable levels and investing in colorful store displays and coolers, the company has been able to build market share as demand and consumption both increase.[4]

SELECT THE SEGMENTATION APPROACH

PATHFINDER'S TIP

Use marketing research to profile the customers in the market and identify appropriate variables for grouping customers into meaningful segments.

Now marketers start to search for segments within the general markets they have defined. People and businesses differ in many ways, but not every difference is meaningful from a marketing perspective. The purpose of segment identification is to form customer groupings that are internally similar yet sufficiently different that each grouping will not react in exactly the same way to the same marketing activities. If all customer groupings were similar or responded in the same way to marketing, there would be no need for segmentation—the company could simply use one marketing plan for the entire market.

Customer groupings are created by applying one or more segmentation variables to the entire market.

Variables for Consumer Markets

Marketers can isolate groupings within consumer markets using demographic, geographic, psychographic, and behavioral segmentation variables (see Exhibit 4.2). Consumer markets can be segmented with just about every one of these variables; the choice for a specific marketing plan depends on the marketer's detailed marketing research profiling customers and analyzing their buying behavior. Sophisticated marketers often apply geographic, demographic, and psychographic or behavioral variables in combination to create extremely well-defined market segments or niches for marketing attention.

EXHIBIT 4.2   Major Segmentation Variables for Consumer Markets

Type of Variable	*Examples*
Demographic	Age, gender, family status, household size, income, occupation, education, religion, race, nationality, social class
Geographic	Nation, region, state, city, climate
Psychographic	Lifestyle, activities, interests
Behavioral	Benefits expected, usage occasion, user status, loyalty status, technological orientation

---

Common sense also plays a role: some variables simply don't lend themselves to certain markets. For example, the consumer market for paper towels can certainly be segmented in terms of education, but will the resulting groupings reveal differing needs or responses to marketing efforts? On the other hand, income and household size are likely to be better variables for segmenting this market, since either (or both) may result in groupings that have different needs or respond differently to marketing activities. The following sections take a closer look at the main categories of consumer segmentation variables.

Demographic Variables   Demographic variables are popular for segmenting markets because they are common and easily identified consumer characteristics. In addition, they often point to meaningful differences in consumer needs, wants, and product consumption, as well as media usage. For instance, it is no surprise that L'eggs and other pantyhose manufacturers segment on the basis of gender when grouping consumers into segments. Yet marketers must be careful to avoid stereotyping customers when using demographic variables such as race and nationality; behavioral and psychographic variables are often more powerful factors for segmentation because they are linked to underlying needs and benefit requirements.

Segmenting on the basis of family status and age (in combination with other variables) helps Kimberly-Clark identify the segments most interested in its disposable diaper products:

Kimberly-Clark. Kimberly-Clark offers a range of disposable diaper products for children and adults. The company targets families with infants from newborn to toddler ages for its Huggies line and has set up a parenting Web site (www.parent stages.com) aimed at this segment, posting tips for young parents and showcasing its infant products. Its Pull-Ups product line is geared for the segment of families with toddlers who are being toilet trained, while its Little Swimmers line is geared for families that want to outfit their toddlers with disposable swimpants. Both Depend and Poise are Kimberly-Clark products for adults dealing with incontinence. Each of these groups responds to a different set of marketing-mix activities, which is why segmentation is effective for Kimberly-Clark.[5]

Sears has been extremely successful in building customer relationships by segmenting U.S. markets using nationality and language to reach out to Asian customers surrounding 30 of its department stores. The retailer organizes Moon Festival celebrations every fall and promotes them through advertisements in Mandarin, Cantonese,

Vietnamese, or Korean, depending on the demographics of each store's market. These celebrations bring customers in and start the cash registers ringing, say Sears officials.[6]

Segmenting on the basis of income can help marketers of upscale goods and services focus on consumer segments with the means to buy; it also can help marketers of lower-priced goods and services focus on segments with a stronger need to stretch their dollars. As a result, income segmentation is as valuable for Saks Fifth Avenue as it is for Dollar General stores. In recent years, the volume of sales in discount stores has grown so rapidly that Procter & Gamble and other manufacturers have decided to maintain or create products and brands specifically for the lower-income segment.[7] Combining demographic variables can help a company focus even further. For example, cosmetics marketer Fashion Fair segments on the basis of race and gender to identify African-American women who need makeup keyed to their skin tones.

Marketers can check numerous sources for demographic details on different segments. For example, Marketsegment.com (www.marketsegment.com/home/Home.htm) provides data on different U.S. subcultures. Economics.com's Free Lunch page (www.freelunch.com) contains links to reports and statistics covering consumer markets, economic trends, industry analyses, and other demographic issues. As the name implies, *Hispanic Business* (www.hispanicbusiness.com) offers statistics and articles about Hispanic businesses. In addition, many of the sources listed in Chapters 2 and 3 include demographic information for segmentation.

Geographic Variables As shown in the earlier Coca-Cola example, companies routinely use geography to segment consumer markets. The decision to use geographic variables may be based on a company's ability to sell and service products in certain areas or climates, its interest in entering promising new markets, or its reluctance to sell in certain areas due to environmental threats or unfavorable climate. For instance, Somerfield, the fifth-largest grocery chain in Great Britain, segments on the basis of neighborhood to identify local locations for its smaller Kwik Save food stores. Tesco, the dominant grocery chain in Great Britain, is using segmentation to find profitable locations for opening supermarkets in other countries—and, competing with Somerfield, to identify new U.K. neighborhood locations for its smaller Tesco Extra food stores.[8]

Still, companies that segment by geography must take care to avoid overlooking meaningful differences within each area or similarities that cross geographic boundaries. Waitrose, a Southern England grocery chain, competes with Tesco, Somerfield, and other rivals by featuring organic foods and emphasizing quality and service. Because customers all over the United Kingdom are interested in organic foods, Waitrose can broaden its segmentation beyond the boundaries of current store locations, serving a wider geographic area through its online shopping sites.[9]

Psychographic Variables Segmenting on the basis of psychographic variables such as lifestyle, activities, and interests can help companies gain a deeper understanding of what and why consumers buy. In some cases, psychographic segmentation is the only way to identify a consumer group for special marketing attention, because activities and interests tend to cross demographic and geographic lines. People who share an interest in sports, for instance, may live anywhere in the United States—or in another country—and be of almost any age or gender. As another example, the segment of two-career couples may cover a broad geographic area.

Despite these similarities, a marketer who applies both psychographic and demographic variables may be able to create one or multiple segments (such as men who follow college basketball) that respond to different marketing initiatives. Marketers of soft drinks, beer, and other products therefore tie in with sports events like the NCAA

Tournament as a way of reaching such segments. The key is to identify the specific psychographic variables (and any other variables) that will create segments with meaningful differences. Hershey, for example, has applied demographic, psychographic, and behavioral variables to identify a segment consisting of women (big buyers of chocolate) who follow the sport of figure skating. Then Hershey creates television commercials linking its chocolate candies to the sport and reaches the segment by buying advertising time during figure-skating programs. Thus, segmentation not only identifies the segment but also provides clues to how it can be reached through marketing.

Behavioral Variables As with psychographic variables, behavioral variables are often the best way to identify a consumer group for special marketing attention, because benefits expected, usage occasion and status, loyalty status, and technological orientation generally cross demographic and geographic lines. Benefits segmentation helps marketers think about what, exactly, a group of consumers expects from a particular good or service. For example, air travelers look for different benefits: business travelers may put more value on convenient schedules, while vacation travelers may put more value on affordability, so marketers will use a different marketing message for each segment. Thus, airline marketers could segment first on the basis of behavior and then further segment by demographics or other variables, putting the emphasis on what people need rather than who they are.

Segmenting by usage occasion helps marketers group consumers based on the occasion(s) when they buy or use a particular product. General Motors (GM), for instance, knows that consumers frequently need directions when they drive. Based on its knowledge of this occasion usage, GM installs its OnStar wireless communication system as optional equipment on basic car models and as standard equipment on upscale models, delivering maps, directions, and travel-related information to GM drivers.[10]

User status—whether a consumer has ever used the product, is a first-time user, or is a regular user—is particularly important when a company wants to increase sales by selling to nonusers or selling more to first-time or light users. Loyalty status refers to the degree of loyalty: does the consumer always buy one particular brand or constantly switch—and why? Companies often mount one marketing program to reinforce loyalty and another to court switchers who are currently buying a different brand.

Technological orientation—whether consumers like or use technology such as the Internet—is a key behavioral variable for marketers that connect with customers via the Internet or that sell tech-related products. For example, the San Francisco Opera found a meaningful marketing opportunity by segmenting psychographically (interest in opera) and behaviorally (affinity for buying online). When it debuted the opera *Dead Man Walking*, first-day ticket sales broke a record, with fully half of the tickets sold online.[11] As another example, Volvo uses affinity for online activities coupled with car ownership to define a consumer segment that responds well to online marketing promotions. "Volvo's target customers are among the earliest adopters of new technology," says the CEO of Volvo of North America. "Just as we created the first automotive Web site back in 1994, we've continued to use new technology in a practical, targeted way to qualify potential buyers and initiate a deeper relationship with them."[12]

Variables for Business Markets

As Exhibit 4.3 shows, business marketers can segment their markets using three major categories of variables: demographic, geographic, and behavioral. In many cases, marketers use a combination of variables, including definition of the industry (a demographic variable) and adding one or more variables for further segmentation, such as

---

CHECKLIST 4.1   Applying Consumer Segmentation Variables

Sample Questions for Demographic Variables: Do Consumer Needs or Responses Differ . . .
- ❏   by gender—and how?
- ❏   according to household size—and how?
- ❏   at different income levels—and how?
- ❏   by occupation—and how?
- ❏   by educational background—and how?
- ❏   by religion—and how?
- ❏   by race—and how?
- ❏   by nationality—and how?
- ❏   according to social class—and how?

Sample Questions for Geographic Variables: Do Consumer Needs or Responses Differ . . .
- ❏   by nation—and how?
- ❏   by region—and how?
- ❏   by state—and how?
- ❏   by city—and how?
- ❏   by climate—and how?

Sample Questions for Psychographic Variables: Do Consumer Needs or Responses Differ . . .
- ❏   according to lifestyle—and how?
- ❏   according to activities—and how?
- ❏   according to interests—and how?

Sample Questions for Behavioral Variables: Do Consumer Needs or Responses Differ . . .
- ❏   by benefits expected—and how?
- ❏   by occasion of usage—and how?
- ❏   by user status—and how?
- ❏   by loyalty status—and how?
- ❏   by technological orientation—and how?

---

size of business (another demographic variable) and location (a geographic variable). Again, the object is to create segments that are internally similar but don't have the same needs or don't respond exactly the same as other segments when exposed to the company's marketing activities.

Demographic Variables   The main demographic variables used to segment business markets are industry, business size, business age, and ownership structure. Industry segmentation is a good starting point, but doesn't necessarily result in groupings that

EXHIBIT 4.3   Major Segmentation Variables for Business Markets

Type of Variable	Examples
Demographic	Industry, business size, business age, ownership structure
Geographic	Nation, region, state, city, climate, distance
Behavioral	Purchasing patterns, user status, usage occasions, technological orientation, loyalty status, benefits expected

are sufficiently different from each other to warrant different marketing approaches. Therefore, marketers typically segment further on the basis of size (as measured by annual revenues or unit sales, number of employees, or number of branches) or even rate of growth in size, reasoning that business of different sizes have different needs. America Online's Netscape division, for example, segments the market for e-commerce services according to business size. Its Netbusiness Web portal service is specifically designed to serve the e-commerce needs of the 28 million U.S. businesses with fewer than 10 employees.[13]

Marketers that segment according to business age are looking for differing needs or purchasing patterns that relate to how long the business has been in existence. Businesses in the formation stage often have a higher need for office or factory space, computers and equipment, accounting and legal services, and many other products. In contrast, older businesses may have a higher need for repair services, upgraded computers and equipment, and other goods and services. Segmenting by ownership structure also can point up meaningful differences. For instance, the insurance and accounting needs of sole proprietorships are not the same as those of corporations. Only by segmenting the market can marketers identify these differences for appropriate marketing attention.

Geographic Variables   Business marketers, like their consumer counterparts, can use geographic variables such as nation, region, state, city, and climate to segment their markets. In this way, they can group business customers according to concentration of outlets or location of headquarters. They can also create segments with special needs or responses based on geography, as eRoom Technology has done (see Exhibit 4.4):

eRoom Technology. Specializing in technology for virtual collaboration, eRoom segments its market according to geographic distance. National and international corporations such as Hewlett-Packard, Pfizer, and Ford, with offices spread across vast distances, need a cost-effective way of enabling farflung personnel to work together. That's where eRoom comes in. Ford wanted to offer special training to a group of 47 managers, based in different countries, by assigning them to work as a team on specific company problems. So eRoom built a secure online environment for the Ford managers to log in at any time from any location, share documents and files, and exchange ideas using instant messaging and chat rooms.[14]

Behavioral Variables   Segmenting on the basis of purchasing patterns, user status, technological orientation, loyalty status, or benefits expected—or some combination of these—can help a company better understand and satisfy specific segments within business markets. Purchasing patterns can vary widely; for example, companies use a variety of policies and practices and make purchases at certain times or intervals. Knowing the buying cycle or policy of a business customer can help marketers design and deliver the right offer at the right time. Similarly, companies that are frequent users of a good or service may require a different offer or message than companies that are trying it for the first time.

Just as consumer markets can be effectively segmented according to benefits expected, so too can business markets. Adding technological orientation as another segmentation variable can result in even more precise customer groupings. Avaya, a

EXHIBIT 4.4 ERoom Technology

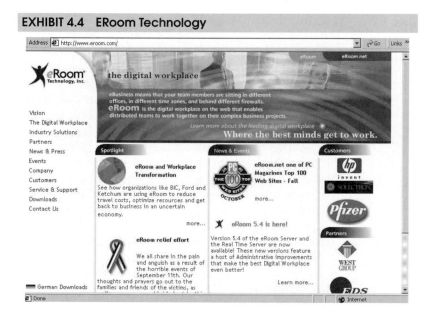

$7.7 billion networking company, uses both variables to identify groups of businesses that need help designing and implementing high-tech systems (technological orientation) to simplify customer service communications (benefit expected). For Banco del Estado de Chile, Chile's state bank, Avaya created a sophisticated network that allows Web-based banking customers to connect with service representatives.[15]

ASSESS AND SELECT SEGMENTS FOR TARGETING

Once the company has applied segmentation variables to group customers within the overall market, it must evaluate each segment based on attractiveness and fit with the firm's resources and core competencies, goals and objectives, and offerings (identified during the analysis of the current situation). The purpose is to screen out unattractive or unsuitable segments and gauge the attractiveness of the remaining segments.

One key measure of attractiveness is the current and future opportunity for sales and profits. Large, more profitable, or faster-growing segments are generally more attractive than smaller, less profitable, or slower-growing segments. In the course of assessing opportunity, marketers also must look at how entering each segment would affect the company's ability to reach its overall goals, such as growth or profitability.

A second measure is the potential for competitive superiority. Can the company effectively compete or achieve a leadership position in the segment, given its core competencies and competitive situation? A third measure is the fit with company resources and core competencies. Segments that need more money or attention than the company can invest will be less attractive. And a fourth measure is the extent of environmental threats. Based on the environmental scanning and analysis, what macroenvironmental threats—such as more restrictive regulatory guidelines—exist now or could emerge to hamper the company's performance in the segment?

Consider Wal-Mart's approach to segmentation. Early on, the company used geographic and demographic variables to segment the United States, identifying smaller towns that were underserved by other retailers. Evaluating these segments, Wal-Mart realized that it could profit by opening stores in many of these towns; that it would face

---

CHECKLIST 4.2   Applying Business Segmentation Variables

Sample Questions for Demographic Variables: Do Business Customers' Needs or Responses Differ . . .
- ❑   by industry—and how?
- ❑   according to business size—and how?
- ❑   according to business age—and how?
- ❑   by ownership structure—and how?

Sample Questions for Geographic Variables: Do Business Customers' Needs or Responses Differ . . .
- ❑   by nation—and how?
- ❑   by region—and how?
- ❑   by state—and how?
- ❑   by city—and how?
- ❑   by climate—and how?
- ❑   by geographic distance—and how?

Sample Questions for Behavioral Variables: Do Business Customers' Needs or Responses Differ . . .
- ❑   by benefits expected—and how?
- ❑   according to purchasing patterns—and how?
- ❑   by user status—and how?
- ❑   according to technological orientation—and how?
- ❑   by usage occasions—and how?
- ❑   by loyalty status—and how?

---

little competition in smaller towns; that it had the resources and ability to build stores in smaller towns; and that it faced no insurmountable macroenvironmental threats. This segmentation yielded an abundance of attractive small-town segments, leading the way for Wal-Mart to embark on a growth strategy that made it the dominant retailer in small-town America. Over the years, it changed its segmentation methods and evaluation criteria in line with the evolution of its markets and customers, its competitors, and the macroenvironment.

Targeting Segments and Choosing Coverage Strategies

PATHFINDER'S TIP

A thorough marketing plan should explain the system used to rank segments for targeting and the coverage strategy used for segment entry.

At the end of the segmentation process, the company has identified various segments within the larger consumer or business market and screened out segments it will not enter. Now it must rank the remaining segments and arrange them in order of priority for entry.

Some marketers do this by weighting the evaluation criteria to come up with a composite score for each segment. This will show which segments are more attractive and will allow comparisons of segments based on higher profit potential, for instance, faster projected growth, or lower competitive pressure. As shown in the simplified sample ranking in Exhibit 4.5, some segments may score higher for competitive superiority but lower for fit with organizational resources. The overall score generally determines which segments are entered first; in this example, segment B has the highest overall score and will be entered first.

Other marketers prefer to rank segments according to similar customer needs or product usage. Different marketers plan for different ranking systems and weighting criteria, based on their own companies' mission and goals, resources, core competencies, and other considerations.

	Score for Future Sales/Profits	Score for Competitive Superiority	Score for Fit with Resources	Score for Environmental Threats	Overall Score
EXHIBIT 4.5 Sample Segment Ranking					
Segment	*Score for Future Sales/Profits*	*Score for Competitive Superiority*	*Score for Fit with Resources*	*Score for Environmental Threats*	*Overall Score*
A	3	5	2	3	13
B	5	4	4	2	15
C	4	2	3	3	12

Scoring key: 5, highly attractive; 4, moderately attractive; 3, average; 2, moderately unattractive; 1, highly unattractive.

CONCENTRATED MARKETING
Focusing one marketing strategy on one attractive market segment.

On the basis of this ranking, the company can now determine which segments to enter and what coverage strategy to use. Many companies identify the most attractive segment and concentrate their marketing efforts only on that one—**concentrated marketing.** This approach has the advantage of allowing the company to focus all its resources and marketing muscle on just one customer grouping, the way Loserkids.com, an online retailer of clothing and accessories, focuses only on teens. However, if the segment stops growing, attracts more competition, or undergoes other changes, it can become unattractive almost overnight.

UNDIFFERENTI-ATED MARKETING
Targeting all market segments with the same marketing strategy, as in mass marketing.

At the other extreme, a company may decide to cover the market by targeting all segments with the same marketing strategy—**undifferentiated marketing.** This mass-marketing approach ignores any segment differences, assuming that a single marketing strategy covering the entire market will yield results in all segments. Although undifferentiated marketing requires less investment in product development, advertising, and other tactics, it is rarely used today because it doesn't adequately address the needs of fragmented, diverse markets.

DIFFERENTIATED MARKETING
Creating a separate marketing strategy for each targeted segment.

Instead, companies that target multiple segments generally use **differentiated marketing** to create a separate marketing strategy for each segment. Even Coca-Cola, long known for mass marketing, now uses differentiated marketing to target segments such as dieters, caffeine-lovers, and non–caffeine lovers. Thanks to technology, more companies can design marketing programs for individual customers in targeted segments; the customizable cereal products available on General Mills' My Cereal Web site illustrate individualized marketing.

Differentiated marketing requires considerable investment in marketing research to understand each segment's needs, as well as higher costs due to different products, different advertising campaigns, and so on. These costs must be taken into account when preparing the marketing plan and related budgets. If the company's resources won't stretch to cover all the targeted segments, the marketer should devise a rollout strategy for entering segments over time, in order of priority.

Positioning for Competitive Advantage

PATHFINDER'S TIP

Use the brand's positioning to drive the entire marketing effort, because it taps into what customers value and differentiates the brand from competitors.

At this point, the company has identified and selected segments for entry and settled on a coverage strategy. Now the marketing pathfinder must decide on an overall positioning strategy to differentiate the brand or product from the competition on the basis of attributes that are meaningful to customers. Marketing research can uncover customers' views of the brand and its competitors, and indicate which key attributes are important factors in customer buying decisions. Then the marketer must determine which attribute (or combination of attributes) leads to the most meaningful differentiation and, ultimately, a competitive advantage that translates into sales.

MEANINGFUL DIFFERENTIATION

Companies can differentiate their brands and products in many ways. Three examples: by stressing physical attributes such as product features; by highlighting service attributes such as convenient installation; or by emphasizing channel attributes such as wide availability. The choice of attribute depends on what customers value and how competitors are perceived. If customers don't value wide availability of a product, that point of differentiation won't be a meaningful basis for positioning. On the other hand, even if wide availability is valued, it won't be meaningful for the company if a competitor has already used that attribute to differentiate its product or brand. Also, it would not be meaningful for the company if the positioning conflicted with its mission, goals, or resources.

Here are some examples of effective positioning based on meaningful differentiation:

- FedEx: fast, reliable on-time delivery
- Southwest Airlines: affordable, no-frills air travel
- Rolex: status-symbol fashion accessory
- Site 59 (on the Web): last-minute travel for less

In each case, the positioning not only conveys the value that the brand provides, but also sets the brand apart from competitors. FedEx's positioning on the attribute of on-time delivery—backed up by day-in, day-out performance—has given the company a distinct image and competitive edge, compared with rivals like Airborne Express and UPS. Southwest's positioning on the attribute of affordable air travel—backed up by low fares—has given it a distinct image and helped it build market share in a highly turbulent industry. In contrast, JetBlue, a Southwest competitor in Northeast markets, also stresses low fares but its new jets, leather seats, and personal video screens add a dimension of comfort that sets the airline apart from other low-price carriers. Because they have clearly differentiated their services, both JetBlue and Southwest have succeeded in a difficult industry.

POSITIONING AND MARKETING LEVERAGE

Positioning alone won't build competitive advantage. It will, however, act as the driving force for all marketing strategies and tactics, setting the direction and tone for the rest of the marketing plan. Thus, to leverage the company's investment in marketing, all marketing programs should support and reinforce the differentiation expressed in the positioning.

Consider how the U.S. division of Agfa, a photographic and digital imaging firm, supported its positioning as a problem-solving provider of imaging solutions for businesses:

Agfa. When Agfa wanted to convey its positioning as a specialist in "heavy-thinking as opposed to heavy metal," the company created a Web-based tool called a "1 to 1 Profiler" to help businesses evaluate their imaging technology needs. Business managers answer a series of questions and then receive a response geared specifically to their answers. In the first 2 years, more than 1,500 businesses used the profiling system to gauge their needs. "It's not a sales proposal," explains the director of marketing communications. "What they get back is an objective and highly refined document. It generates a large amount of goodwill and brands us as a leader in our industry." Agfa's campaign tagline, "A Smarter

Way," and all its marketing messages contribute to communicating the problem-solver positioning.[16]

Once the company has established its differentiation, it needs to reevaluate this positioning when the environment changes. For example, Spirian Technologies of Chicago initially used a positioning of speedy implementation to differentiate itself from rival software-services firms. Corporate customers relied on Spirian to quickly upgrade their PC software and install new programs as needed. However, when an economic downturn began cutting into customers' revenues, Spirian found that its customers were now putting cost efficiency above other benefits. Spirian's CEO realized the company had to make a positioning change: "Suddenly, we had to change to a message that you could use our services to cut cost," he remembers. After Spirian repositioned itself to emphasize the cost-cutting value of its services, the company found its marketing efforts had much more leverage with prospects.[17]

Refer to Appendix 3 for instructions on how to use *Marketing Plan Pro* software to document the data you have gathered and your decisions in the appropriate sections of a written marketing plan.

Chapter Summary

More marketers are using segmentation, targeting, and positioning to compete more effectively by serving specific customer groups with differentiated offerings. Market segmentation is the process of grouping customers within a market according to similar needs, habits, or attitudes that can be addressed through marketing. The purpose is to form groupings that are internally similar yet sufficiently different that each grouping will not react in exactly the same way to the same marketing activities. Segmentation is the basis for targeting decisions about which market segments to enter and the segment coverage strategy to use. Once segments have been chosen, the company creates a positioning strategy for effective differentiation.

The market segmentation process consists of three main steps: (1) select the market, (2) select the segmentation approach, and (3) assess and select segments for targeting. Marketers can segment consumer markets using demographic, geographic, psychographic, and behavioral segmentation variables. Marketers can segment business markets using demographic, geographic, and behavioral variables. After segmentation, marketers must evaluate each segment based on attractiveness and fit with the firm's resources, goals, and offerings. Having identified various segments within the larger consumer or business market and screened out segments it will not enter, the company must rank the remaining segments and arrange them in order of entry priority, using concentrated marketing, undifferentiated marketing, or differentiated marketing. Finally, the company must create an overall positioning strategy to differentiate the brand or product from the competition on the basis of attributes that are meaningful to customers. In turn, this positioning must be supported and reinforced by the company's marketing mix.

5

Determining Objectives and Strategic Direction

Chapter Contents

MARKETING PATHFINDER'S QUOTE

"Objectives to raise profit, increase market share, or change stakeholder attitudes and behaviors are meaningless unless companies make effective plans to manage their most valuable asset: customer relationships."

—DR. JUDY STRAUSS, COAUTHOR OF *E-MARKETING*[1]

Determining Strategic Direction

PATHFINDER'S TIP

The firm's strategic direction must build on the foundation of the organizational mission and overall goals examined in the analysis of the internal environment.

The ultimate purpose of the marketing plan is to help the organization achieve *objectives*—shorter-term performance targets—that will, in turn, bring it closer to achieving its *goals,* longer-term performance targets tied to the mission. Marketers must start with a thorough examination of environmental factors, strengths and weaknesses, the company's mission, the market, and the customers in targeted segments; then they can begin determining the strategic direction for their company's marketing plan. This direction must be consistent with corporate priorities and resource allocations set by the organization's overall strategic direction.

Most organizations create marketing plans to support growth strategies. However, some strive to sustain current sales levels and others may follow a downsizing strategy for survival or as a prelude to going out of business (see Exhibit 5.1).

EXHIBIT 5.1 Strategic Direction Options

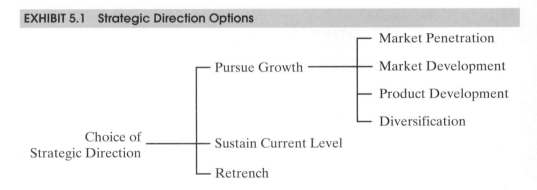

GROWTH STRATEGIES

Marketing pathfinders can pursue growth by following one of these four broad strategies:[2]

MARKET PENETRATION
Growth strategy in which the company sells more of its existing products to customers in existing markets or segments.

Market penetration is a growth strategy in which the company sells more of its existing products to customers in existing markets or segments. This is the strategy followed by retailer J.C. Penney, which uses specialized catalogs and strategically placed store branches to bring shoppers back again and again. At the J.C. Penney branch in Plaza Las Americas, Puerto Rico, 40 percent of the customers return to the store to shop every week.[3] Clearly, market penetration is a viable option for companies that can build on an established, profitable customer base.

MARKET DEVELOPMENT
Growth strategy in which the company identifies and taps new segments or markets for existing products.

Market development involves identifying and tapping new segments or markets for existing products. Telecommunications giant Verizon is doing this by expanding its data and wireless operations beyond consumers into small business and corporate markets in the Northeast United States, using customer service as a key differentiator. The company will soon expand its wireless offerings for businesses through new networks in Europe, Asia, and Latin America.[4] PayMaxx, a payroll services firm, also has achieved rapid growth by expanding its market reach through the Internet. In just 2 years, its revenues from Web customers grew by 400 percent, compared with 25 percent revenue growth from other customers.[5]

PRODUCT DEVELOPMENT
Growth strategy in which the company sells new products to customers in existing markets or segments.

Product development is a growth strategy in which the company sells new products to customers in existing markets or segments. Amazon.com has followed this strategy in expanding online sales by adding electronics, kitchen items, home improvement products, and a broad array of products unrelated to books. California-based Vans, which began as a manufacturer of shoes for skateboarders, has expanded into related apparel and opened skateboard parks to attract more revenue from its current customer base.[6] Colgate-Palmolive also has used product development to grow sales and profits. Based in part on the introduction of its Total multibenefit toothpaste—which targets customers in existing segments and markets—Colgate was able to boost its share of the U.S. toothpaste market from 24.7 percent to 31.8 percent in just 3 years.[7]

DIVERSIFICATION
Growth strategy of offering new products to new markets through internal product development capabilities or by starting (or buying) a business for diversification purposes.

Diversification is a growth strategy of offering new products to new markets, through internal product development capabilities or by starting or buying a business for diversification purposes. The purpose is to take advantage of new opportunities. Citigroup is well known for this strategy; it buys companies with complementary products and develops new products to serve new segments and markets.

Remember that environmental developments can affect the company's ability to follow a growth strategy and achieve ambitious goals and objectives, as Cisco Systems learned not long ago:

Cisco Systems. Cisco was aware that its telecommunications customers were establishing challenging goals for selling high-speed Internet access to households and businesses, indicating high future demand for Cisco's networking equipment. So Cisco set its own high sales objectives and made marketing and production investments predicated on an aggressive penetration strategy. Within a year, Cisco's customers eased up on purchases because the economy was slowing, leaving Cisco to deal with an enormous inventory stockpile and an obsolete marketing plan. Even an unexpected influx of orders from companies replacing equipment destroyed when New York's World Trade Center was attacked by terrorists didn't significantly improve Cisco's sales situation.[8]

OTHER STRATEGIES

Growth is not always desirable or even possible. In tough economic times, for instance, organizations often look for ways to marshal their resources and simply maintain current sales or boost profitability. Sometimes rising costs, slower sales, or lower profits (or a combination of all three) can force companies into a period of strategic retrenchment, which calls for different goals and tactics than growth.

For example, Motorola's CEO realized that the company's growth strategy was not working as its share of the global mobile phone market shrank from 26 percent to 14 percent in just 4 years. After the mobile phone unit had reported lower quarterly sales and gross margins, lost $400 million, and annoyed big customers by missing deadlines for introducing new phones, the CEO laid out a new strategic direction to prepare for future growth, backed by new goals for cost cutting and product development. One goal was to streamline the diverse product line by eliminating more than 100 phones; another was to simplify development and production by using only 100 silicon components instead of the 500-plus formerly used; and a third was to speed new products to market within 6 to 9 months, instead of 18 months.[9] If Motorola reached all these goals, it would be more efficient, more responsive, and better primed for growth in the coming years.

Even the most drastic strategic direction—downsizing leading to bankruptcy—isn't necessarily an exit strategy, although turnarounds take considerable time, management attention, and investment. Consider the turnaround strategy being implemented at the chicken chain Boston Market:

Boston Market. After McDonald's bought Boston Market's 860 restaurants and brand for just $173.5 million following the chain's bankruptcy, top management began downsizing, closing some outlets, and converting others to McDonald's restaurants. Then marketing research revealed that the chain still enjoyed a high level of customer loyalty and brand preference. So McDonald's conducted a test, revamping four outlets with new decor, additional menu items, and stronger promotional support. The resulting sales gains of over 15 percent convinced management to change strategic direction and pursue a growth strategy, aiming for double-digit sales increases in the coming years—yet recognizing that the turnaround may be slow and require substantial marketing investment.[10]

Setting Marketing Plan Objectives

PATHFINDER'S TIP

Review the SWOT analysis to identify potential pitfalls and sources of strength for achieving marketing plan objectives.

Strategic direction indicates a general route for the marketing plan but without specifics. Now marketers have to set marketing and financial objectives as short-term destinations along the path toward longer-term organizational goals. Step by step, the achievement of each marketing and financial objective brings the organization closer to fulfilling its ultimate purpose. The exact objectives set will depend on the marketer's knowledge of the current situation, environmental issues and keys to success, customers in targeted segments, and the organization's mission, goals, and positioning.

Objectives will be effective for guiding marketing progress only if they are:

- *Specific, time-defined, and measurable.* Objectives must be specific and include both deadlines and quantitative measures so marketers can plan the timing of activities and evaluate results to check progress. Marketers also must be able to measure progress by looking at sales figures, customer counts, satisfaction surveys, or through some other method.
- *Realistic but challenging.* To move the organization closer to its long-range goals, marketing objectives should be rooted in reality yet aggressive enough to inspire high performance.
- *Consistent with the mission and overall organizational goals.* Objectives set for the marketing plan should support the organization in fulfilling its ultimate purpose—as stated in the mission—and take the organization closer to its long-range goals.
- *Consistent with internal resources and core competencies.* Challenging objectives will be empty words unless the organization has the resources, core competencies, and strengths to further their achievement. A thorough internal environmental analysis should indicate whether the organization is capable of driving toward the marketing plan objectives.
- *Appropriate in light of external environmental opportunities and threats.* Objectives must make sense in the face of market and competitive realities and other opportunities and threats uncovered during the external environmental analysis.

Objective setting ties together planning at different organizational levels, as General Electric's (GE) experience illustrates:

General Electric. Every January, GE sets 1-year "stretch targets" to stimulate major gains in key areas during the coming 12 months. Each unit then develops a

---

CHECKLIST 5.1   Do Your Objectives Measure Up?

❑   Is the objective specific?

❑   Is the objective time defined?

❑   Is the objective measurable?

❑   Is the objective realistic?

❑   Is the objective challenging?

❑   Is the objective consistent with the organization's mission?

❑   Is the objective consistent with the organization's overall goals?

❑   Is the objective consistent with the organization's internal resources and core competencies?

❑   Is the objective appropriate given external environmental opportunities and threats?

marketing plan with objectives that contribute to achieving that year's stretch targets. Recently, the GE Financial Assurance division, which specializes in insurance and investment products, took steps to support increased sales potential by setting a year-long objective calling for 50 percent of sales to be generated by products that are less than 18 months old.[11] Other units have set 1-year objectives for increasing sales, speeding order fulfillment, and improving quality, among many other targets.

Yet long-range goals can change over the time, necessitating a change in marketing objectives and direction, as well. Several years ago, GE realized that its long-range goal of being number 1 or 2 in every business area was limiting its opportunities and growth potential. As a result, the corporation asked its business managers to redefine their markets without using dominant market share as the goal, and to refocus on growth opportunities by creating and delivering value in new ways to new segments. In turn, each business unit had to develop new marketing plans with objectives to support the new long-term strategic direction of growth.

Marketers usually set two types of objectives in their marketing plans. **Marketing objectives** are targets for managing specific marketing relationships and activities, whereas **financial objectives** are targets for managing specific financial results. Here's a closer look at each (see Exhibit 5.2).

MARKETING OBJECTIVES

Marketing objectives should include targets for managing customer relationships because these are so critical to company success. Depending on the industry, the strategic direction, and the organization's mission and resources, marketers may set targets for acquiring new customers, retaining customers, increasing customer loyalty, and increasing customer satisfaction. Some firms go further, setting objectives for managing relationships with other stakeholders, such as channel partners. Nonprofits would set marketing objectives for managing relationships with members or contributors,

MARKETING OBJECTIVES
Targets for short-term performance in managing specific marketing relationships and activities.

FINANCIAL OBJECTIVES
Targets for short-term performance in managing specific financial results.

 **PATHFINDER'S TIP**
Ensure that marketing objectives can be achieved using the combination of marketing-mix tools, strengths, and resources available to the company.

EXHIBIT 5.2   Marketing and Financial Objectives

Type of Objective	*Purpose*	*Samples*
Marketing	Provide targets for managing specific marketing relationships and activities.	• Customer acquisition • Customer retention • Customer satisfaction • Channel relationships • Unit sales • Market share • Product development • Order fulfillment
Financial	Provide targets for managing specific financial results.	• Sales volume • Product sales • Channel sales • Profitability • Return on investment • Break-even

corporate sponsors, and so on. E-businesses would set objectives for managing relationships with registered customers or users, linked affiliates, and others. Here are some sample goals for managing marketing relationships:

- *Customer acquisition:* Expand the customer base by adding 200 small business customers during each month next year.
- *Customer retention:* Reduce the annual customer defection rate to 15 percent by the end of the year.
- *Customer satisfaction:* Score 95 percent or above on all of next year's quarterly customer satisfaction surveys.
- *Channel relationships:* Expand distribution by signing with 4 supermarket chains during next year.

In addition, marketers need to set objectives for sales, market share, and related activities. Similarly, nonprofits would set objectives for donations, grants, and related activities, just as e-businesses would set goals for sales, traffic, transactions, fulfillment, and so on. Office Depot, for example, recently set—and achieved—the goal of becoming the largest online retailer of office supplies (see home page in Exhibit 5.3). Now it has set growth objectives for boosting online sales and profits by increasing the proportion of store customers who buy online from 40 percent to 50 percent. "Our success is measured not by traffic to the site, but by sales," comments Monica Luechtefeld, executive vice president of e-commerce.[12]

Here are some sample objectives for managing marketing activities:

- *Unit sales:* Sell 500 units in each targeted segment during every month next year.
- *Market share:* Capture 3 percent of the U.S. frozen orange juice market by March 31.
- *Product development:* Develop and introduce two new products by December 31.
- *Order fulfillment:* Cut the time needed to fulfill online orders to 1 day by May 15.

EXHIBIT 5.3   OfficeDepot.com

FINANCIAL OBJECTIVES

PATHFINDER'S TIP

Set reasonable financial objectives that link to long-term organizational goals yet can be supported by practical schedules and budgets.

Although the exact financial objectives will vary from organization to organization, businesses and e-businesses generally quantify sales volume and product targets, profitability targets such as margin or pretax profit, return on investment (ROI) targets for marketing, and break-even targets. Nonprofits might set targets for fund raising, among other financial objectives.

To be effective, financial and marketing objectives must work together and be consistent in guiding decisions about marketing strategy and tactics. In practical terms, this means that a marketing objective of achieving a certain market share must be accompanied by a financial objective of achieving the equivalent sales volume. On the other hand, key financial objectives may have to give way if a company is to achieve a particularly coveted marketing objective. For example, Dell wanted to grab market share and surpass Compaq to become the market leader in global PC sales. To do this, it lowered PC prices while simultaneously cutting costs. Dell achieved its market leadership, but it also registered a drop in gross profit margins, despite the lower costs.[13]

Here are some sample financial objectives:

* *Sales volume:* Achieve $150,000 yearly sales volume by December 31.
* *Product sales:* Sell $3,000 worth of Product A every month.
* *Channel sales:* Increase monthly Internet sales to $50,000 by end of year.
* *Profitability:* Increase the gross profit margin to 25 percent by end of year.
* *Return on investment:* Achieve 17 percent ROI on funds invested in direct marketing activities.
* *Break-even:* Manage sales and costs to reach the break-even point by June 30.

LINKING STRATEGY, GOALS AND OBJECTIVES, TACTICS, AND PROGRAMS

PATHFINDER'S TIP

Think about the customer value the organization must create and deliver—through strategic direction, marketing tactics, and programs—to accomplish its goals and objectives.

The marketing plan becomes a practical map for action only when the strategic direction, overall goals, and objectives are translated into appropriate marketing mix tools and tactics, which in turn must be translated into day-to-day marketing programs. Exhibit 5.4 illustrates this strategy pyramid.

Strategic direction, goals, and objectives are shown at the top of the pyramid, because they are the guiding force behind the decisions made at lower levels of the pyramid and they indicate corporate priorities and allocation of resources. All the tactics and programs developed during the remainder of the marketing planning process must not only be consistent with the strategic direction, goals, and objectives in the marketing plan—they must actually support them.

Thus, by properly implementing the programs in the marketing plan and measuring its progress, the organization should find that it is moving in the chosen strategic direction and getting closer to accomplishing its financial and marketing objectives. Understanding this vital link between strategy, goals, objectives, tactics, and programs can help marketers avoid programs that are not appropriate for the strategic direction or that don't lead to the fulfillment of objectives and goals.

Refer to Appendix 3 for instructions on how to use *Marketing Plan Pro* software to document the decisions you have made about objectives, goals, and strategic direction in your written marketing plan.

EXHIBIT 5.4 Strategy Pyramid

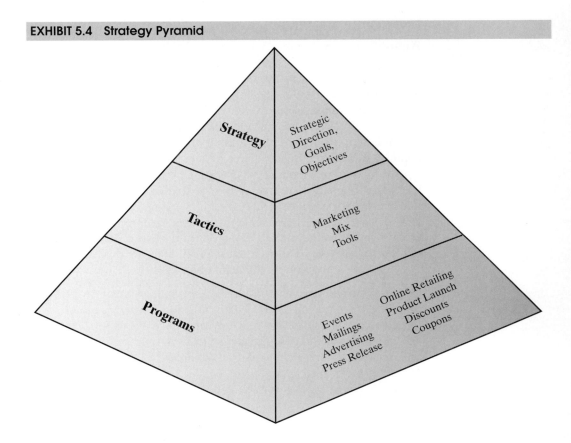

Chapter Summary

The organization's strengths and weaknesses, as well as its mission and goals, market and customer analysis, and environmental analysis are the backdrop against which marketers determine the strategic direction for the marketing plan. Among the strategic direction options are the pursuit of growth (including market penetration, market development, product development, and diversification), maintenance of current sales levels, and retrenchment (including, in the extreme, a strategy of downsizing). The chosen strategic direction must be consistent with priorities and resource allocations established by the organization.

Once the strategic direction is set, marketers have to establish marketing and financial objectives as short-term targets that will lead the organization toward its longer-term goals. Objectives are effective only if they are specific, time defined, and measurable; realistic but challenging; consistent with the mission and overall organizational goals; consistent with internal resources and core competencies; and appropriate for external environmental opportunities and threats. Marketing objectives are short-term performance targets for managing marketing relationships and activities; financial objectives are short-term performance targets for managing financial results. The strategy pyramid illustrates the principle that marketing tactics and programs must support the strategic direction, goals, and objectives documented in the marketing plan.

CHAPTER

6

Developing Marketing Strategies and Programs

Chapter Contents

- Overview of Marketing Mix Strategies and Programs
- Product Strategy
    - Features and Benefits
    - Quality
    - Packaging and Labeling
    - Related Services
    - Branding
    - Product Development and Management
- Place (Channel) Strategy
    - Channel Levels
    - Channel Members
    - Channel Functions
    - Logistics
- Pricing Strategy
    - Choice of Pricing Objective
    - Costs and Break-Even Analysis
    - Customer Perceptions and Demand
    - Competitive Situation
    - Price Adaptation
- Promotion Strategy
    - Promotion Tools
    - Choice of Target Audience
    - Choice of Promotion Objective
    - Message and Media
- Supporting the Marketing Mix
    - Customer Service Strategy
    - Internal Marketing Strategy
- Chapter Summary

MARKETING PATHFINDER'S QUOTE

"Achieving marketing excellence and delivering superior service are two sides of the same success coin."

—DR. A. PARASURAMAN, COAUTHOR OF *TECHNO-READY MARKETING: HOW AND WHY YOUR CUSTOMERS ADOPT TECHNOLOGY*[1]

Overview of Marketing Mix Strategies and Programs

 **PATHFINDER'S TIP**

In planning strategies and programs, marketers must remember the strategy pyramid and think about how progress will be measured using budgets, sales forecasts, and schedules.

All the earlier marketing planning steps provided vital background and direction for developing product, place, price, and promotion strategies to create and deliver value based on the needs and behavior of the targeted segments. These four marketing-mix elements must be supported with coordinated strategies for customer service and internal marketing—two factors that can make the difference in effectively implementing any marketing plan (Exhibit 6.1).

Consider how Rafael Alvarado, founder of Better Bags in Houston, developed and supported a marketing mix strategy to fuel the rapid growth of his small business:

Better Bags. Rafael Alvarado started Better Bags after he invented a better plastic bag and dispenser for the supermarket produce aisle. In total, the U.S. produce bag market is worth $170 million, with one competitor dominating nearly half the market. This means Alvarado must target carefully to compete. "We don't have the economy of scale to have the best price, so we've chosen to focus on value-added features," he says. The firm targets smaller grocery chains interested in customized imprinting and easy-use dispensers—key elements in the product offering. The channel strategy is to sell directly to the chains. The pricing strategy is to justify pricing 20 percent above competing bags by demonstrating valued benefits like lower waste. The promotion strategy is to invite chains to sample Better Bags' dispensers and bags at special trial discounts. Supporting this marketing mix, Alvarado provides attentive customer service and an internal marketing strategy of motivating employees—mainly new immigrants—through a full package of benefits and rewards. These strategies have helped Better Bags increase sales by 25 percent every year since 1996, to its current annual sales level of $15 million.[2]

EXHIBIT 6.1 Marketing Mix Strategy

Marketing Mix Strategies	**Targeted Customer Segments**	**Support Strategies**
• Product • Place • Pricing • Promotion		• Customer Service • Internal Marketing

Marketers must make decisions about key issues to customize each marketing mix strategy to the unique needs, circumstances, and environments of their customers. For example, product strategy is formulated through decisions about features and benefits, quality, packaging and labeling, related services, and branding. The other three marketing-mix strategies require decisions about other key issues, as outlined in this chapter.

Once marketing mix strategies have been formulated, the marketer can design and document individual marketing programs. These programs translate the strategies into action by outlining specific steps that will help the organization achieve its marketing and financial objectives. Programs indicate what will be done; as discussed in the next chapter, metrics, budgets, and schedules indicate exactly who will do it, and how and when.

The following sections look at the specific areas and issues that marketing pathfinders need to consider when making decisions about product, place, price, and promotion strategies. In the course of planning these strategies, companies often supplement their market and customer analyses with specific marketing research studies to answer questions about customer and competitive attributes, perceptions, and reactions. They also look at the results of previous years' strategies and programs to see what worked, what costs they incurred, and what returns they achieved. And they examine any environmental issues, such as legal and regulatory constraints, that can affect the use of a particular strategy or program.

Product Strategy

PATHFINDER'S TIP

Start with an analysis of existing goods and services and consider how each provides value to the customer segment being targeted.

This strategy covers the development and management of the company's tangible goods and intangible services to meet the needs of customers in targeted segments. The starting point is the analysis of current offerings, conducted earlier in the planning process as part of the internal environmental scan. This analysis puts the company's current offerings in the context of financial and marketing objectives and highlights strong and weak products in terms of age, share, geography, and distribution channels. Checklist 6.1 summarizes key questions to be asked in analyzing the current offerings and planning the product strategy for the marketing plan.

In the course of developing product strategy, marketers must look at the value of each good or service from the customer's perspective as well as the organization's perspective. In other words, the marketer must ask what value each product provides and to which customer segment, while simultaneously asking how the product helps the organization reach its marketing and financial objectives. From the customer's perspective, a product's value derives from the benefits delivered by its features; from its quality; from its packaging and labeling; from related services; and from its branding. The marketer must therefore make decisions about each of these elements to formulate a product strategy customized to its customers and circumstances.

FEATURES AND BENEFITS

FEATURES Specific attributes that enable the product to perform its function.

BENEFITS Need-satisfaction outcomes that customers desire from the product.

Features are specific attributes that enable the product to perform its function. In physical goods such as backpacks, features include padded shoulder straps and strong zippers; in intangible services such as Web-based banking, features include integrated display of all account information and one-click funds transfer. Features exist to deliver **benefits,** the need-satisfaction outcomes customers desire from a product. For example, a customer who buys an electric drill is seeking the benefit of creating holes for nails and screws.

CHECKLIST 6.1   Analyzing and Planning Product Strategy

Current Offerings

❑   What products are being offered, at what price points, and for what customer segments?

❑   What are the unit sales, revenues, and profit trends of each product over the years?

❑   What is the age of each product? How are newer products faring in relation to older products?

❑   What is the market share of each product or line?

❑   How does each product support sales of the line, i.e., are some sold only as supplements or add-ons to others?

❑   How does each product contribute to the company's overall performance and goals?

❑   Which product accounts for the largest proportion of sales and profits?

❑   How do product sales vary according to geography?

❑   How do product sales vary according to channel?

❑   What are the strengths and weaknesses of the current offerings?

Product Plans

❑   How does each product support the organization's objectives and strategic direction?

❑   What opportunities for adding value through product modifications or introductions exist in each segment?

❑   What strengths and core competencies apply to product strategy?

❑   What weaknesses and threats pose risks to product strategy? How can these be minimized or overcome?

❑   How do each product's features and benefits, quality, packaging, services, and branding provide value for customers? What enhancements would add value and help the company achieve its goals?

❑   How do each product's features and benefits, quality, packaging, services, and branding compare with competitive offerings?

❑   Where is each product in the life cycle, and what is required to align its stage and sales with the strategic direction and marketing plan objectives?

❑   How can product introductions be managed to minimize cannibalization?

❑   What changes to product lines and product mixes will help the company pursue its goals?

Consumers and business customers buy products not for their features alone but for the way those features provide valuable benefits in solving particular problems or fulfilling certain needs. Thus, marketing pathfinders need to be sure that the products they offer or plan to offer have features that deliver valued benefits to their targeted segments. Marketing research often reveals opportunities to compete and serve segments by adding value. Exhibit 6.2 shows how the Sonic personal digital assistant (PDA), a hypothetical competitor to Palm, matches some of its main features and benefits to key needs of two targeted segments.

Companies can compete more effectively when they design or promote features linked to benefits that better satisfy customer needs. Consider the Nintendo GameCube video game console:

Nintendo GameCube. Nintendo has long targeted the children's segment of the video game market. With its introduction of the GameCube console, however, the company shifted its targeting to the teen and twenty-something segment of

EXHIBIT 6.2 Needs, Features, and Benefits for Sonic Personal Digital Assistant			
Targeted Segment	*Need*	*Feature*	*Benefit*
Business travelers	Stay in touch while away from the office	Wireless e-mail	Conveniently send and receive messages from anywhere
Business travelers	Record information while away from the office	Voice recognition	Simple, no-hands to record information
College and graduate students	Express individuality	Case wardrobe of different colors and patterns	Change the case to make a fashion statement
College and graduate students	Perform multiple functions without carrying multiple gadgets	Works with Palm-compatible cameras, software, and other peripherals	Convenient, cost-effective way to do more

avid video game players. To satisfy the needs of this segment, GameCube included features such as a wireless controller (benefit: players have the freedom to move farther from the console) and connections for high-definition television and digital video cable (benefit: players can take advantage of advanced technology when and where available). It also offered consoles in blue, orange, or black (benefit: consumers can express their personalities or match other entertainment equipment colors). These features were designed to help Nintendo compete against Sony's PlayStation 2 and Microsoft's Xbox game consoles.[3]

E-businesses can use technology to provide valued benefits through features that are not easily duplicated by offline businesses. Consider the registry feature of Babiesrus.com:

Babiesrus.com. An online retailing joint venture of Amazon.com and Toys 'R' Us, Babiesrus.com offers an online baby registry feature, allowing parents to request gifts of products sold anywhere on Amazon.com, not just from the baby products pages.[4] This benefit, valued by the targeted segment of Net-savvy parents and their families and friends, helps to differentiate Babiesrus.com from rivals that lack such a broad registry feature. And by attracting more parents and more shoppers, the feature helps Babiesrus.com achieve financial and marketing objectives such as sales growth and market share targets.

QUALITY

QUALITY How well the product satisfies customer needs.

Although product **quality** is often defined in terms of performance capabilities, the most important definition is how well the product satisfies customers. By this definition, a high-quality product is one that does a competitively superior job of fulfilling customer needs. Savvy marketers know that the basic functionality of acceptable quality is only the price of entry in today's global, interconnected marketplace. Word-of-mouth (or word-of-mouse on the Web) can quickly sink a product with inferior quality—and just as quickly generate interest in a product with excellent quality. Good quality is no guarantee of success, but it can help companies attract new customers, retain existing customers, capture market share, charge higher prices, earn higher profits, or meet other financial and marketing objectives.

Yet overdesigning quality can lead to higher costs and higher prices. When *Smart Business* magazine evaluated PDAs on the basis of durability, performance, and price, it judged the Casio Cassiopeia to be overly rugged—making it bulkier and more expensive than less durable competing models.[5] In the race to differentiate a product, companies may wind up incorporating too many features at too high a price, dampening demand, sales, and profits. This is why companies need customer research to determine the optimal level of quality for each product and market segment.

PACKAGING AND LABELING

From the customer's perspective, packaging adds value by keeping tangible products safe and in convenient containers until they are used, while labeling adds value by communicating product contents, uses, and warnings. Thus, Kellogg's Corn Flakes stay fresh and uncrushed in the plastic-lined cardboard packaging, and Advil pain reliever tablets are kept out of tiny hands by child-resistant containers; both packages bear labels with information about product ingredients and consumption. Going beyond legal and regulatory requirements, a growing number of companies are planning environmentally friendly packaging and labeling to burnish brand image and demonstrate good corporate citizenship.

But design for functionality and ecological impact is only part of the story. Packaging and labeling also play an important marketing role for the company by creating competitive differentiation, highlighting the product's features and benefits, reinforcing the brand and its image, and attracting attention among customers and channel partners. In planning packaging, marketing pathfinders should aim for a design that sells the product from the shelf. Here's how Heinz Frozen Foods used new packaging to add value for customers and channel partners while boosting product sales:

> **Heinz Frozen Foods.** When Heinz repackaged Ore-Ida frozen potato products in bright red, resealable standup plastic bags, it wanted to allow customers the convenience of zipping bags closed after shaking out part of the contents. At the same time, the company reasoned that colorful packaging standing upright in the frozen food case would be more visible than packages lying flat, leading to higher product and retailer sales and higher market share: "We think we can improve sales by as much as 14 percent and the retailer's gross margin return on investment by 12 percent," said a Heinz executive.[6]

RELATED SERVICES

Service is part of nearly every product offering. In some cases, the service is itself the product; in other cases, one or more services are offered to complement a physical good. Based on marketing research into customer needs and expectations, more organizations are adding services to their product offerings as a way to enhance customer value, strengthen customer relationships, and achieve marketing and financial objectives. For example, General Motors (GM) created the OnStar wireless communication system as a fee-based option to add value to its vehicles by allowing customers to obtain driving directions, trade stocks, and handle other in-vehicle tasks. This unique service, which attracts up to 4,000 new subscribers daily, is helping GM satisfy more of its customers' needs while bringing in additional revenue month after month.[7]

Even marketers of services are planning new services to enhance the features and benefits of their offerings for targeted segments:

> **Charles Schwab.** The brokerage firm Charles Schwab researched the needs of two market segments it was targeting for its online brokerage services: active online traders and customers of traditional brokerage firms. It found that active online traders like to click and research securities before buying and selling, whereas customers of traditional brokerages want detailed answers to their investment questions. In response, Schwab added online service features such as easier access to investment research reports, more sophisticated stock screening tools, and customized, automated responses to individual investors' questions.[8]

BRANDING

 **PATHFINDER'S TIP**

Use branding to support growth strategies and related objectives by planning a line extension or a brand extension.

BRANDING Using words, designs, or symbols to give a product a distinct identity and differentiate it from competing products.

CUSTOMER LIFE-TIME VALUE Total amount a customer spends with a company over the course of a long-term relationship.

LINE EXTENSION Putting an established brand on a new product added to the existing product line.

BRAND (CATE-GORY) EXTENSION Putting an established brand on a new product in a different category, aimed at a new customer segment.

Branding gives a product a distinct identity and differentiates it from competing products using words, designs, and symbols. After customers learn to associate a brand with a particular set of features, benefits, and quality, they simplify the decision-making process by routinely buying that brand rather than stopping to evaluate every alternative on every shopping trip. Thus, a strong brand encourages customer loyalty and increases **customer lifetime value,** the total amount a customer spends with a company over the course of a long-term relationship. Because of this loyalty, a strong brand also can provide some insulation against competitive threats.

The brand may include the company name (Kellogg's Corn Flakes) or rely on individual names for different products, categories, or channels (Kmart for the store name, bluelight.com for the online retail brand). Brands should be recognizable and memorable, capable of being legally protected, and suitable for international markets if the company pursues future global expansion. Online brands are not immune to these basic branding guidelines. Yahoo! and Amazon.com have become strong and distinctive brands through constant and consistent marketing communication, whereas Books.com and many other nonspecific brands have struggled or have been acquired.

Marketers need to be careful when establishing what their brand stands for, because a strong brand image is not easily changed. GM has been trying for years to broaden the appeal of its venerable Cadillac brand, a favorite of older auto buyers. But lower quality and cost-cutting model designs—coupled with strong competition from Lexus, BMW, and other luxury cars—have hurt Cadillac's sales and market share. Now GM is introducing bolder model designs, improving quality, and adding features in a high-stakes bid to get its brand noticed by the younger, more affluent segment of car buyers.[9]

In marketing planning, a company may choose to support a growth strategy by putting an established brand on a new product added to the existing product line, creating a **line extension**. Nabisco did this when it extended the Oreo line by introducing Chocolate Creme Oreo cookies to capitalize on the brand's continued sales growth within a stagnant cookie category.

Another path to growth is a **brand (or category) extension,** putting an established brand on a new product in a different category, aimed at a new customer segment. The

Canadian apparel chain Roots did this when it started Roots Air, an airline aimed at business travelers who want to fly in style for less. Similarly, Motley Fool has leveraged its personal finance brand to expand into new categories such as newsletters, books, seminars, and e-commerce (on fool.com).[10] Either extension strategy can help a new good or service achieve customer acceptance, if marketing research shows that the brand has a positive image consistent with the segment's needs, expectations, and perceptions.

PRODUCT DEVELOPMENT AND MANAGEMENT

PRODUCT LIFE CYCLE Theory that identifies the stages of introduction, growth, maturity, and decline through which a product moves in the marketplace.

Marketing pathfinders use product strategy to manage the progress of a product through the **product life cycle** of introduction, growth, maturity, and decline (Exhibit 6.3). Even experts have difficulty predicting the exact length and shape of a product's life cycle, which limits the practical application of this theory. However, marketers can look at sales trends for clues to a particular product's life cycle stage: new products with low but growing sales are considered in the introduction stage; young products with rapidly increasing sales are in the growth stage; existing products with relatively level sales are in maturity; and older products with decreasing sales are in decline. These stages can be influenced by environmental factors such as competition and customer needs, so marketers need to carefully monitor the environment as they interpret sales trends.

Deciding to do away with a product or line in decline is not an easy decision, and it has a ripple effect far beyond the targeted segments, GM learned from its Oldsmobile experience:

> **Oldsmobile.** The Oldsmobile line was 103 years old when GM finally gave up on plans to revive it. Big hits like the Cutlass helped sell more than 1 million Olds vehicles annually at the peak in the 1980s, but 1990s products like the Aurora and Bravada just didn't attract enough buyers. Late in 2000, GM finally announced its decision to drop the Olds line because it was unprofitable and selling only 289,000 vehicles per year. GM knew its customers would be concerned, so it promised to continue servicing Olds vehicles and to make critical parts available for at least 15 years. GM's financing division said it would arrange loans and leases as long as Olds vehicles were being sold, but Bank of America and others stopped writing Olds leases because of concerns over lower resale values. Dealers also felt the effects of GM's decision. Some dedicated Olds dealerships expected to close, while others planned to sell other lines. Still, GM CEO Rick Wagoner says that phasing out Olds was the right decision: "We've devoted a lot of resources in bringing out new Olds products over the last several years. I have a clear conscience that we gave it a chance."[11]

Just as GM's future marketing plans will map every step leading to the eventual phase-out of the Oldsmobile line, its plans will also lay out the steps needed to complete the product development process for new vehicles. This critical process starts with the generation and screening of new ideas, followed by initial concept testing, business analysis, prototype design, market testing, and the ultimate commercialization of the new product.

CANNIBALIZATION Allowing a new product to cut into sales of one or more existing products.

Companies generally make decisions about new products and life cycle movement to avoid or minimize **cannibalization**—allowing a new product to eat into sales of one

EXHIBIT 6.3   Product Strategy from Development through the Life Cycle

Idea Generation and Screening	Initial Concept Testing	Business Analysis	Design Prototype	Market Testing	Commercialization
• Based on customer needs and wants, identify new product ideas	• Research customer value of product concepts	• Estimate development, production, and marketing-mix costs	• Design and produce working prototypes	• Test customer reaction through limited market trials or simulated testing	• Plan targeting and timing of launch
• Screen out unprofitable or unsuitable ideas	• Refine concept based on research	• Compare costs with potential share, sales, profitability to identify good candidates	• Test prototype functionality, customer appeal	• Test different marketing-mix combinations for support	• Plan production and marketing-mix support for launch

Introduction	Growth	Maturity	Decline
• Launch the new product	• Enhance product (new features, improved quality, added services, new packaging)	• Add brand or line extensions	• Reposition, reformulate, or cut struggling products
• Support launch with marketing-mix programs to build customer awareness, make product available, and encourage trial	• Support rising sales with expanded channel coverage, pricing for market penetration, and communications to start and reinforce customer relationships	• Defend market share through competitive pricing, channel expansion, communicating differentiation, and promotion to reinforce customer loyalty	• Manage profitability through careful pricing, pruning channel outlets, and minimal or highly targeted communications

or more existing products. Some cannibalization is inevitable in high-tech markets, where life cycles are relatively short because competitors race to launch the next breakthrough product. Companies in these markets often take the view that if they don't cannibalize their own products, rivals will seize the opportunity to grab both sales and customer relationships. Rather than completely cannibalize a product, however, the firm may prefer to reposition it for other uses or segments. In the computer world, for example, expensive chips that were state-of-the-art last year may be priced lower than today's top performing chips and repositioned for use in stripped-down computers designed for segments where computing power is less of a priority and customers are more price sensitive.

New technology is causing music publishers to consider cannibalization issues:

> **Virgin Records and EMI Recorded Music.** These two music publishers are testing the digital release of single songs that consumers can download and burn onto CDs using their personal computers. Concerned that releasing the singles in the regular (nondigital) formats could cannibalize sales of the albums, the publishers chose to allow only digital downloads, which are being distributed by Liquid Audio to online retailers for sale at $3.49 per song. One advantage is that consumers will be able to buy and download versions of songs that are not available on albums; another is that consumers who like the single may be encouraged to buy the entire album. On the other hand, "if you give a track away as a free download, that may lead to cannibalization," observes a Liquid Audio executive. The publishers will be closely monitoring sales for signs of significant cannibalization.[12]

In planning for new products, marketers need to look closely at potential opportunities for providing value in each segment. They also must consider how to build on internal strengths and core competencies to create and launch competitively superior products for targeted segments, while finding ways to compensate for internal weaknesses and overcome external threats.

Marketing planning also covers the management of all products in the line and all lines in the mix. As Exhibit 6.4 indicates, decisions about product strategy affect the length and width of product lines and mixes. Longer product lines and wider product mixes typically require more resources to develop and sustain, but they help companies grow and pursue ambitious financial and marketing objectives. In contrast, shortening and narrowing lines and mixes can help the firm concentrate its resources on the most promising products and segments for survival, maintenance, or future growth.

EXHIBIT 6.4   Product Line and Mix Decisions

Decision	*Result*
New product	Lengthens product line
Line extension	Lengthens product line
New line	Widens product mix
Brand extension	Widens product mix
Product deletion	Shortens product line
Line deletion	Narrows product mix

Place (Channel) Strategy

PATHFINDER'S TIP

Design the channel strategy based on customer and market analysis and the product, pricing, and promotion strategies.

The second major component of the marketing mix is place strategy, covering the company's use of channel intermediaries such as wholesalers, retailers, and agents, to make goods and services available to customers. This strategy must be carefully coordinated with the product's progression through the life cycle and with pricing and promotion decisions. It also must be based on a thorough understanding of the customer (how do customers expect or prefer to gain access to the product?) and the market (how are channel choices affected by competition, legal issues, geographic considerations, channel costs, and other realities?). Checklist 6.2 highlights the main questions to ask when formulating channel strategy.

Michael Dell's experience shows how channel strategy can provide an effective competitive edge, even for a start-up battling established industry giants:

Dell Computer. Michael Dell began by custom building PCs and selling directly to customers via mail and telephone. He priced his PCs lower than comparable computers sold in stores because he built only as needed and ordered, and he

---

CHECKLIST 6.2 Planning Channel Strategy

Channel Issues

❑ How do customers expect or prefer to gain access to the product? How do these customer requirements affect channel choices?

❑ How are current channel arrangements contributing to financial and marketing objectives for sales, profits, and so on?

❑ Which channels and members perform the best, and at what cost to the company?

❑ Does the product have any unique characteristics that affect channel plans and costs?

❑ How do product life cycle, positioning, and market targeting affect channel choices?

❑ How do environmental issues such as competition, legal limitations, and geographical constraints affect channel choices?

❑ How do internal capabilities and product plans affect channel choices?

❑ How many channel levels are needed or desirable to make products available to targeted segments? What resources and issues are connected with channel level choices?

❑ How many channel members are needed at each channel level and each life-cycle stage? What resources and issues are connected with channel member choices?

Logistical Issues

❑ What logistical functions must be performed and by which channel members?

❑ Who will transport and store supplies, parts, and finished products—and how and when?

❑ How will inventory levels be managed—and by whom?

❑ Who will collect, analyze, and exchange data about orders, billing, and payment—and how and when?

❑ How do production- and sales-related objectives affect logistical plans?

❑ How are logistics affected by customer requirements and preferences, channel and company capabilities, and product plans?

❑ Will the organization handle its own logistics or hire others to handle some or all of these functions?

didn't have to factor in profits for retailers. This channel strategy enabled Dell to successfully challenge larger, more established rivals like IBM and Compaq. When Dell began selling PCs via the Internet, it was able to cut costs even more and let customers configure their own PCs by choosing among dozens of features and options. Now the leading PC marketer in the world, Dell uses its direct marketing model to sell as much as $50 million worth of PCs and related products via the Web every day.[13]

The Internet has revolutionized channel arrangements in a number of industries by opening new paths for connections between marketers and customers. Now marketers can offer software or music files for immediate download, a cheaper alternative to requiring customers to buy physical products. Marketers for travel services, insurance policies, and other intangibles are also finding the online channel a cost-effective way to reach targeted customer segments. In fact, the online channel has already altered the channel structure of several industries. For example, within 3 years of the emergence of Expedia, Travelocity, and other popular travel sites, the number of non-Web travel agents had dropped by 15 percent.[14]

Among the key decisions marketers must make when developing channel strategy are the number of channel levels, number of channel members, channel functions, and logistics. In making these decisions, marketers take into account their need for control, the company's ability to handle different channel functions, the size and composition of the market, and the availability of interested and suitable intermediaries.

CHANNEL LEVELS

How many channel levels are needed or desirable to make products available to targeted segments? The higher the number of channel levels, the more intermediaries are involved in making the product available. A zero-level channel refers to a direct channel linking seller and buyer. Dell used this type of channel when it bypassed wholesalers and retailers to sell directly to customers. However, Dell entered the market during the growth stage of the product life cycle, when PCs were still selling strongly and were already fairly commonplace—so customers knew enough about the product to risk placing an order without a demonstration.

New products often need considerable support from channel members, which means marketers launching something new must plan on using a one-level, two-level, or even three-level channel to reach their customers. In a one-level channel, the seller works with a single intermediary, usually a retailer in consumer markets or an industrial distributor in business markets. Each level in the channel adds value in some way, by making the product available in a convenient place or providing information and samples of how to use it. In exchange, each level expects to profit from the sale to the next level or to the final customer, costs that must be factored into the ultimate selling price.

Some products, such as automotive parts and accessories, are customarily distributed through established two- or three-level channels, so manufacturers with new products must find ways of breaking into those channels to reach targeted segments, not always easy with an unproven product or brand. The marketing plan also should allow for reverse channels when needed to return products for exchange, repair, or recycling. This is particularly critical for e-businesses that have no physical presence and for any business offering products that can be recycled or that need proper disposal to protect the environment. That's why Hewlett-Packard, for example, includes a prepaid label with each laser toner cartridge so customers can easily return empty cartridges for recycling.

CHANNEL MEMBERS

How many and what type of channel members will be needed at each channel level? The answer depends on the product's life-cycle stage, its positioning, and the segment being targeted. At introduction, an innovative new product may be offered in just a limited number of outlets to reinforce its novelty and allow sales staff to learn about its features and benefits. In the decline stage, companies may sell through fewer channel members to minimize shipping and distribution costs. Moreover, products with a luxury positioning would cheapen their image if sold in many stores or in discount stores; conversely, impulse items like gum would not achieve high sales volumes if sold only in exclusive specialty stores. Also, each channel member has certain profit expectations, which affects the company's cost of distributing its product.

How customers buy or use the product is a major factor in decisions about channel members. Products that are bought frequently and on impulse should be distributed as widely as possible, whereas products bought after a lengthy evaluation process and with intense sales support need only be distributed through a limited number of more specialized outlets. Clearly, marketers must analyze customers' needs and habits to uncover new channel opportunities. Consider the experience of Commonwealth Bank of Australia (CBA):

Commonwealth Bank of Australia. CBA wanted to start banking relationships with more segments within the Australian market, so it partnered with the Woolworth chain to reach a broad cross-section of shoppers by opening bank branches inside stores. The venture, known as Woolworth's Ezy Banking, attracted 150,000 customers before the national rollout ended, a good start toward CBA's longer-term goal of serving 1 million customers in store-based branches within 5 years. "A quarter of the customer base is aged between 15 and 28 and a further quarter is aged 45 and over, which further confirms customers of all ages are attracted to this unique offer," notes a CBA executive. And 40 percent of the new customers had no prior relationship with CBA. Woolworth is also profiting, because Ezy Banking customers spend 20 percent more yearly in the store than nonbanking customers spend.[15]

PATHFINDER'S TIP

Consider how much cost and control must be exchanged for the value added by each channel level and intermediary.

CHANNEL FUNCTIONS

What functions should each channel member handle? The channel as a whole must perform a variety of functions to make the right assortment of products, in the right sizes, available to consumers or business customers at the right time and in the right place, with the right touch of service. These value-added functions include matching the volume, amount, or offer to customer needs; providing customers and other channel members with product and market information; contacting and negotiating with customers to maintain relationships and complete sales; and transporting and storing products prior to purchase.

During the marketing planning process, companies must determine which channel functions each intermediary will handle, and how each will be compensated for the value it adds. There are marketers who handle many functions themselves because they want to control the quality and the customer relationship; others delegate selected functions to reduce costs and unnecessary movement of goods. Amazon.com, for example, recently arranged for Ingram Book Group, a wholesaler, to fulfill some orders by shipping books directly to customers. "You won't be able to tell if a book is sent from our center in Fernley, Nevada, or Ingram in La Vergne, Tennessee," says an Amazon vice president. On the other hand, rival Barnesandnoble.com's CEO is against such arrangements, noting, "I can't see entrusting our customer relationships to an outside company. If things go wrong, you are in for a pot of trouble."[16]

LOGISTICS

LOGISTICS
Managing the movement of goods, services, and related information from the point of origin to the point of sale or consumption.

Logistics covers the movement of goods, services, and related information from the point of origin to the point of sale or consumption. In the marketing plan, the company's channel strategy should address these key logistical decisions:

- who will transport and store supplies, parts, and finished products—and how and when
- how inventory levels will be managed, and by whom
- who will collect, analyze, and share data on customer orders, billing, and payment—and how and when

Ideally, the company wants to make its logistical arrangements both effective and efficient, so it doesn't overspend to get supplies, products, and information where and when they should be. It might choose to handle all these logistical functions, or ask intermediaries or specialized firms to handle selected functions. For example, new e-businesses and other start-ups often outsource logistical operations to avoid the initial expense of building and managing warehouses and distribution centers. Such decisions should be made in the context of customer requirements and preferences, channel and company capabilities, product plans, and production- and sales-related objectives.

Logistics can help companies strengthen relationships with channel partners while making the right product available to customers at the right time. Campbell Soup, for example, collects sales and inventory data from major retail chains every business day, then uses an automatic replenishment system to ship replacement stock to the chains as needed. The retailers save money, because they have less inventory sitting idle in their distribution centers and don't run out of popular products; for its part, Campbell can more efficiently allocate stock to the right locations.[17]

Few companies have logistical budgets as large or requirements as complex as that of General Mills, which annually spends $400 million just for shipping goods in volume from factories to distribution centers to stores. Still, its approach to logistics management shows how creative thinking about a function as routine as shipping can boost the bottom line. General Mills knows that shipping costs of products account for a whopping 60 percent of the expense of getting its products to the supermarket. Searching for additional paths to profitability, General Mills marketers found they could cut trucking costs by $24 million by sharing truck space for supermarket deliveries with other consumer products manufacturers.[18]

Pricing Strategy

 **PATHFINDER'S TIP**

Look for ways to avoid price-only competition by highlighting the value being provided through product, promotion, or channel differentiation.

Pricing strategy, the third major marketing mix component, is complex but crucial because it is the only component that directly produces revenue. Savvy pricing has helped upstarts successfully enter highly competitive markets, the way Amazon.com has taken on Barnes and Noble and Borders in the book market and JetBlue Airways has challenged American Airlines and other carriers in the air travel market. Although Amazon.com and JetBlue use lower prices as a major customer appeal, higher prices can be an effective tool for marketers aiming at affluent segments. Neiman Marcus and Saks Fifth Avenue support their upscale retail positioning with relatively high prices, while Mercedes-Benz reinforces its top-quality image through relatively high prices. Thus, pricing strategy is inextricably linked to both positioning and targeting.

In addition, pricing is closely connected to marketing mix decisions about product, channel, and promotion strategies. Marketers use pricing as one of the tools to manage the product life cycle and achieve specific objectives. Some companies use *skimming pricing* during the introduction stage of the life cycle, setting an initial high price to establish a high-end image and more quickly recover development costs in line with profitability objectives. Others prefer *penetration pricing,* pricing products relatively low to gain market share in a short period.

Cutting price will often help a company with a mature product defend market share or quickly clear declining products to make way for new ones. Pricing also helps recoup product development costs and distinguish the value of the features and benefits of different products in the overall product line. In terms of channel strategy, pricing influences decisions about suppliers, logistics, and channel members. In terms of promotion strategy, higher-priced products aimed at affluent segments are often promoted in different media and with different messages than lower-priced products aimed at lower-income segments.

Pricing is frequently the marketing weapon of choice for companies battling rivals in the airline industry or in telecommunications, to name just two intensely competitive markets. Yet nonprice competition—through product, promotion, or channel differentiation—can provide an even more powerful advantage, because these strategies are not as easily matched. Prices can be changed in an instant, but product, promotion, and distribution changes take much longer and require more resources to execute.

DYNAMIC PRICING A strategy in which prices are varied from customer to customer or situation to situation.

FIXED PRICING A strategy in which prices do not vary from customer to customer or situation to situation.

In fact, price changes are becoming much more commonplace with the rising popularity of **dynamic pricing**, a strategy in which prices are varied from customer to customer or situation to situation, unlike **fixed pricing**, where the prices do not vary. Dynamic pricing is used by eBay, Priceline.com, and other online auction and reverse-auction sites in the consumer market; it is also used by numerous industrial marketplaces in the business market. Some retailers are even selling selected products through dynamic pricing. JCPenney.com uses dynamic pricing on its Auction and Falling Prices pages, where prices may go up or down depending on inventory supply and customer demand.[19]

However, fixed pricing is still the norm in most markets, especially for companies selling consumer products through retailers and other intermediaries; nonetheless, firms serving business markets are finding that a growing number of large industrial customers favor dynamic pricing when buying commodities and certain supplies and parts. Such pricing policies are an important factor in making pricing decisions, although marketers can get around industry pricing customs with offers that are particularly unique or compelling.

When making decisions about pricing strategy, marketing pathfinders need to consider internal factors such as the company's choice of pricing objective and its costs and break-even calculations. They also need to examine external factors such as customers' perceptions of value—which affect demand—and the competitive situation, both particularly important when entering new segments or marketing new products.[20] These internal and external factors help the marketer zero in on an appropriate price range, while price adaptations help the company modify the price for a specific product. Legal and regulatory considerations apply, as well, although those are not covered here but are mentioned in Checklist 6.3, which summarizes questions to be explored in the process of planning pricing strategy.

CHOICE OF PRICING OBJECTIVE

What does the organization want its pricing strategy to achieve? Pricing objectives, the first internal factor, should be tied to the marketing and financial objectives and the strategic direction and objectives examined earlier in the marketing planning process (see Exhibit 6.5). However, due to market realities, organizations may have to trade off one type of pricing objective for another. Rarely can a company achieve stunningly high profitability while simultaneously raising its market share to a much higher level.

CHECKLIST 6.3 Planning Pricing Strategy

Internal Factors

❑ What does the organization want its pricing strategy to achieve?
❑ How can pricing be used to support positioning and targeting decisions?
❑ How can pricing be used to manage the product life cycle and product line objectives?
❑ How can pricing support the marketing and financial objectives?
❑ How do channel decisions affect pricing?
❑ How do promotion decisions affect pricing?
❑ Is the emphasis going to be on price or nonprice competition?
❑ What are the product's costs, and how do they affect the price floor?
❑ What is the break-even point at different volume levels? How do different prices affect revenues, volume, and break-even?

External Factors

❑ How do industry customs affect pricing?
❑ How do customers perceive the balance between a product's price and its benefits?
❑ Are customers in the targeted segment price-sensitive? Are customers in other segments less price-sensitive?
❑ What are the prices and costs of competing products, and how do they affect the price ceiling?
❑ What nonprice alternatives exist for reacting to competitive price changes?

Price Adaptation

❑ Are discounts an appropriate tactic for achieving pricing objectives?
❑ Are allowances an appropriate tactic for achieving pricing objectives?
❑ Is bundling an appropriate tactic for achieving pricing objectives?
❑ Is product enhancement an appropriate tactic for achieving pricing objectives?
❑ Is loss-leader pricing an appropriate tactic for achieving pricing objectives?
❑ Is it necessary or advisable to raise prices, and if so, how?
❑ How do organizational resources, capabilities, goals, and strategic direction affect pricing and price adjustments?

As Amazon.com, Dell, and others have learned, such market share gains often depend on low prices or price reductions, which in turn can mean lower profits. Thus, pricing objectives should be consistent with each other and with the overall marketing plan objectives.

Repsol Petroleum, which operates a chain of gasoline stations in the United Kingdom, recently had to resolve a conflict between pricing and financial objectives:

> **Repsol.** Repsol, based in Chelmsford, competes with Esso, among other gasoline giants. When Esso announced a policy of matching any price in its market area— no matter how low—every competitor felt the downward pricing pressure. Repsol analyzed price and volume trade-offs at each of its 56 company-owned stations and found that 14 could not price competitively without returning profit margins below the level set in the financial objectives. As a result of this analysis, Repsol decided to close those 14 stations. "We now sell more volume with 42 sites than we did with 56, and see higher gross profits," says a Repsol manager.[21]

COSTS AND BREAK-EVEN ANALYSIS

PATHFINDER'S TIP

If the company doesn't know or hasn't measured exact costs, use close estimates and start tracking and refining the figures so the company will have more accurate data for next year's marketing plan.

Another internal pricing factor is an understanding of the organization's costs and its break-even point—the sales level at which revenue covers costs. The point is to define the theoretical floor of the pricing range, the lowest price at which the company will cover its costs. Costs and break-even are more easily calculated for existing products in existing market segments, where marketers can use historical results as a basis for future projections. For new products and segments, marketers must rely on research-based forecasts and expert estimates of costs and sales volume. In either case, marketers may only be able to make an educated guess about the company's costs and future sales.

Now marketers have to look more closely at total costs, which are made up of fixed costs—overhead expenses such as rent and payroll, which don't vary with volume—and variable costs—expenses such as raw materials. Knowing total costs, the company can calculate the average cost of producing a single item (total costs divided by production) at different output levels, corresponding to different assumptions about

EXHIBIT 6.5 Sample Pricing Objectives	
Type of Objective	*Sample Pricing Objectives*
Financial	• To support profitability: Set prices to achieve a gross profit margin of 40% on this year's sales.
	• To support return on investment: Set prices to achieve ROI of 18% for the full year.
	• To cover costs: Set prices to break-even on sales within 2 months.
Marketing	• To support higher market share: Set prices to achieve a market share of 7% within 6 months.
	• To support higher sales: Set prices to achieve a sales increase of 12% over last year.
	• To support customer acquisition: Set prices to attract 1,500 new customers from January to June.

demand. This reveals cost changes at different output levels and indicates how low the company might price the product at each level to at least cover its costs.

A more sophisticated but complex way to manage costs and pricing is by **target costing.** This entails the use of research to determine what customers want in a product and the price they will pay for it. Then the company works backward from that price to find ways of producing the product at a reasonable cost while returning a reasonable profit.

TARGET COSTING Using research to determine what customers want in a product and the price they will pay, then finding ways of producing the product at a cost that will accommodate that price and return a profit.

Knowing its costs, the company can now calculate the break-even point and see how a price will affect revenues and profits at different sales levels. The formula for calculating the break-even volume is:

$$\text{Break-even volume} = \frac{\text{fixed cost}}{\text{price} - \text{variable cost}}$$

Exhibit 6.6 illustrates a sample break-even analysis for a company that manufactures specialized software for dentists. In this example, the price (unit revenue) is $995, the variable cost is $45 per unit, and the fixed cost totals $40,500. Thus, the calculation is:

$$\text{Break-even volume} = \frac{40,500}{995 - 45} = \frac{40,500}{950} = 42.6 \text{ units (rounded up to 43)}$$

The charting function in *Marketing Plan Pro* (or the graph function in a spreadsheet program) visually indicates this point and shows how profits increase as sales volume rises beyond the break-even volume of 43 units.

CUSTOMER PERCEPTIONS AND DEMAND

How do customers perceive the balance between a product's price and its benefits? This is one of the major external factors affecting pricing. As noted in Chapter 1, value is the difference between perceived benefits and perceived price. The higher the benefits in relation to price, the higher the value. Thus, the marketer must research and analyze customers' perceptions of the total price—including shipping and any other additional or hidden costs—as well as perceptions of the product's benefits when planning pricing strategy. If customers deem the price too high in relation to the benefits, they simply won't buy, which will lower demand. On the other hand, if the price is perceived as too low for the level of quality that the customer expects, demand also will suffer.

On the Web, where customers can compare prices at the click of a mouse, high perceived value is helping many e-businesses compete. Consider how Overstock.com has combined below-wholesale pricing with good service to profitably attract and serve price-sensitive consumers:

Overstock.com. When an e-business is about to go under, Overstock.com personnel show up, checkbook in hand, offering to buy its inventory for a fraction of the original wholesale price. That's how Overstock.com was able to buy $12 million worth of jewelry from Miadora.com and Jewelry.com for just $2.5 million, and $11.5 million worth of toys from ToyTime.com for just $3.7 million. Because its cost is so low, Overstock.com can often sell the product for less than the usual wholesale price, a bona fide bargain in any customer's value equation. Add in free shipping, a money-back guarantee, and responsive customer service, and the value package looks even better to the customer—and extremely profitable for Overstock.com.[22]

EXHIBIT 6.6   Break-Even Analysis

Fixed Costs		
Creation of printed material graphics and text	$	3,200
Creation of CD-ROM graphics	$	650
Initial set up fee for CD	$	1,600
Initial set up fee for printed materials	$	1,250
Production of 2,000 demo units	$	30,750
Estimated Fixed Costs	$	40,550
Per–unit variable costs (to fulfill orders sold)	$	45
Per–unit revenue	$	995
Break-even (in Units)		43

Break-Even Analysis:		
Assumptions:		
Average Per–Unit Revenue	$	995
Average Per–Unit Variable Cost	$	45
Estimated Fixed Costs	$	40,550
Units Break–even		43
Sales Break–even	$	42,471

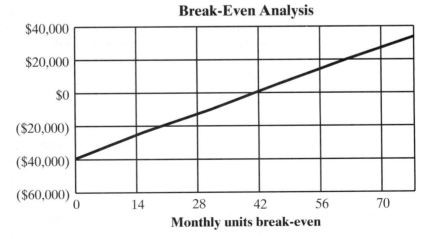

Break-Even Analysis

Units break-even point = where line intersects with $0

Through research, companies can determine customers' price sensitivity, which affects the level of demand for a product at different price points. Such research is faster and easier for products offered on the Web. In general, customers look at more than price when making a buying decision, and they are less sensitive to a product's price when they:

- are unaware of or can't easily compare substitutes
- are unaware of the price of substitutes
- perceive the product to be highly differentiated
- would incur costs or difficulties in switching
- perceive that the quality or prestige justifies the price
- are spending a relatively insignificant amount or are sharing the cost[23]

Clearly, the challenge is to identify a price range that is acceptable to customers and simultaneously allows the company to achieve its marketing plan objectives. Overstock.com does this by using bargain prices to serve the price-sensitive segment of the consumer market with a healthy profit margin. However, other companies like Repsol may choose to ignore the price-sensitive segment and focus instead on segments that will pay prices above the rock-bottom range. Companies also may decide to focus on customer segments that perceive value in the product but cost less for the company to serve, thereby delivering better profit margins.

COMPETITIVE SITUATION

Understanding customers' perceptions and the impact on demand is one external clue to an acceptable price range (the ceiling, in particular). The competitive situation provides another external clue. By analyzing the prices, special deals, and probable costs of competing products, a company can get a better sense of the alternatives that are available to customers and the pricing objectives and strategies set by rivals.

Repsol found that Esso's price-matching policy forced it to lower prices to compete or risk losing customers and sales. Esso appeared to be emphasizing the marketing objectives of market share and customer acquisition over the financial objective of profitability; it was also a much larger corporation and could spread its costs over a higher overall volume. Repsol was more concerned with its profit objective, so it responded by closing 14 gas stations where it could not profitably compete, keeping a close eye on the competitive situation surrounding the remaining stations.

Thus, competitors' pricing strategies can not only set the effective ceiling for the product's price in a given segment, they can affect more than just price. In response to competitive price changes, a company can withdraw from a particular market or segment (as Repsol did) or take one of the alternative actions shown in Exhibit 6.7. These possible responses can be analyzed in the pricing strategy and contingency planning sections of the marketing plan.

PRICE ADAPTATION

If internal factors indicate the price floor and external factors indicate the price ceiling, price adaptation helps companies modify and fine-tune prices within the range—or even beyond. Marketers may use price adaptation to lower the price (such as discounts and allowances) or add value (such as bundling and product enhancements), or both:

- *Discounts.* Many companies offer quantity discounts for buying in volume and seasonal discounts for buying out of season. Business customers also may earn a cash discount for prompt payment; intermediaries may earn a functional discount for performing specific channel functions.

EXHIBIT 6.7 Alternative Reactions to Competitive Price Cuts		
Strategic Options	*Reasoning*	*Consequences*
1. Maintain price and perceived quality. Engage in selective customer pruning.	Firm has higher customer loyalty. It is willing to lose poorer customers to competitors.	Smaller market share Lowered profitability
2. Raise price and perceived quality.	Raise price to cover rising costs. Improve quality to justify higher prices.	Smaller market share Maintained profitability
3. Maintain price and raise perceived quality.	It is cheaper to maintain price and raise perceived quality.	Smaller market share Short-term decline in profitability Long-term increase in profitability
4. Cut price partly and raise perceived quality.	Must give customers some price reduction but stress higher value of offer.	Maintained market share Short-term decline in profitability Long-term maintained profitability
5. Cut price fully and maintain perceived quality.	Discipline and discourage price competition.	Maintained market share Short-term decline in profitability
6. Cut price fully and reduce perceived quality.	Discipline and discourage price competition and maintain profit margin.	Maintained market share Maintained margin Reduced long-term profitability
7. Maintain price and reduce perceived quality.	Cut marketing expense to combat rising costs.	Smaller market share Maintained margin Reduced long-term profitability
8. Introduce an economy model.	Give the market what it wants.	Some cannibalization but higher total volume

- *Allowances.* Intermediaries often receive discounts, extra payment, or extra product allocations for participating in a special promotion. Companies often offer trade-in allowances for businesses or consumers who turn in an older product and buy a new one.
- *Bundling.* The company may enhance customer perceptions of a product's value by bundling it with another good or service at one price. McDonald's meal deals, for example, are priced lower than the sum of the individual menu items but help the firm sell more soft drinks and fries, boosting overall profit margin. Unbundling can be used if the bundle price is perceived as too high and individual products will sell well on their own.
- *Product enhancement.* Enhancing the product to raise its perceived value can help the company maintain or raise price. As an example, Goodyear developed specialized tires for better performance in rain or snow. Because of higher perceived value, these tires could be priced higher, returning higher profits.[24]

Specific pricing tactics can help marketers achieve specific marketing or financial objectives. Loss-leader pricing, for instance, with popular or new items priced near cost, is a common way to build store or Web site traffic and encourage impulse purchasing of higher-margin products. Objectives for product line sales can be supported by establishing distinct price points for each product in the line, keyed to the perceived feature and benefit differences between products. Objectives for customer acquisition during specific periods can be supported by short-term pricing cuts or tactics that temporarily enhance value, such as low interest rates. The choice of pricing tactic depends on the company's resources and capabilities, its goals and strategic direction, and its specific marketing plan objectives.

How can marketers plan to raise prices to cover higher costs or achieve higher profitability? Here's how Mi8 Corporation handled this delicate task:

> **Mi8.** Mi8 is an e-business that sells corporate customers access to software over the Internet. When Mi8 found out that a key supplier was about to raise its prices, the company planned a price hike of 14 percent so it could maintain its own profit margin. To soften the blow of the announcement, Mi8 allowed customers a 90-day window before applying the higher price. It also offered a lower-price option for customers who signed a 1-year contract. Thanks to its sensitivity to customer reaction, Mi8 lost no customers and heard no complaints after raising its price.[25]

Promotion Strategy

 **PATHFINDER'S TIP**
Review the market and customer analyses and plan for additional marketing research if needed to learn more about the target audience.

INTEGRATED MARKETING COMMUNICATION
Coordinating the content and delivery so all marketing messages are consistent and support the positioning and strategic direction outlined in the marketing plan.

Marketing pathfinders develop promotion strategy, the fourth component of the marketing mix, to communicate with their customers and other stakeholders. This strategy requires decisions about five basic promotion tools: advertising, sales promotion, public relations, direct marketing, and personal selling. Although promotion was traditionally a monologue initiated by the organization, today marketers are opening dialogues with their customers by designing messages and using media with interactive properties.

For maximum effect, marketers must integrate all marketing communications to ensure that the messages are consistent and support the positioning and strategic direction outlined in the marketing plan, an approach known as **integrated marketing communication**. That's how Rensselaer Polytechnic Institute (RPI) supported its brand-building efforts:

> **Rensselaer Polytechnic.** RPI, in Troy, New York, learned through research that it had no strong image among business and community leaders, two key stakeholder groups for fund-raising, even though it ranked 17th among U.S. engineering schools and stressed applied, not theoretical, education. The school realized its brand-building communications—not intended as a recruiting campaign—also had to appeal to faculty, alumni, and current and prospective students. Based on its analysis of the market and targeted stakeholder groups, RPI decided to emphasize that its students become problem solvers, using the tagline, "Why not change the world?" RPI's ad agency created standardized communication graphics for all messages and placed ads in media that reach the stakeholder targets, such as *Time,* CNN, and CNBC. The campaign was successful: After nearly 2 years and almost $1 million in promotion spending, RPI's research found that 86 percent of the surveyed corporate leaders and alumni rated the school "excellent" on graduate programs, quality of research, and technological creativity.[26]

Promotion strategies can be characterized in terms of "push" or "pull." In a "push" strategy, the company targets intermediaries, encouraging them to carry and *push* the product to business customers or consumers. Push strategies often emphasize personal selling and sales promotion aimed at intermediaries. In a "pull strategy," the company targets customers, encouraging them to ask intermediaries for the product and thereby *pull* it through the channel. Pull strategies frequently emphasize advertising and sales promotion aimed at consumers and business customers.

More companies are reaching out to target audiences through *viral marketing*, the use of promotional e-mail messages that encourage recipients to send the message to others. For example, Webreleaf, a Web site operated by a nonprofit environmental conservation group, offers free e-mail postcards that visitors can address and send to their friends. This helps Webreleaf's message get to a wider audience and, just as important, it adds a personal touch that prevents the postcards from being perceived as *spam*, unsolicited e-mail messages that marketers often transmit in bulk.[27]

The choice of promotion tool depends on who the organization wants to reach, what it wants to accomplish, what it wants to communicate, and how the audience prefers to receive the message. It also depends on the organization's internal strengths and weaknesses (such as financial resources) as well as external opportunities and threats. As with all the other marketing mix strategies, marketers need research to understand their audience and its communication needs and preferences; they also can use research to pretest possible actions and evaluate the results after implementation. See Checklist 6.4 for a summary of questions to ask when planning promotion strategy for a marketing plan.

PROMOTION TOOLS

Marketers can choose among a wide variety of techniques in the five basic categories of promotion tools, as shown in Exhibit 6.8. Advertising, perhaps the most ubiquitous form of promotion, is a cost-effective way of communicating with a large audience. Marketers generally include advertising in the promotion strategy when they want to introduce and differentiate a product; build a brand; burnish organizational image; communicate competitive superiority; or convey an idea. U.S. drug manufacturers have been enormously successful in using television and print advertising to drive pull strategies in which consumers are encouraged to visit doctors and request prescriptions for Claritin, Allegra, Prilosec, and other brand-name drugs.[28]

Sales promotion is geared toward eliciting fast action from the audience and rewarding customers for continuing to purchase. Marketers generally include sales promotion in the strategy when they want to accelerate short-term sales results; combat competitive pressure; address customer price sensitivity; start or reinforce a relationship with customers or channel members; increase the perceived value of the offer. Phoenix-based Itz-Toys, for example, returns every year to the American International Toy Fair in New York to demonstrate new products for buyers from Toys 'R' Us, FAO Schwarz, and other toy chains.[29] The Brooklyn Cyclones, a minor league baseball team in New York City, uses special events like Russian Night and Kids Club Day to appeal to specific segments of its extremely diverse consumer market.[30]

Public relations has more credibility than other promotion tools because the audience receives the message through media channels that are seen as more objective than the organization itself. However, the outcome is unpredictable: marketers cannot control what members of the media report, nor can they guarantee that the company and its products will actually get any media coverage at all. This tool is part of the promotion strategy when marketers want to present the product and company in a positive light; build goodwill and trust; and educate customers, channel members, and other stakeholders about the product and its benefits. As one example, the home improve-

---

CHECKLIST 6.4 Planning Promotion Strategy

Audience Analysis

❑ What does research reveal about the segment and its communication needs, preferences, habits, profile, and media usage?

❑ Who is in the target audience, and what is the profile of a typical audience member?

❑ What does the audience analysis suggest about appropriate promotion tools, message strategy, media strategy, and timing of communication?

Objectives

❑ What does the organization want to achieve through marketing communication?

❑ How do the promotion objectives support the organization's marketing and financial objectives?

❑ Is the organization going to use a push or pull promotion strategy to achieve its objectives?

Promotion Tools

❑ Which promotion tools would be most efficient and effective, given the target audience, promotion objectives, message and media, internal strengths and weaknesses, and external opportunities and threats?

❑ How can advertising be used to support the marketing mix and promotion objectives?

❑ How can sales promotion be used to support the marketing mix and accelerate or reward purchasing?

❑ How can public relations be used to build image and stakeholder relationships in support of the marketing mix?

❑ How can direct marketing facilitate two-way interaction with customers and support promotion objectives?

❑ How can personal selling generate one-on-one dialogue and help achieve promotion objectives?

Message and Media

❑ How can message content attract audience attention, hold interest, create desire, and motivate the action desired by the company?

❑ Is a rational or an emotional appeal more appropriate, given the product, the audience, and the message and media?

❑ How can the message be communicated through format and design, wording, graphics, sound, and other media decisions?

❑ What are the cost and characteristics of each medium and media vehicle under consideration?

❑ What is the most effective and efficient balance between reach and frequency?

❑ What is the most appropriate media schedule for the message?

❑ What geographic area should the media cover?

---

ment chain Lowe's sponsors a race-car team and has paid to put its name on a NASCAR race track. Public relations builds both goodwill and sales: "The typical NASCAR fan that shops our store spends 25 percent more than the average customer does," says Lowe's CEO.[31]

Direct marketing is a highly targeted communication tool that allows for two-way interaction between buyer and seller. When the company has a comprehensive database of customer and prospect characteristics and preferences, direct marketing can be a very effective way of conveying an offer tailored to each recipient's needs and behav-

EXHIBIT 6.8   Major Promotion Tools

Tool	Use	Examples
Advertising	Efficiently get messages to large audience	Television and radio commercials; Internet banner ads; magazine and newspaper ads; product and company brochures; billboards; CD- and video-based ads
Sales promotion	Stimulate immediate purchase, reward repeat purchases, motivate sales personnel	Samples; coupons; premiums; contests, games, sweepstakes; displays; demonstrations; trade shows; trade incentives
Public relations	Build positive image and strengthen ties with stakeholders	Event sponsorship; news releases and briefings; speeches; public appearances
Direct marketing	Reach targeted audiences and encourage direct response	E-mail campaigns; printed and online catalogs; telemarketing; direct mail letters and brochures; direct response television
Personal selling	Reach customers one-to-one to make sales, strengthen relationships	Sales appointments; sales meetings and presentations

ior. Just as important, the company can easily tally the results and compare with the objectives. Marketers use direct marketing when they want to start, reinforce, or renew relationships with very specific audiences; increase sales of specific products among specific customers; or test the appeal of new or repositioned products; or test alternate marketing-mix tactics such as different prices.

Personal selling is an excellent tool for reaching business customers and consumers on a one-to-one basis to generate dialogue, learn more about customer needs, and present complex or customized information. This is an especially vital tool when the company is selling expensive goods or services or needs to customize the product for individual customers. However, personal selling is labor intensive and therefore expensive; a single sales call can cost $500 or more.[32] Through sales-force automation technology, sales personnel can access customer and prospect databases, market data, product data, product presentations and other information they need to start or strengthen relationships, work on solutions to customer problems, explain product specifications and usage, enter orders, and check on inventory and deliveries. Personal selling through home-based sales parties has helped Tomboy Tools market specially designed hammers plus other tools and accessories to women who like tackling do-it-yourself projects. "Women are more comfortable in their own environment. We wanted to focus on where the women are, rather than where they're not—like, the hardware store," explains one of the founders.[33]

 **PATHFINDER'S TIP**

Profiling helps marketers think about the audience's receptivity to different promotion tools and likely reaction to message content, media delivery, and timing of communications.

CHOICE OF TARGET AUDIENCE

Just as marketing pathfinders narrow the focus of the marketing plan to more effectively target specific market segments, they also need to select specific audiences for the promotion strategy, based on their marketing and financial objectives. If the marketing objective is to initiate new customer relationships, the target audience will be prospects in the targeted segments. If, like RPI, the marketing objective is to build a strong brand, the target audience will consist of noncustomer stakeholders, such as employees and community leaders. If, as in GM's Oldsmobile situation, the marketing objective is to phase out a product line while retaining goodwill for future relationships, the target audience will be current and prospective customers, dealers, and suppliers.

The choice of target audience directly affects the company's choices about the type of promotion tool, the message content, the media used, and the timing of communication activities. That's why marketers go beyond generalities to research and profile the typical member of the target audience in as much detail as possible, including gender; age; lifestyle choices; media, product, and payment preferences; timing of buying decisions; and so on. These detailed profiles help companies learn enough about the audience to determine exactly what the communication should say and how, when, and where to say it.

CHOICE OF PROMOTION OBJECTIVE

What, specifically, does the organization want to achieve through marketing communication? Promotion objectives need to be closely tied to the marketing and financial objectives in the marketing plan. If the company wants to acquire new customers, it must first make the segment aware of its offer. Thus, one objective might be to "achieve 25 percent awareness of Product A among the target segment within 4 months," with the exact percentage and timing dependent on the marketing objective, the promotion investment, and knowledge of the customer's buying decision process. Related objectives might be to "have 900 prospects request an information package about Product D before June 30" and "generate 300 qualified leads for the sales staff by March 15."

If research shows that the segment is already aware of the product but has no strong preference for it, the promotion strategy might aim to "achieve 18 percent preference for Product E among the target segment within 3 months." If research indicates that customers like the product enough to try it, the objective might be to "achieve 9 percent trial of Product C among the target segment within 6 months" or "have 200 customers request samples of Product B during January."

Marketers should be ready to adjust their priorities and tactics to achieve promotion objectives both efficiently and effectively. Consider the experience of Smarter Kids.com:

SmarterKids.com. SmarterKids.com, an online retailer of educational books and software, initially used its promotion strategy to build customer traffic through a costly combination of broadcast advertising and deals with Web portals to reach a fairly broad audience. At the time, "the most important thing we could do was prove we could get people to the site and get them to buy," explains Al Noyes, executive vice president of sales and marketing. Within months, the site pulled its broadcast ads and let the portal arrangements lapse "because the cost per new customer was unacceptable," Noyes says. Now SmarterKids.com is emphasizing efficiency by targeting more narrowly and using less-expensive online advertising and promotional partnerships with Junior Achievement and other groups.[34]

MESSAGE AND MEDIA

When planning strategy to achieve the promotion objectives, marketers must coordinate their use of message and media, because decisions about one directly affect decisions about the other. At the same time, both message and media must be in line with the target audience's needs, wants, behavior, and receptivity, while encouraging the action desired by the company (e.g., awareness or purchase of the product).

Many marketers formulate message content following the AIDA framework: *A*ttract the audience's attention, hold its *i*nterest, create *d*esire, and motivate *a*ction. The idea is to break through the clutter of promotional messages to grab attention and, by the time audience members have finished digesting the message, move them to respond by taking the desired action. For example, the UPS magazine ad in Exhibit 6.9 attracts business buyers' attention with a head-on photo of a jumbo jet and the head-line "China's 1.26 billion people can't wait to get your products. (Good thing we fly six jumbos there each week.)" The ad's wording holds interest and creates desire by explaining how quickly and frequently UPS delivers to major cities in China. Then the ad ends with a sentence to motivate action: "To find out more, visit ups.com or call us at 1-800-782-7892."

RATIONAL APPEAL Message strategy that relies on facts or logic to motivate audience response.

EMOTIONAL APPEAL Message strategy that relies on feelings rather than facts to motivate audience response.

This UPS ad uses a **rational appeal**, in which the message focuses on facts and logic by showing how the delivery service's features and benefits solve the problem of selling in Chinese markets, to motivate audience action. Many business ads use rational appeals. In contrast, an **emotional appeal** relies on feelings rather than facts to motivate audience response. Martha Stewart.com uses emotional appeal in Valentine's Day consumer ads headlined "Living is loving: Give to your heart's content."

Executing the message strategy requires decisions about format and design, wording, graphics, sound, and elements specific to the chosen medium. The UPS print ad, for instance, uses both the wording and size of the headline and the dramatic head-on photo of a jet to capture attention. Marketers who choose other media can use a wide range of elements to implement their AIDA message strategy.

When matching message and media, companies must consider the cost and characteristics of each medium and research the audience of each media vehicle. Each medium has specific characteristics that convey the message in a different way; the Internet offers sight, sound, motion, and interactivity, whereas print ads in magazines and newspapers offer color, longer life, and the ability to communicate more details. To be effective in achieving the promotion objectives, even the most creative message must be presented in a medium or vehicle (such as a particular magazine or television program) that reaches the target audience. For example, Golden Books found the Internet an excellent medium for reaching its target audience and stimulating sales through sampling:

Golden Books Publishing. When Golden Books was getting ready to launch a new book series called *Finditquick.com*, it targeted mothers with school-age children. The company decided to use the sales promotion tactic of sampling to encourage mothers to try and then order a copy. So it advertised free samples on the site of StartSampling, an e-business that sends samples to consumers who register online and provide household demographics and other data, because the site's audience matched the segment it wanted to reach. The promotion objective was to receive orders from 25 percent of those who requested samples. Golden Books actually achieved a 67 percent response rate—and gained enormous insight into its audience through the research gathered at the site.[35]

REACH How many people in the target audience are exposed to the message during a particular period.

Marketers also need to decide how many people they want to reach during a certain period (known as **reach**) and how often they want to repeat the message during

EXHIBIT 6.9 UPS Ad

CHINA'S 1.26 BILLION PEOPLE CAN'T WAIT TO GET YOUR PRODUCTS.

(GOOD THING WE FLY SIX JUMBOS THERE EACH WEEK.)

No one delivers China faster. Why keep the world's biggest market waiting when you don't have to? UPS now offers more shipping options and shorter transit times than ever before. In fact, with six weekly, direct flights to Beijing, connecting to Shanghai, there's no faster way to reach every major city in China. So next time you get a big order from Xi'an, think fast. Think UPS. To find out more, visit ups.com or call us at 1-800-782-7892.

UPS

MOVING at the SPEED *of* BUSINESS®

FREQUENCY How many times, on average, the target audience is exposed to the message during a given period.

that period (known as **frequency**). Reaching more people is costly, as is repeating the message many more times. Thus, the company must determine the best way to allocate its budget by balancing reach with frequency.

Two final media decisions are when and where to schedule the messages. A message or campaign can run continuously (as constant reminders of the product's benefits or availability), during periods of seasonal or peak demand (to reach customers when they are most interested in buying), or steadily but with more intensity during brief periods (to coincide with other marketing mix tactics such as sales promotions or expanded distribution). The choice of where to advertise—in geographic terms—depends on where the product is currently being sold or will be introduced during the course of the marketing plan. As with reach and frequency, decisions about where and when are directly linked to budget decisions.

Supporting the Marketing Mix

PATHFINDER'S TIP

The organization's ability to deliver superior customer service depends on a well-planned internal marketing strategy to build strong relationships inside the organization.

INTERNAL MARKETING Marketing that targets managers and employees inside the organization.

Regardless of product or market, no marketing-mix strategy is complete without a strategy for customer service and a strategy for internal marketing. Superior customer service is a major differentiator, enabling companies to build strong customer relationships while maintaining or even raising prices despite intense competitive pressure or other environmental issues. **Internal marketing**—marketing to managers and employees inside the organization—allows the company to build internal relationships as a foundation for building external relationships and satisfying customers by implementing the marketing plan. Decisions to be made in formulating these two support strategies are discussed in the following sections.

CUSTOMER SERVICE STRATEGY

Marketing pathfinders can approach customer service strategy in terms of the needs that customers have at different points in the buying process:

- *Customer service before the sale.* Before they buy, customers often need assistance obtaining information about the product and its usage, features, benefits, and warranty; matching the right product to the right situation or need; researching add-ons like availability and pricing of replacement parts; and planning installation, training, or other postsale services.
- *Customer service at the moment or point of sale.* When they are about to buy, customers may need help choosing a specific model; scheduling delivery, pick-up, or use; choosing among payment options or preparing purchase orders; arranging trade-ins or taking advantage of other promotional offers; completing paperwork for warranty registration; or handling other sale-related issues. At FinestWine. com, for instance, when the Webmaster notices customers checking out expensive wines, he opens a small chat window and offers advice and tips about complementary foods or other related information.[36]
- *Customer service after the sale.* After the purchase has been completed, customers sometimes need assistance installing a product; reordering refills or spare parts; scheduling maintenance or repair service; training users; or dealing with other postsale needs. Bank of America calls new customers a few weeks after they open accounts to answer questions and follow up on emerging problems or needs. "It's low-tech, but it can have a tremendous impact on the quality of new customer relationships," says the senior vice president of consumer marketing.[37]

The marketing plan should also specify the level of customer service to be provided to each segment. Marketers frequently offer a lower level of customer service support to less profitable segments, while providing more profitable segments with a higher level of support. Some marketers vary their service support according to the complexity of the good or service, the product price, the location of the sale, and other factors. Dell, for example, provides service for its computer equipment at four levels. Larger and more complex installations that must be operational at all times qualify for round-the-clock support and personal service visits, while installations that are less complex or time-sensitive receive telephone service support.[38]

Customer service is a key element in the fulfillment plans that all e-businesses must prepare to ensure that online buyers receive what they ordered on the expected schedule. This means arranging for timely shipping and convenient returns as well as maintaining the right inventory level and having personnel available to answer questions or respond to complaints. Several years ago, Toysrus.com (www.toysrus.com) was unprepared for the huge consumer response to its nationally distributed holiday flyer—and customers were furious when the company could not fill orders in time for Christmas. In contrast, the online retailer RedEnvelope (www.redenvelope.com) provides both phone and Web-based ordering and maintains a suitable staffing level even at peak periods. As a result, 99 percent of its shipments go out on time.[39]

INTERNAL MARKETING STRATEGY

The internal marketing strategy is a way of focusing the entire organization on the customer and generating support for the marketing plan. At the very least, a good internal marketing strategy ensures the appropriate staffing levels and organization structure to carry out the marketing plan. It also helps the marketing department secure cooperation from other departments that are involved in implementing the marketing plan, such as operations and research and development.

In addition, the internal marketing strategy should outline how employees will get the expertise to help customers, learn about the organization's marketing objectives and strategies, and obtain information so they can communicate with customers and with each other to support external marketing initiatives. Depending on the company's resources and priorities, internal marketing communication can take place through internal newsletters and Web pages; training and marketing or sales meetings; and other techniques.

Internal marketing programs can be designed to go beyond communication by motivating a higher level of employee commitment and involvement. At Commerce Bancorp of Cherry Hill, New Jersey, a "Wow team" shows up at any of the 150 branches without warning to reward staff members for special service achievement. In turn, branch personnel are encouraged to find opportunities and situations in which they can "wow" their customers. Superior customer service is this bank's most powerful competitive weapon, fueling rapid growth in new customers and new deposits even though the bank pays relatively low rates on savings and certificates of deposit.[40]

Here's how Green Hills Farms Store, a family-owned supermarket in Syracuse, New York, uses internal marketing to support its marketing programs:

Green Hills Farms Store. Managers at the Green Hills Farms Store use their knowledge of the customer and the market—in particular, the years of purchasing details gathered from the 10,000 customers in the frequent buyer program—to create marketing mix programs that reinforce customer loyalty and boost sales and profits. The first Great Gobbler Giveaway promotion program was meant to boost sales by giving a free turkey to every customer who spent $500 in the 10 weeks before Thanksgiving. Although overall sales didn't rise, gross margins did, because good customers bought more high-profit products. The store continued modifying this promotion program and now offers four different levels of rewards for pre-Thanksgiving shoppers. Another promotion program is the weekly advertising flyer, inserted in local newspapers. Because the store knows who its best customers are and where they live, it can restrict this program to selected neighborhoods and save more than $3,000 a week. When two competitors opened nearby, managers fought back with a program in which every loyal shopper received a customized letter of appreciation and a certificate redeem-

able for a gift basket in that shopper's favorite department (as indicated by purchasing patterns). The result: Customers remained loyal, sales rose, and the store even gained a few new shoppers. As part of its internal marketing, the supermarket tests promotions on its 200 full- and part-time employees before targeting customers. This lets the store see how employees react and allows for adjustments when the program is introduced to customers. Employees also serve as goodwill ambassadors, telling their friends and family about exciting new promotions.[41]

See Appendix 3 for instructions on how to use *Marketing Plan Pro* software to document the marketing-mix strategies and support strategies you have devised in a marketing plan format.

Chapter Summary

Marketers make decisions about each element in the marketing mix to satisfy customer needs, accommodate environmental circumstances, and achieve financial and marketing objectives. They also support product, place, price, and promotion decisions with coordinated strategies for customer service and internal marketing, which affect implementation. Among the considerations in formulating product strategy are decisions about features and benefits, quality, packaging and labeling, related services, branding, and product development and management. Among the considerations in formulating place strategy are decisions about channel levels, channel members, channel functions, and logistics.

Pricing strategy entails decisions about the choice of pricing objective; analysis of costs and break-even volume; customer perceptions and demand; competitive issues; and price adaptation. Promotion strategy entails decisions about specific promotion tools; choice of target audience; choice of promotion objective; and message and media.

Rounding out the marketing-mix strategy, marketers require a strategy for customer service and a strategy for internal marketing. Customer service can be provided before, during, and after the sale, with the level of service geared to the customer segment and marketing plan objectives. Internal marketing involves marketing to people inside the organization, a necessary prerequisite to building external relationships and implementing the marketing plan. Internal marketing strategy addresses the appropriate staffing levels and the organization structure needed to carry out marketing activities and support profitable, effective customer relationship management.

Budgeting, Forecasting, and Tracking Progress

Chapter Contents

MARKETING PATHFINDER'S QUOTE

"The future will bring many surprises—both favorable and unfavorable—so be prepared by using systematic techniques for forecasting, budgeting, and measurement."
—DR. ARVIND RANGASWAMY, COAUTHOR OF *MARKETING ENGINEERING*[1]

Tools for Measuring Marketing Progress

PATHFINDER'S TIP

Marketers can't manage what they can't measure, which is why forecasts, budgets, schedules, and metrics are important tools for tracking the progress of marketing plan activities.

FORECAST Future projection of what sales and costs are likely to look like in the period covered by the plan.

BUDGET Time-defined allocation of financial outlays for a specific function or program.

SCHEDULE Time-defined plan for completing work that relates to a specific purpose or program.

METRICS Numerical measures of specific performance-related activities and outcomes.

In plotting the path toward marketing and financial objectives, marketers need to be able to predict how far their companies might go during each leg of the marketing journey. After they set the marketing plan in motion and the journey begins, marketers begin to periodically measure how far the company is progressing along the planned path and how far it still has to go. The time to establish concrete checkpoints and rules for measuring progress is before the marketing plan is implemented, so the organization can build in quantifiable standards and practices to measure outcomes on a regular schedule. Once implementation is underway, marketers can monitor these measures and analyze changes over time, comparing actual results with expected, historic, and competitive or industry results to diagnose performance. These comparisons help marketers spot significant variations that require control intervention, as discussed in Chapter 8.

Marketing plans should include four key tools for measuring progress: forecasts, budgets, schedules, and metrics (see Exhibit 7.1):

- **Forecasts** are future projections of what sales and costs are likely to look like in the months and years covered by the plan. Linked to market demand and to overall goals and objectives, forecasts show the direction in which marketers expect sales and costs to move over time. Marketing plans usually include forecasts of market and product sales and costs, among other forecasts.
- **Budgets** are time-defined allocations of financial outlays for specific functions or programs. Marketers use budgets to plan and then track the expenses of marketing plan programs and activities. Marketing plans generally include budgets for each marketing program or activity; sometimes budgets for each targeted segment and each manager or department are also prepared.
- **Schedules** are time-defined plans for completing work that relates to a specific purpose or program. Marketers create schedules to coordinate and then track the timing of key tasks and the allocation of resources to implement marketing programs. Marketing plans should include a schedule with key milestones for each major program or activity.
- **Metrics** are numerical measures of specific performance-related activities and outcomes. These measures track specific marketing elements so the company can see whether they are bringing the organization closer to its objectives and goals. Metrics also focus employees and managers on activities that make a real difference; set up performance expectations that can be objectively measured; and form a foundation for employee accountability and pride in accomplishments. Typically, marketing plans include metrics measuring new customer acquisition, customer satisfaction, sales volume, profitability, and other outcomes.

EXHIBIT 7.1 Tools for Measuring Marketing Progress

Tool	*Application*
Forecasts	Used to predict future sales and costs as checkpoints for measuring progress
Budgets	Used to allocate funding across programs in specified periods and then track expenditures during implementation
Schedules	Used to plan and coordinate the timing of tasks and programs
Metrics	Used to establish measures for specific performance-related outcomes and activities and then track results against measures

Although marketing managers can get the big picture by measuring overall results such as monthly sales volume, they use forecasts, budgets, schedules, and metrics to follow the mountain of details that can make or break performance. This chapter discusses how to apply all four tools in a marketing plan.

FORECASTING SALES AND COSTS

PATHFINDER'S TIP

Marketers must use the information uncovered through environmental scanning and their understanding of markets and customers to devise forecasts that are as realistic as possible.

Marketers use forecasts to predict what sales and costs will look like in the period covered by the marketing plan and just beyond. To do a good job of forecasting, companies must weigh a variety of external factors like demand and environmental threats and opportunities as well as internal factors like goals, capabilities, and constraints. Many companies prepare forecasts for the best-case, the worst-case, and the most likely scenario. Even though forecasts can never be more than good estimates, they should be as accurate as possible, because the organization relies on them when fine-tuning objectives and strategies and when planning the resources needed to properly carry out the marketing plan.

For example, restaurant owners must forecast sales at different times of the day and different days of the week, so they can project costs and plan staffing levels and order sufficient food and supplies to meet demand. In preparing their forecasts, restaurants take into account holidays, seasonality, economic conditions, competitive actions, and other elements that can have an effect on demand. Nonprofit organizations may prepare forecasts of future contributions, overall need for services, and projected service utilization, along with future estimates of associated costs. Many companies also use forecasts when evaluating possible product or company acquisitions that affect marketing planning. Procter & Gamble, for instance, arranged to buy Clairol from Bristol-Myers Squibb because it forecast significant growth for the hair-care market, where P&G has considerable strength and experience.[2]

Making decisions based on a forecast that underestimates sales could leave a company without sufficient inventory and staffing to satisfy customers; on the other hand, making decisions based on a forecast that overestimates sales could lead to overproduction and other costly problems. Even the most carefully prepared forecast can be overtaken by environmental shifts, as Cisco Systems learned the hard way:

Cisco Systems. Economic conditions and new technology are two key drivers of demand for networking equipment—a market that Cisco had profitably served for years. Yet Cisco management continued to implement marketing programs based on forecasts of ever-higher sales despite an ongoing economic slowdown that dampened corporate spending and slowed market adoption of its new telecommunications technology. Inventory levels soon became a problem, because Cisco had stockpiled inventory and parts based on forecasts of continued sales growth. Finally, the firm was forced to write down $2.5 billion in excess inventory and revise its forecasts and activities in line with lower sales projections.[3]

Clearly, marketers need to review and revise forecasts often, especially in light of the many internal or external changes that can influence sales, costs, and marketing performance. Ford managers, for instance, constantly scan the environment for clues that their sales forecasts need to be updated. Having felt the effects of sudden and dramatic economic downturns, they not only look at daily vehicle sales but also check informal sources such as Internet chat rooms to get a sense of consumer confidence. "When you have this month-to-month volatility, it creates a certain level of anxiety," says Ford's director of sales analysis. "You've got to really pay attention."[4]

Forecasting is complicated by the fact that the company's marketing-mix strategies will influence the direction and velocity of sales. For example, the company will probably forecast higher initial sales for a new product if it plans to use penetration pricing, a pricing approach specifically designed to encourage rapid adoption of a product. On the other hand, if it uses skimming pricing, which is designed to skim profits from the market, the forecast for introductory sales volume will probably be lower than with penetration pricing.

Types of Forecasts

Although marketing plans vary, most include these types of forecasts:

- *Forecasts of market and segment sales.* The company should start by projecting full-year sales of the overall market for the next 1 to 5 years, using the market definition created during the market analysis. This helps the company size the market overall so it can plan for the share it wants to achieve and estimate the share its competitors will have in future years. If possible, the company should also break out segment forecasts so it can project how sales in each segment are likely to change year by year.
- *Forecasts of company product sales.* Based on market and segment forecasts, market and customer analysis, and on decisions about strategic direction, goals, and marketing strategies, the company now projects the number and dollar amount of product (or product line) sales for each market or segment. These are usually presented month by month for 1 year or for the period covered by the marketing plan. Some companies create separate forecasts of new product sales so they can track them more closely.
- *Forecasts of cost of sales.* Here, management forecasts the costs associated with forecasts of company product sales, based on data gathered for the analysis of the current situation and data about cost trends. These cost forecasts may be adjusted after budgets have been prepared for marketing plan activities.
- *Forecasts of sales and costs by channel.* When companies sell through more than one channel level or intermediary, they may want to project monthly unit and dollar sales by product by channel and, if feasible, costs per channel. These forecasts focus attention on the predicted sales and cost trends of each channel and provide a yardstick for measuring and analyzing actual channel results and expenses.

Creating this series of forecasts is only part of the task. Next, the marketer calculates the month-to-month and year-to-year change for the figures in each forecast to examine trends (such as how much growth in sales is being projected for the coming 12 months) and rate of change (such as how quickly costs are rising). Marketers use both their forecast projections and these trend calculations when checking on target markets, setting and reviewing goals and objectives, allocating resources for action programs, and measuring actual against expected results.

Sources and Tools for Forecasting Data

Forecasting sales and costs requires research and judgment. Marketers will uncover many sources of forecasting data in the course of scanning the environment and conducting the market and customer analysis. Primary research sources such as studies of buying patterns and intentions can suggest possible demand levels and provide insights into the potential direction of market, segment, and product sales. However, when working with buyer research, marketers must use judgment, remembering that customers may not buy in the future as they have in the past, nor will they necessarily make future purchases even though they told researchers they would do so.[5]

Secondary sources such as trade associations, government statistics, and industry analysts' reports also can be valuable sources of data for sales and cost estimates. In particular, data on high-tech markets and products can vary widely from source to source—and change quite rapidly—so marketers must again use judgment, weighing the knowledge and credibility of the source and the age of the data when using information for forecasting. Exhibit 7.2 shows selected sources of forecasts for high-tech products and markets; some free information is available on all sites, although in-depth studies and detailed forecasts often require a fee.

In addition, some marketers predict future sales by applying causal analysis methods such as regression analysis, econometric models, and neural networks; or using time series methods such as smoothing and decomposition. In many cases, they then apply judgmental forecasting methods to adjust their statistical analyses and arrive at a final set of forecasts for the marketing plan. Judgmental forecasting tools include sales force estimates, executive opinion, and the Delphi method, as shown in Exhibit 7.3. These tools may be subject to human error or bias, which is why marketers generally combine the results of judgmental methods with statistical analyses and estimates from knowledgeable sources for increased accuracy.

As difficult as forecasting can be for existing products, marketing planners face even more challenges in developing forecasts for new products. Some companies use the Bass model for forecasting initial purchases of new products; this is appropriate when (1) the company has been able to collect sales data for even a brief period, or (2) the product is similar to an existing product or technology with a known sales history.[6] When a product is so innovative that it establishes an entirely new product category—such as the Palm Pilot—marketers have no historical or industry data to factor into their forecasts. Instead, some predict sales using the results of test market research, while others look at sales patterns of products with similar market behavior for clues to the new product's future sales. To forecast sales of first-generation digital cameras, for

EXHIBIT 7.2	Selected Sources of Forecast Data for High-Tech Products and Markets
Source	*Information*
Forrester Research (www.forrester.com)	Research highlights, projections, and news analysis about high-tech products and markets
Gartner Group (www.gartnergroup.com)	Analyses, projections, and commentary about high-tech products and markets
Giga Information Group (www.gigaweb.com)	E-business research and projections
IDC (www.idc.com)	Snapshots and analyses of high-tech trends and projections
Jupiter Media Metrix (www.jmm.com)	Analytical reports about the Internet's impact on marketing and commerce
NUA (www.nua.ie/surveys)	Surveys and projections of Internet usage around the world
ZDNet Research Center (researchcenter.zdnet. com/index.html)	Links to free and fee-based studies of e-commerce and high-tech products and markets

EXHIBIT 7.3 Judgmental Tools for Forecasting	
Forecasting Tool	*Use*
Sales force estimates	Composite projection based on estimates made by sales personnel; convenient but accuracy depends on instincts, experience, and objectivity of salespeople.
Executive opinion	Composite projection based on estimates made by managers; convenient but accuracy depends on instincts, experience, and objectivity of managers.
Delphi method	Composite projection based on successive rounds of input from outside experts, who ultimately come to consensus on estimates; time consuming but sometimes helpful when forecasting sales of new products or new markets.

example, a marketer might look at sales of CD-ROM drives rather than examining sales of traditional camera products.

Once forecasts are in place in the marketing plan, the next step is to prepare budgets that will be used to track expenses after marketing programs are implemented.

BUDGETING: PLANNING AND TRACKING EXPENSES

PATHFINDER'S TIP
Be guided by the priorities established by the strategic direction, goals, and objectives in the marketing plan when allocating the marketing budget among all the programs and activities being planned.

AFFORDABILITY BUDGETING
Method in which company budgets for marketing based on what it can afford.

Budgeting enables marketing managers to allocate expenses by program or activity over specific periods in the marketing plan and then track actual expenditures compared with forecast costs. Many companies have proprietary procedures for developing budgets. Some require that budget preparation follow internal financial calendars; some specify profit hurdles or particular assumptions about expenses and allocation; some mandate particular formats or supporting documentation; and some require budgets based on best-case, worst-case, and most likely scenarios.

Budgeting Methods for Marketing Spending

How much money should be budgeted for implementation of marketing programs? Smaller companies often deal with this question using **affordability budgeting,** simply budgeting what they believe they can afford, given other urgent expenses:

Cincinnati Custom Cleaning. When Dave and Christine McAdams founded Cincinnati Custom Cleaning, they phased in a direct-mail campaign to acquire new customers, targeting medical offices as their first segment. As they grew, they continued to prospect by mail every month; "every time we had a little extra money, we spent it on postage," says Christine McAdams. By bootstrapping, the company has grown monthly revenues to $30,000 and expanded to serve more segments of the corporate market.[7]

Affordability budgeting worked for Cincinnati Customer Cleaning in its early days, when the cofounders had very little to spend. However, this is generally not a good way to set budgets, because it doesn't allow for the kind of significant, ongoing investments that are often needed to launch major new products or enter pressured markets. In effect, budgeting based on affordability ignores the profit payback that comes from spending on marketing to build sales.

Ideally, the size of the marketing budget should be based on careful analysis of the link between spending and sales (or, for nonprofits, donations). By building a sophisticated model of how sales actually react to different spending levels, the company can determine exactly how big the marketing budget must be to achieve the sales results outlined in its financial objectives. Companies without these kinds of models tend to rely on rule-of-thumb methods that don't directly correlate spending with sales results, such as the percentage-of-sales method, the competitive-parity method, and the objective-and-task method.

PERCENTAGE-OF-SALES BUDGETING Method in which company allocates a certain percentage of sales revenues to fund marketing programs.

With **percentage-of-sales budgeting,** management sets aside a certain percentage of dollar sales to fund marketing programs, based on internal budgeting guidelines or previous marketing experience. Although this is a simple method to implement, one disadvantage is that sales are seen as the source of marketing funding, rather than being seen as the result of budget investments. Another is that the company may have no justification (other than tradition) for choosing the percentage devoted to marketing. Finally, if the budget is continually adjusted based on month-by-month sales, lower sales may lead to a lower marketing budget—just when the company needs to maintain or even increase the budget to stimulate higher sales.

COMPETITIVE-PARITY BUDGETING Method in which company creates a budget by matching what competitors spend, as a percentage of sales or a specific dollar amount.

When companies use **competitive-parity budgeting,** they fund marketing by matching what competitors spend (as a percentage of sales or specific dollar amount). Again, this is a simple method, but it ignores even major differences between companies and doesn't allow for adjustments to find the best spending level for achieving the organization's goals.

OBJECTIVE-AND-TASK BUDGETING Method in which budget is determined by totaling the cost of completing all marketing tasks needed to achieve the marketing mix objectives and marketing plan objectives.

With the widely used **objective-and-task budgeting** method, budget size is determined by adding up the cost of completing all the marketing tasks needed to achieve the marketing-mix objectives and marketing plan objectives. In the absence of a proven model showing how sales levels respond to marketing spending, the objective-and-task method provides a reasonable way to build a budget by examining the cost of the individual programs that contribute to marketing performance—as long as the appropriate objectives have been set.

Budgets Within the Marketing Budget

Once the overall budget has been established, marketers start to allocate marketing funding across the various activities in the time period covered by the marketing plan. Then, when they implement the marketing plan, they can input actual expenditures for comparison with planned expenditures. The most common budgets developed for marketing plans are:

- *Budgets for each marketing mix program.* These budgets list costs for each program's tasks or expense items, presented month by month and with year-end totals. Depending on the company's preferred format, marketing mix budgets also may show expected sales, gross or net margins, and other objectives and profitability measures. Tracking expenses by program reinforces accountability and helps management weigh expected costs against actual costs—and results.
- *Budgets for each segment or market.* Creating budgets segment by segment forces companies to understand their segment-specific costs; it also shows which segments are most costly to serve and which yield the best returns.
- *Budgets for each region or geographic division.* As with budgeting by segment or market, budgeting by region or geography focuses management attention on the cost of marketing in each location and allows easy comparisons between outlays and returns.

- *Budgets for each division or product manager.* These budgets help divisional and product managers track the costs for which they are responsible, compare spending with results achieved, and pinpoint problems or opportunities for further investigation.
- *Budget summarizing overall marketing expenses.* This summary budget may be arranged by marketing program or tool, by segment or region, or using another organizational pattern appropriate for the organization. Typically, this budget shows month-by-month spending and a year-end total; in some cases, companies may project spending for multiple years in one summary budget. And this budget may include expected gross or net margins and other calculations based on sales and expenditures.

All these budgets act like checkpoints against which actual spending can be measured. In this way, marketers can quickly spot overspending and calculate margins and other profitability measures to check on progress toward financial objectives. The next step is to coordinate the timing of each activity through scheduling.

SCHEDULING MARKETING PLAN PROGRAMS

PATHFINDER'S TIP

Be sure to mention the timing and progress of ongoing programs or activities in the analysis of the current situation and include updated schedules in the current marketing plan.

Every marketing program consists of a series of tasks or activities (*milestones*) that must be completed to move the company closer to the desired objective. Scheduling helps the company define the timing of these tasks and coordinate implementation to avoid conflicts and measure progress toward completion. To create a detailed program-by-program schedule, the marketing pathfinder lists the major tasks and activities for one program at a time and, through research or experience, assigns each a projected start and end date. Some companies create a series of schedules, based on best case, worst case, and most likely scenarios. Next, the marketer notes who is responsible for supervising or completing each task in that program.

Depending on the company's chosen format and management preferences, the marketing plan may not have to contain lots of detail about each program (such as Gantt charts, critical path schedules, or other project management devices). In fact, some companies include only one summary schedule showing the timing and responsibility for each planned program, rather than including separate schedules of activities for each program. Either way, the point is to make the timing as concrete as possible so management can track progress by seeing whether programs and activities are on schedule. Then they use metrics to monitor progress of key performance-related activities and outcomes.

MEASURING WHAT MATTERS: METRICS

PATHFINDER'S TIP

Review the progress represented by last year's metrics measurements in the analysis of the current situation and use the lessons learned when planning objectives and measurements for new programs.

Marketers use metrics as windows into the mechanics that drive performance, checking progress on a regular basis so they can spot and correct problems early. The marketing plan need not include detailed metrics for every activity, just the key activities that significantly affect performance and keep the organization moving in the desired strategic direction. For example, Nationwide Financial monitors customer retention and 11 other metrics to measure its progress toward overall goals—and links management compensation to achieving preset metrics measures.[8]

Metrics must cover activities that are relevant to the mission, as the nonprofit Nature Conservancy found when it reevaluated what its metrics actually measured:

The Nature Conservancy. The mission of the Nature Conservancy is to preserve the global diversity of animals and plants by protecting rare species habitats. For decades, the organization measured progress toward fulfilling this mission using two simple metrics: (1) the amount of money raised and (2) the number of acres preserved. By these standards, the Conservancy was performing very well: it had increased paid memberships from 28,000 to more than 1 million in less than 30 years, was annually raising more than $750 million, and was protecting more than 66 million acres around the world. Yet top management realized that these metrics weren't measuring progress toward the biodiversity part of the nonprofit's mission. After testing as many as 98 different metrics, the Conservancy established a group of measures organized around effectiveness in (1) halting extinction threats and preserving biodiversity, (2) launching programs and reaching goals for preservation, and (3) developing the resources and capabilities to carry out its mission.[9]

Checklist 7.1 summarizes some important questions to ask when planning metrics.

Identifying Metrics

The Nature Conservancy identified its key metrics by working backward from its mission and long-term goals to find specific outcomes and activities that signal progress. Many businesses follow the same reasoning, matching their metrics to their goals and marketing program objectives. For example, companies pursuing a strategic direction of overall growth need metrics to measure changes in customer relationships and sales. Such metrics might include measurements of customer acquisition, customer retention, customer defection, customer satisfaction, customer lifetime value, and sales trends by customer or segment. In turn, customer relationship metrics that reveal increases in the customer base and in customer satisfaction serve as early indicators of future sales performance.[10] The exact metrics depend on the company, its goals and objectives, and the strategies outlined in the marketing plan. The point is to focus on progress in satisfying customers, overtaking competitors, and other nonfinancial measures that are important to long-term strategic goals and competitive strength, while remaining aware that striving for good performance on such measures may mean accepting lower financial performance in the short term.[11]

CHECKLIST 7.1   Planning Metrics

❑ What activities and outcomes are important to the organization's mission—and what components can be measured to track progress toward fulfilling the mission?

❑ Which activities and outcomes contribute the most to marketing performance—and what components can be measured to track progress toward marketing objectives?

❑ Which activities and outcomes contribute the most to financial goals—and what components can be measured to track progress toward these goals?

❑ What metrics will help the organization follow the progress of marketing mix programs toward achieving their objectives?

❑ What metrics will help the organization track customer movement toward a purchase?

❑ What metrics will help the organization track the way marketing programs influence customer movement toward first-time buying, satisfaction, and repeat buying?

❑ What metrics will help the organization measure movement in the sales pipeline?

❑ What additional metrics are needed to monitor activities and outcomes that signal progress in other areas that are important to the organization?

Companies also need metrics to track outcomes related to objectives and programs that affect sustained profitability and other financial goals. These metrics usually measure overall gross or net margin and margins for each product and product line, channel, promotion, and price adjustment, among other profitability measures. Consider the metric of gross profit margin, which the giant chip-maker Intel watches closely as it balances financial metrics with non-financial metrics:

Intel. Intel achieved a 64 percent gross profit margin on sales of computer chips during one recent year. The following year, its metrics showed that gross margins were much lower, the result of a decision to slash the price of Pentium 4 chips to regain market share lost to a competitor—a key nonfinancial metric. Still, in line with the need to boost profit margins, Intel is also using metrics to measure progress toward cost reduction targets.[12]

Exhibit 7.4 shows a few sample metrics for these and other common marketing and financial objectives.

EXHIBIT 7.4   Sample Metrics for Common Marketing Plan Objectives

Type of Objective	Sample Metrics
Marketing	• To acquire new customers: Measure number or percentage of new customers acquired per month, quarter, or year.
	• To retain current customers: Measure number or percentage of customers who continue purchasing during a set period.
	• To increase customer satisfaction: Measure percentage of customers who are satisfied or very satisfied.
	• To increase distribution: Measure number or percentage of new channel relationships acquired during a set period.
	• To increase unit sales: Measure number of products sold per week, month, quarter, or year.
	• To increase market share: Measure company's dollar or unit sales divided by total industry sales during the month, quarter, or year.
	• To accelerate product development: Measure the amount of time needed to bring a new product to market.
	• To expedite order fulfillment: Measure number of days needed to process a customer order and ship the product.
Financial	• To increase sales volume: Measure dollar sales per week, month, quarter, or year.
	• To increase product sales: Measure dollar sales per product per week, month, quarter, or year.
	• To improve channel productivity: Compare sales and costs for each channel per week, month, quarter, or year.
	• To improve profitability: Measure gross or net margin by product, line, channel, promotion, price adjustment, segment, or customer by week, month, quarter, or year.
	• To reach break-even: Measure number of weeks or months until revenues equal and then begin to exceed costs.

Nonprofits frequently work backward from their objectives to create metrics that quantify periodic results and trends for:

- donations received (metrics such as donations by source and productivity of fundraising by program or source)
- number of people being helped (metrics such as utilization of service by segment, service, or location)
- public image (metrics such as awareness by stakeholder segment and attitude by stakeholder segment)

A second way to identify metrics is by looking for key components or activities related to customer buying behavior (using research gathered during the analysis of markets and customers). This means finding measurements that signal customer movement toward a purchase. For example, the company might start by measuring awareness and attitudes to find out whether the target audience knows about the product or brand and has a positive attitude toward it. The company could also measure the audience's efforts to research and try the product by looking at store or Web site traffic, number of customers test-driving a car, number of information packets requested, and so on. When the target makes a purchase, the company can use metrics to measure sales by transaction or by segment, customer or segment purchase frequency, sales by channel or intermediary, and so forth. Exhibit 7.5 presents sample metrics keyed to some basic stages in the buying process.

Many companies use metrics to track how each program in the marketing plan influences the customer's movement toward the initial purchase, satisfaction, and repeat purchases. For example, software manufacturer Oracle uses media-specific metrics to find out how well its online advertising campaigns perform in attracting prospects and facilitating sales:

EXHIBIT 7.5 Metrics Based on Customer Buying Behavior

Behavior	*Sample Metrics*
Customer becomes aware of a product.	Measure customer awareness of product and competing products, by segment.
Customer learns more about the product.	Measure number of information packets or catalogs requested; number of hits on Web site; number of people who visit store; number who subscribe to e-mail newsletter.
Customer has a positive attitude toward the product.	Measure customer attitudes toward the product and competing products, by segment; feedback from hotlines, letters and e-mail, channel and sales sources, etc.
Customer tries the product.	Measure number of people who receive free samples; number who redeem coupons for trial sizes.
Customer buys the product.	Measure sales by transaction, segment, product, channel, payment method; conversion from trials and information requests.
Customer is satisfied.	Measure customer satisfaction by product and by segment; satisfaction feedback from hotlines, letters and e-mails, channel sources, etc.
Customer becomes a loyal customer.	Measure customer retention; size and frequency of repeat purchases; utilization of frequent buyer program.

Oracle. Oracle uses several metrics to follow the progress of online advertising programs targeting businesses. First, the company measures click-through rates to find out how many people click on one of its banner ads to go to the Oracle site for more information. Then it measures the promotional cost to acquire a new registrant at the Web site and the online conversion rate to determine how many prospects who click through actually buy. These metrics helped Oracle discover that larger, flashier banners were generating a better response than smaller, simpler banners.[13]

Similarly, Air2Web, which makes software for secure wireless access to corporate systems, asked its ad agency to design an online campaign with an objective of efficiently bringing qualified prospects to its Web site. The agency first analyzed two Web-site metrics: the way visitors clicked around the Web site and which pages generated the highest number of sales leads. Then it created different messages to drive recipients to those pages. Using metrics to track advertising click-through, conversion rates, and costs, the agency found that this campaign was more cost efficient than earlier programs: it reduced the cost per new customer acquired by 50 percent compared with the previous quarter.[14] Exhibit 7.6 shows some common online marketing metrics.

When a company wants to be able to track program-by-program performance progress toward specific objectives and goals, it can define its metrics even more narrowly. For example, if The Nature Conservancy set a target of increasing contributions

EXHIBIT 7.6   Common Online Marketing Metrics

Metric	*Outcome or Activity Being Measured*	*Comments on Metric*
Hits	How many times the files at a certain Web site are accessed.	Only a broad indicator of site popularity.
Impressions	How many times a banner ad was presented.	One Web page may include multiple banner ads and therefore generate multiple impressions.
Click-through	How many times someone clicks on a banner ad to get more information at the sponsor's site.	General indication of interest but not necessarily linked to sales.
Page views	How many times a certain Web page is accessed.	Doesn't indicate whether one visitor accessed the page multiple times or multiple visitors accessed the page once.
Visitors (eyeballs)	How many people visit a certain Web site.	To be more precise, should measure unique visitors and repeat visitors.
Stickiness	How long people remain at a Web site during one visit.	Suggests the attractiveness of a site.
Entry and exit	Pages where someone enters and exits the site during a visit.	Indicates online referral sources and clues to site usage.
Registrations	How many people become registered users of a Web site.	Indicates strong interest and encourages two-way communication.
Transactions	How many people perform a particular action, such as buying or downloading from a site.	Specific metrics depend on goals and customer buying process.

from corporate donors, it could track the ratio of corporate to personal contributions received from each of its marketing programs. This metric would help the nonprofit pinpoint which programs yielded a higher percentage of corporate contributions. Then it could use this knowledge to fine-tune programs in progress and develop more effective programs for future marketing plans.

Businesses that rely on the promotional tool of personal selling usually set up metrics to measure the sales pipeline. Such metrics include number of prospect inquiries, number of qualified leads generated, number of sales presentations, number of bids accepted, percentage of prospects converted to customers, and number of orders received. Businesses that sell through intermediaries can gauge channel productivity using metrics such as number or percentage of customers or sales generated per channel or intermediary, cost and profits per sale by channel or intermediary, speed of order fulfillment, and percentage of stock-outs. Of course, the exact metrics depend on each organization's particular situation and priorities.

Using Metrics

To use metrics, marketers must find practical ways to measure meaningful outcomes and activities. Not every outcome or activity can be measured, nor is every possible metric actually meaningful. If a company lacks the budget to conduct valid attitudinal research, it can't use customer attitudes as a metric, for example.

Likewise, the company may be able to measure Web site hits but not need the information because it has learned, through research, that registrations and transactions are much better indicators of movement toward a purchase. In fact, online activity and productivity metrics such as click-through are easily measured, but e-businesses now rely more on sales-oriented metrics to track progress. "For most [business-to-business] advertising, the key metric is generating qualified sales leads," says one agency executive. The head of OfficeDepot.com goes further, stating that sales metrics, not traffic and other activity metrics, are the way she measures her site's success.[15] ClassMates Online and other e-businesses use sophisticated systems to determine the return on investment performance of individual banner ads through metrics that measure sales of particular products to particular customer segments.[16]

However, metrics can become so overused that they get in the way of other activities and performance targets:

> **Florida Light and Power.** When Florida Light and Power decided to focus on quality improvement, it established a huge battery of metrics to track performance using different quality indicators. The utility did achieve its quality objectives and went on to win a prestigious national quality award. After a time, however, management decided to slash the number of metrics because employees protested that the time spent on measurement and reporting could be better invested in delivering good customer service.[17]

Although metrics start with periodic measurements of specific marketing plan activities and outcomes, they're most valuable to marketing pathfinders when viewed in the context of:

- *Expected outcomes.* How do the outcomes measured by metrics compare with the expected outcomes documented in the marketing plan? If the metric is dollar sales by segment, the marketer will compare actual segment sales over a given period with expected segment sales for that period. This shows whether the organization is making the expected progress.

- *Historical results.* How do the outcomes measured by metrics compare with the actual outcomes in previous periods? Because marketing pathfinders review previous results as part of their analysis of the internal environment, they have the data to weigh current outcomes against previous outcomes. This comparison can reveal unusual trends and suggest possible problems that could affect performance.

- *Competitive or industry outcomes.* How do the outcomes measured by metrics compare with competitors' outcomes or average outcomes for the industry? When comparable competitive or industry information is available, marketers can check these against their current outcomes to gauge relative performance and reveal strengths and weaknesses. However, marketers must bear in mind that competitors are operating under different circumstances and may have very different goals, costs, and outcomes, so competitive comparisons are only useful in relative terms.

- *Environmental influences.* How do the outcomes measured by metrics appear in relation to environmental trends and pressures, such as an economic boom or a parts shortage? Marketers need to interpret metrics in the context of everything else that's affecting the organization. If metrics indicate that sales objectives are barely being achieved when an economic boom has dramatically boosted demand, the organization should dig deeper and examine or create other metrics to find out why sales aren't higher still.

Many companies check performance progress using metrics on a monthly basis, although some check weekly and some daily—or more often, when they have access to fresh data and know they can gain or lose a sale at the click of a mouse. Gateway Computer, for instance, uses a sophisticated monitoring system to update sales metrics from its Web site and its retail chain every 2 hours.[18] RedEnvelope monitors metrics even more frequently:

RedEnvelope Gifts Online. RedEnvelope is an upscale Web retailer specializing in distinctive lifestyle gifts such as gourmet gift baskets and sports-themed accessories. Online competition is fierce, and customers can click in or away in an instant, so RedEnvelope marketers take advantage of technology to monitor key performance metrics hour by hour. This way, they can see which products are selling more slowly than projected and respond by substituting other products that better match the very latest customer buying trends.[19]

As RedEnvelope's managers know, metrics are tools to track the progress of programs after implementation, nothing more—it is up to management to make decisions and take action when metrics show that the expected results are not being achieved.

Appendix 3 includes instructions on how to use *Marketing Plan Pro* software to document the decisions you have made in the appropriate sections of a written marketing plan. Although the spreadsheets and formats shown in the *Marketing Plan Pro* software are suitable for straightforward budgets and schedules, they can be modified in different ways.

Chapter Summary

Companies need to establish specific checkpoints, practices, and standards for measuring progress so they can accurately track marketing plan implementation and be ready with control intervention if necessary. The four key tools for measuring progress are: (1) forecasts, future projections of what sales and costs are likely to look like in the period covered by the plan; (2) budgets, time-defined allocations of financial outlays for specific functions or programs; (3) schedules, time-defined plans for completing work that relates to a specific purpose or program; and (4) metrics, numerical measures of specific performance-related activities and outcomes.

To make forecasts as accurate as possible, companies must consider a variety of external factors like demand and environmental threats and opportunities as well as internal factors like goals, capabilities, and constraints. They must also review and revise forecasts in line with changes that affect marketing performance. Preparing a series of budgets enables companies to allocate expenses by program or activity over specific periods in the marketing plan and then track actual expenditures compared with forecast costs. Budgets can be prepared following the affordability method, the percentage-of-sales method, according to competitive parity, or by the objective-and-task method. Scheduling helps marketers define the timing of each marketing plan task and coordinate its implementation to avoid conflicts and measure progress toward completion. Metrics enable marketers to check the progress of key marketing plan activities using measures that are relevant to the organization and its goals, objectives, and strategic direction.

Controlling Plan Implementation

Chapter Contents

MARKETING PATHFINDER'S QUOTE

"Key to demonstrating the effectiveness of a marketing program is experimentation—driving the organization to set objectives, capture data, and measure results; firms that don't experiment, don't learn."
—DR. GARY L. LILIEN, COAUTHOR OF MARKETING ENGINEERING[1]

Types of Marketing Plan Control

PATHFINDER'S TIP

The time to plan for implementation is before the organization's marketing plan goes into effect.

At this point in the marketing planning process, the marketing plan is nearly complete. The final step is to plan how the company will control the plan's implementation. As noted in Chapter 1, marketing control keeps both employees and activities on the proper path so the organization continues moving in the direction outlined in the marketing plan.

In preparing a marketing plan, marketers need to plan for four types of marketing control: annual plan, profitability, productivity, and strategic control (see Exhibit 8.1).

EXHIBIT 8.1 Types of Marketing Plan Control	
Control	*Use*
Annual plan control	Gauge the organization's progress toward achieving the marketing and financial objectives and the program objectives outlined in the marketing plan.
Profitability control	Gauge the organization's performance in achieving profit-related objectives through measures such as return on investment, return on equity, return on assets, contribution margin, gross/net profit margin.
Productivity control	Gauge the organization's efficiency in managing the sales force, channels, marketing communications, and products.
Strategic control	Gauge the organization's effectiveness in managing marketing, customer relationships, and social responsibility and ethics.

With each type, marketing pathfinders follow the same control process: starting with the objectives set in the marketing plan, they establish standards for measuring progress toward those objectives, measure actual performance and compare the results with planned performance, diagnose any variance, and then determine if corrective action is needed. The control process is discussed in more detail later in this chapter.

ANNUAL PLAN CONTROL

 **PATHFINDER'S TIP**
Look back at what emerged from last year's annual plan control process for clues to issues that may affect this year's marketing performance.

ANNUAL PLAN CONTROL Type of marketing control used to assess the progress and performance of the current year's marketing plan.

Because marketers generally formulate new marketing plans every year, they need **annual plan control** to assess the progress of the current year's marketing plan. This type of control covers:

- *broad performance measures* such as overall sales results, market share results, cost-to-sales results, and overall financial results. Such measures help senior management (and stakeholders such as employees and investors) evaluate the company's overall effectiveness and strengths while pinpointing issues that are impeding this year's performance. Automakers, for instance, look particularly closely at monthly results of vehicle sales and market share, interpreted in the context of overall industry results and environmental influences.
- *performance toward meeting the specific marketing and financial objectives* established in the marketing plan. This aspect of performance is critical: If a company fails to achieve this year's marketing plan objectives, it will have difficulty achieving its longer-term goals and mission. Organizations often examine how specific divisions or activities are doing on their marketing plan objectives. Retailers such as Macy's and Barnes and Noble, for example, set companywide as well as store-by-store marketing and financial objectives, then measure and compare performance with weekly, monthly, and yearly results from previous years.
- *performance toward achieving the more narrowly defined objectives* set for each marketing-mix strategy and program. By measuring interim and year-end performance using forecasts, budgets, schedules, and metrics, management can see whether the organization is meeting program objectives that, in turn, support the year's marketing plan objectives as well as longer-term goals. Managers with line responsibility usually follow these measures most closely and regularly report performance trends to more senior managers.

Although market share measures are driven by sales performance, they reflect relative competitive standing. These measures therefore help senior managers gauge their organization's competitive strength and situation over time. This is why General Motors, Ford, DaimlerChrysler, Honda, Toyota, and other automakers pore over their monthly market share performance for the United States and other major markets, then use the data to adjust future marketing and production activities in line with marketing plan objectives and program objectives.

PROFITABILITY CONTROL

PATHFINDER'S TIP

Be sure the company's profitability measures take into account the goals and objectives identified earlier in the marketing planning process.

PROFITABILITY CONTROL Type of marketing control used to assess the organization's progress and performance based on profitability measures.

As the term implies, **profitability control** assesses the organization's progress and performance based on key profitability measures. The exact measures differ from organization to organization, but often include, among other profitability measures:

- return on investment, return on assets, return on equity, and other return measures
- contribution margin
- gross and net profit margin

Many companies measure the monthly and yearly profit-and-loss results of each product, line, and category, as well as each market or segment and each channel. By comparing profitability results over time, marketers can spot significant strengths and weaknesses and identify problems and opportunities early. Profitability measures have become particularly sensitive in the e-commerce world, where a company may achieve or even exceed marketing objectives such as aggressive market share growth yet remain unprofitable:

> **eToys.** Founded in 1997, online toy retailer eToys set ambitious growth and market objectives and quickly achieved one of the highest traffic counts on the Web. High-profile alliances with America Online, Discovery Toys, the Gap, and other partners fueled eToys' popularity, while expensive marketing campaigns built the brand and increased awareness of the site's products and services. Month after month, the company lost money as it spent heavily to attract customers and, later, to fix problems such as slow order fulfillment. But after eToys missed sales and revenue estimates during the all-important year-end holiday shopping season in 2000, industry analysts downgraded its stock, and its price plummeted. By early 2001, less than 4 years after its debut, eToys closed its site, sold its inventory and other assets, and filed for bankruptcy, never having reported a profit. Then KB Toys bought the eToys Web address, brand, and inventory and reopened the site—as a subsidiary—in time for the 2001 holiday season.[2]

As eToys found out, e-business investors and other stakeholders are keenly interested in profitability and other financial performance measures, not just nonfinancial achievements.

PRODUCTIVITY CONTROL

PATHFINDER'S TIP

Think about how productivity control can help the company achieve both marketing and financial objectives.

PRODUCTIVITY CONTROL Type of marketing control used to assess the organization's performance and progress in managing the efficiency of key marketing areas.

Productivity control assesses the organization's performance and progress in managing the efficiency of key marketing areas. Closely related to profitability control, productivity control usually covers the efficiency of the sales force, promotions, channels and logistics, and product management. The purpose is to measure profitability improvements through reduced costs or higher yield. Productivity is so important to the bottom line that some companies appoint marketing controllers to establish marketing productivity standards, measure performance, and find new ways to wring more efficiency out of marketing operations—without compromising customer satisfaction or other goals and objectives.

By weighing the short- and long-term payback of each marketing activity against its cost, a growing number of companies are finding that they can get much the same results by spending less. Here are some examples of productivity control at work inside Xerox, well-known for its document imaging products:

> **Xerox.** Xerox used to stage dozens of elaborate new product launch meetings each year to educate and motivate sales staff. But responding to severe profit pressure, the company applied new efficiency measures and found it could save $19 million by drastically cutting the number of in-person meetings in favor of less costly conference calls and Web-based presentations. Xerox also set goals for producing "waste-free products from waste-free factories." It systematically reduced or eliminated factory emissions and waste while designing its copiers and other products for easy refurbishing or recycling. These efficiencies saved Xerox $50 million within a decade.[3]

Like Xerox, more companies are using productivity control to boost the efficiency of their product development and manufacturing activities as well as expediting order fulfillment, shipping and delivery, and many other marketing tasks. In many cases, inefficiencies (such as slow product development or slow order fulfillment) lead to poor customer satisfaction, while efficiency improvements lead to higher satisfaction. Clearly, productivity control is connected not only with profitability but with customer relationships as well.

STRATEGIC CONTROL

Strategic control assesses the organization's effectiveness in managing the marketing function, in managing customer relationships, and in managing social responsibility and ethics issues—three areas of strategic importance. Whereas productivity control, profitability control, and annual plan control are applied monthly or more often, strategic control may be applied once or twice a year, or as needed to give top management a clearer picture of the organization's performance in these strategic areas.

Marketing Assessment

To assess the effectiveness of the marketing function, companies should conduct a yearly **marketing audit**—a detailed, systematic analysis of marketing capabilities and performance. This type of audit helps top management gauge the strengths of the marketing function and pinpoint areas needing improvement. It also reinforces that marketing is being held accountable for performance. After an audit is conducted, a summary of the findings should be included in the internal environmental analysis section of the marketing plan.

Checklist 8.1 shows some of the questions to include when planning a marketing audit.

Organizations also can compare their marketing practices to those of the top performers in their industry and to the benchmarks of acknowledged business or nonprofit

PATHFINDER'S TIP
Incorporate the keys to success identified earlier in the marketing planning process when planning for strategic control.

STRATEGIC CONTROL   Type of marketing control used to assess the organization's performance and progress in the strategic areas of marketing effectiveness, customer relationship management, and social responsibility and ethics.

MARKETING AUDIT A detailed, systematic analysis of an organization's marketing capabilities and performance.

CHECKLIST 8.1   Planning a Marketing Audit

Marketing Strategy

❑   Does the mission focus on external market and customer needs?

❑   Is the mission clearly stated and used as the foundation for marketing planning?

❑   Do the marketing objectives and goals relate to the mission, and are they clearly stated and communicated to guide marketing decisions?

❑   Are the strategy, goals, and objectives appropriate in light of macroenvironmental and microenvironmental trends?

❑   Do all marketing programs and activities have clear and appropriate objectives that relate to the organization's strategy, goals, and mission?

❑   Do all marketing personnel understand and have the skills and resources to carry out the marketing strategy?

Marketing Operations

❑   Does the organization have an effective marketing information system to track internal results and make the information available to marketing decision makers?

❑   Does the organization have an effective marketing intelligence system to track competitive developments and external environmental events?

❑   Does the organization have an effective and efficient system for managing and evaluating new product development? For managing and evaluating the entire product portfolio?

❑   Does the organization have an effective and efficient system for setting, managing, and evaluating pricing?

❑   Does the organization have an effective and efficient system for managing and evaluating supply-chain relationships?

❑   Does the organization have an effective and efficient system for managing and evaluating marketing communications and individual promotions?

❑   Does the organization have an effective and efficient system for managing and evaluating the sales force and the sales process?

Stakeholder Relations

❑   Are the organization's policies and procedures customer friendly?

❑   How does the organization solicit, analyze, and respond to customer feedback and comments?

❑   What are customers' perceptions of the company and the brand, compared with competitors? How have these perceptions changed over time?

❑   What is the customer satisfaction level, how is it measured, and how often? How has satisfaction changed over time?

❑   Does the organization have a system for finding out why customers leave and feeding this information back to improve marketing?

❑   What is the organization doing to track the perceptions and reactions of other important stakeholder groups?

Marketing Results

❑   How does management follow up when programs and activities fail to achieve their stated objectives? What analyses are conducted to diagnose and correct problems?

❑   Is the organization achieving the desired return on marketing investments?

❑   How does management prepare for unexpected events that can help or hurt marketing performance?

leaders. This assessment allows management to identify weaknesses to be addressed and strengths that can serve as the foundation for outstanding marketing performance.

Customer Relationship Assessment

Because customers are the lifeblood of every business, management needs to assess the organization's performance in managing customer relationships. This assessment should look at yearly trends in new customer acquisition, customer retention, customer defections, customer satisfaction, and customer perceptions. Sources of data for this assessment include internal records, customer surveys, and other feedback mechanisms that indicate customer attitudes and satisfaction. By tracking these trends over time, management can see where the company needs to improve and design programs to strengthen relationship building with customers.

For example, here is a look at the way Eastman Chemical assesses its performance in customer relationship management:

Eastman Chemical. Eastman Chemical, which sells industrial chemicals to business customers, has developed a three-pronged approach to evaluating customer relations. First, it measures overall customer satisfaction and compares the results with competitive satisfaction levels; next, it examines customer complaints; and finally, it conducts a "win-loss analysis" to determine what caused an individual business customer to change its level of purchasing with Eastman.[4]

Social Responsibility and Ethics Assessment

What is the organization doing to demonstrate its commitment to social responsibility and ethical marketing? Customers and other stakeholders are increasingly interested in doing business with organizations that earn their trust by protecting the environment; behaving ethically toward customers, suppliers, investors, employees, and other stakeholders; and supporting their local communities. For this reason, management should plan for a periodic assessment of the organization's performance on these and other measures of social responsibility and ethical marketing.

No objective standards exist for measuring corporate performance in social responsibility and ethics, although the Council on Economic Priorities Accreditation Agency suggests standards covering use of child and forced labor, discrimination, health and safety, and other issues. For the most part, organizations make their own decisions about how to incorporate social responsibility and ethics into their plans and what results to measure. Most measure the results on a yearly basis and report progress to top management.[5] Some organizations, such as the Co-operative Bank, choose to publicize the results of their social responsibility and ethics assessments:

The Co-operative Bank. The United Kingdom–based Co-operative Bank has worked hard to establish a good reputation for ethical and socially responsible marketing. Every year since 1997, management has issued a "Partnership Report" showing how the bank's activities during the previous year affected key stakeholders such as customers, employees, and the community. This report also indicates improvements the bank intends to make in areas such as customer sat-

EXHIBIT 8.2   Environmental Affairs at Starbucks

isfaction, ecologically sustainable practices, workforce management practices, community involvement, and commitment to ethical marketing practices.[6]

Starbucks and other companies sometimes establish separate mission statements regarding their support of socially responsible causes and environmental protection; then they periodically report to stakeholders about their progress in these important areas (see Exhibit 8.2).

Analyzing Progress and Controlling Implementation

PATHFINDER'S TIP

The budgets, forecasts, metrics, and standards formulated for the marketing plan serve as the foundation for measurements used in controlling implementation.

The control process, introduced in Chapter 1, is essential for guiding the implementation of any marketing plan. Without control, marketers are unable to determine whether their programs are working out as planned. On the other hand, a well-planned control process gives marketers the information they need to make decisions about continuing, revamping, or abandoning marketing programs or products that fall short of performance measures. Consider 3Com's speedy reaction when applying profitability control to the marketing of its Audrey Internet appliance:

3Com. Although technology analysts forecast a rosy future for sales of Internet appliances—small, non-PC products that allow consumers to access the Web— 3Com kept its Audrey model on the market for only 5 months. Audrey enabled family members to check e-mail with the touch of a button, surf Web channels, and update a household calendar and address book. But 3Com was facing profitability problems and needed to cut costs quickly. After analyzing sales trends in the months following Audrey's introduction, 3Com managers concluded that the growth in sales would not allow the company to turn a profit as quickly as needed, so they dropped the product rather than continue investing in its production and promotion.[7]

Managers of public companies feel extra pressure to apply appropriate control methods, because they must regularly disclose key results to investors and analysts and issue warnings if they think actual results will vary from previously announced forecasts. Autobytel.com, Drugstore.com, and Buy.com know this pressure very well:

Dot-com Death Watch. Autobytel.com, a Web-based car retailer, was under such financial pressure in 2000 that Goldman Sachs put it on a dot-com "death watch," along with Drugstore.com, Buy.com, and seven other struggling e-businesses. One year later, three of the ten e-businesses were gone and two others had been absorbed by rivals, but the remaining five—including Autobytel, Drugstore.com, and Buy.com—were still alive. An Autobytel executive explained his firm's survival by saying that it used "old economy key metrics, like the number of customers, revenue, cost of revenue, and expense control." Similarly, Drugstore.com's CEO noted that his firm survived—even as rivals like HealthCentral went bankrupt—because it closely tracked its gross margins, controlled customer acquisition costs, and strived for operating efficiency. Still, Drugstore.com doesn't expect to be profitable until 2004 at the earliest. And Buy.com had another bad year in 2001. By the third quarter, it required an infusion of cash from its founder to continue operating and was reacquired by the founder by year's end.[8]

To plan implementation control, the marketer starts with the objectives set for each strategy or program, as documented in the marketing plan. The next step is to formulate standards for measuring interim progress toward those targets. Then the marketer arranges to periodically measure actual results, compare these results with the preset standards, and analyze any variances. When a program or product is not turning out as expected, the organization must be prepared to take corrective action by making adjustments or implementing a contingency plan formulated in advance. Despite today's highly volatile marketing environment, however, fewer than 25 percent of companies responding to a recent survey said they always develop plans for corrective action.[9]

The remainder of this chapter discusses how marketers can tackle each step in the marketing control process to assure smooth implementation of the marketing plan.

SET STANDARDS AND MEASUREMENT TIMING

With the goals and objectives in the marketing plan as the starting point, marketers need to set standards for the results expected at specific intervals after a program or product is launched. Typically, these standards and measurement intervals are drawn from marketing plan budgets, forecasts, metrics, and schedules.

For example, assume that the company approves a marketing budget based on monthly sales of 1,000 units of Product A at an average price of $40 and an average cost of $25. At the end of every month, the company can compare its actual unit sales, average price, and average cost results with the budgeted performance. Similarly, if customer relationship metrics call for acquiring 2,500 new customers during a 12-month period at an average cost of $75 per acquisition, the company can break that objective down into standards for weekly or monthly customer acquisition (adjusted for seasonal variations if necessary). Then management can measure actual weekly or monthly acquisition results and costs, compare those with the standards, and see where performance fails to meet expectations.

The exact standards and measurement timing vary from organization to organization and industry to industry. Marketers at Macy's and other retailers often measure sales results quarterly, monthly, weekly, and daily, and compare these with planned results and with the previous year's results. They hope to spot products that exceed sales expectations so they can quickly reorder and sell more before demand peaks. And they watch for products selling more slowly than expected so they can take corrective action by rearranging merchandise, adding a special promotion, or cutting the price. Regardless of industry or mission, the key is to find standards and measurement intervals that allow the organization enough time to diagnose the results and make changes to stay on track.

DIAGNOSE RESULTS

Once marketers implement the marketing plan, they prepare to measure actual performance, compare the results to the standards they've set, and identify any variance—upward or downward. To diagnose significant variances, marketers must dig deeper by examining actual performance trends and comparing recent results with historic and competitive or industry results. At times, they may have to commission marketing research to understand the underlying issues that contributed to these variations and determine what corrective action is needed, if any.

This is where astute environmental scanning and analysis comes in. Major competitive moves, sudden economic swings, and other external events can have a profound effect on marketing results. Moreover, changes in personnel, funding, and technology are just some of the internal events that can account for variances. Business-to-business marketers also need to follow the fortunes of their customers, because slowdowns in a customer's business may mean lower or cancelled orders for its suppliers, directly affecting their performance. Although marketers can do little about broad environmental shifts such as economic downturns, they must stay abreast of such developments, consider the possible effect on marketing performance, and be ready to take corrective action—even to the point of dropping a program or product from the marketing plan, as 3Com did with its Audrey Internet appliance.

TAKE CORRECTIVE ACTION

What should marketers do when they find that actual performance doesn't match planned performance? One approach to corrective action is to change the program, the strategy, or the implementation details in a bid to achieve the planned results. For example, if a direct marketing campaign doesn't generate enough sales leads, the company might add telemarketing or e-mail to the schedule as a way of reaching the program's objectives on time.

A second approach is to change the standards or objectives by which performance is measured. This is appropriate when marketers believe that the variance is not a one-time occurrence and see the underlying cause influencing ongoing performance. GM took this type of corrective action recently:

General Motors. Reviewing month-end results, marketers at GM were pleasantly surprised to find that actual vehicle sales were higher than expected sales, and market share had inched up from the same period a year earlier. Digging deeper, they learned that the entire industry was doing better, in part because the economy appeared to be rebounding from a yearlong slump, which was boosting demand. In reaction to their diagnosis of this variance, GM marketers decided to revise their sales forecasts and change their plans to start producing more vehicles.[10]

Although corrective action is the last step in the marketing control process, its outcome feeds back to the beginning of the cycle. Thus, when marketers take any form of corrective action, they'll use this reaction as input for setting or reevaluating goals and objectives at the start of the next control cycle.

PREPARE CONTINGENCY PLANS

PATHFINDER'S TIP

Take time to think about worst-case scenarios and what the organization would have to do to recover as quickly as possible if faced with such an emergency.

Contingency plans serve as alternate paths to guide organizations toward their objectives when one (or more) of the original strategies or programs is disrupted by uncontrollable environmental forces. Financial services firms and other companies that must continue operating without interruption are especially meticulous about contingency planning. As a result, Merrill Lynch and other brokerage firms recovered quickly after terrorists destroyed the World Trade Center in New York City. Merrill Lynch, for example, immediately moved operations to its backup center in New Jersey, where personnel were able to access corporate data and continue to service customers. Despite its preparedness, the company—like many others that had offices in the Twin Towers—saw its financial performance drop as it coped with the expense of replacing equipment, writing off damaged property, and relocating employees to offices outside New York's financial district.[11]

Marketers usually prepare contingency plans showing how their organization will respond in the case of emergencies such as:

- computer systems outages
- prolonged power interruptions
- natural disasters
- sudden bankruptcy of a major customer or supplier
- contamination or other environmental disasters
- sudden technological breakthrough by a competitor
- major failure of a program or strategy
- price war or other extreme competitive development
- major criminal, sabotage, or terrorist activity

PanAmSat, for example, created a contingency plan for keeping its global communications satellites in operation even if onboard systems malfunctioned. DirecTV had contracted with PanAmSat to deliver satellite television service to Latin American customers, so this contingency plan—implemented when one satellite's propulsion system actually experienced problems—was essential for continuing service without a break and keeping customers satisfied.[12]

Checklist 8.2 shows some questions to ask when preparing a contingency plan. Marketers should prepare contingency plans as they develop their marketing plans, then periodically review and update these plans to be sure they are ready to deal with emergencies. When preparing a contingency plan, think creatively about the organization's options, priorities, and resources to come up with alternatives that minimize the impact of the disruption and allow the organization to recover as quickly as possible. And use the lessons learned from dealing with the emergency as input for analyzing the current situation when preparing next year's marketing plan.

Refer to Appendix 3 for instructions on how to use *Marketing Plan Pro* software to document the controls, assessments, standards, measurements, and contingency plans you have formulated in developing your marketing plan.

CHECKLIST 8.2   Preparing a Contingency Plan

❑ What environmental, technical, or competitive occurrences and disasters could significantly disrupt the organization's operations, facilities, and ability to serve customers?

❑ What specific functions, systems, and locations could be affected?

❑ Which internal decision makers should be notified in the event of an emergency? Who will initiate this notification?

❑ What advance preparations can the organization make to minimize the effect of an emergency? Who will be responsible for these preparations? What resources will be needed?

❑ What steps should the organization take—and in what order—to restore normalcy if an emergency occurs? Who will be responsible for taking these actions and monitoring the results?

❑ What steps should the organization take—and in what order—to continue serving customers and keep operations going during the emergency? Who will be responsible for taking these actions and monitoring the results?

❑ How and when should the organization communicate with customers, investors, employees, the media, and other stakeholders about the emergency? Who should be designated to speak for the organization?

Chapter Summary

The purpose of marketing control is to ensure that employees and marketing activities are effectively moving the organization in the direction outlined in the marketing plan. In preparing a marketing plan, marketers need to plan for four types of marketing control: annual plan, profitability, productivity, and strategic control. Annual plan control is used to assess the progress of the current year's marketing plan. Profitability control is used to assess the organization's progress and performance according to key profitability measures. Productivity control is used to assess the organization's performance and progress in managing the efficiency of key marketing areas. And strategic control is used to assess the organization's effectiveness in managing the marketing function, customer relationships, and social responsibility and ethics issues.

A well-planned control process gives marketers the information they need to make decisions about continuing, revamping, or abandoning marketing programs or products that fall short of expectations or performance measures. Starting with the objectives set for each strategy or program, the marketer formulates standards for measuring interim progress toward those targets. Then the marketer plans to periodically measure actual results, compare these results with the preset standards, and analyze any variances. Corrective action (in the form of adjustments or contingency plan implementation) should be taken when a program or product does not measure up to the preset standards.

MARKETING PLAN RESOURCES

Online resources are dynamic and subject to change; if a particular resource is not at the listed Web address, try using a search engine to find the new location.

Selected online marketing plan outlines and guides:

- *Marketing Plan Pro* site for *Marketing Plan Handbook* users (www.paloalto.com/prenticehall/)
- Know this.com's links to marketing plan guides and information (www.knowthis.com/general/marketplan.htm)
- SBA's Online Women's Business Center guide to marketing planning (www.onlinewbc.gov/docs/market/index.html)
- U.S. Small Business Administration marketing plan outline (www.sba.gov/gopher/Business-Development/Business-Initiatives-Education-Training/Marketing-Plan/)

Selected online sources for researching demographic trends:

- *American Demographics* (www.americandemographics.com)
- *CIA World Factbook* (www.cia.gov/cia/publications/factbook)
- Internet Public Library international references (www.ipl.org/ref/RR/static/rci00.00.00.html)
- *Statistical Abstract of the United States* (www.census.gov/prod/www/statistical-abstract-us.html)
- United Nations Population Fund (www.unfpa.org)
- U.S. Bureau of Economic Analysis (www.bea.gov)

Selected online sources for researching economic trends:

- Financial news coverage (such as www.bloomberg.com, money.cnn.com)
- Business Information Solutions (www.infods.com)
- Michigan State University's GlobalEdge (globaledge.msu.edu/ibrd/ibrd.asp)
- *The Economist* (www.economist.com)
- U.S. Department of Commerce statistics (www.stat-usa.gov)

Selected online sources for researching ecological trends:

- Business for Social Responsibility (www.bsr.org)
- Global Network of Environment and Technology (www.gnet.org)
- Management Institute for Environment and Business (www.wri.org/meb)
- U.S. Department of Energy Office of Environmental Management (apps.em.doe.gov/ost)
- U.S. Environmental Protection Agency (www.epa.gov)

Selected online sources for researching technological trends:

- CyberAtlas (cyberatlas.internet.com)
- Smart Business (www.smartbusinessmag.com)
- TechNews World (www.technewsworld.com)
- U.S. Patent and Trademark Office (www.uspto.gov)

Selected online sources for researching political-legal trends:

- *CIA World Factbook* (www.cia.gov/cia/publications/factbook)
- CyberSecurities Law (www.cybersecuritieslaw.com)
- Federal Trade Commission (www.ftc.gov)
- Stateline.org (www.stateline.org)
- Taxsites.com (www.taxsites.com/state.html)
- U.S. Congress (thomas.loc.gov)
- U.S. Federal Trade Commission (www.ftc.gov)

Selected online sources for researching social-cultural trends:

- Social Science Information Gateway (sosig.ac.uk)
- General Social Survey (www.norc.org)
- *PopMatters* magazine of global pop culture (PopMatters.com)
- Information Please (www.infoplease.com)

Selected online sources for researching and analyzing competitors:

- *Gale's Encyclopedia of Associations* (print) or Internet Public Library Associations on the Net (www.ipl.org/ref/AON/)
- Hoover's Online (www.hoovers.com)
- IndustryClick (www.industryclick.com)
- ProductScan (www.productscan.com)
- Society for Competitive Intelligence Professionals (www.scip.org/ci)
- U.S. Securities and Exchange Commission filings (www.sec.gov)

Selected online sources for researching consumer segments and behavior:

- *Academy of Marketing Science Review* (www.amsreview.org)
- CACI U.K. (www.areadata.co.uk/freedata.htm)
- Customer lifetime value calculations (www.ryanandwong.com/lvalue.htm)
- Direct Marketing Association (www.the-dma.org/library)
- Economics.com's Free Lunch (www.freelunch.com)
- Gartner Group (www.gartnergroup.com)
- Global Statistics (www.geohive.com)
- *Hispanic Business* (www.hispanicbusiness.com)
- *Journal of Consumer Research* (www.journals.uchicago.edu/JCR/home.html)
- Marketsegment.com (www.marketsegment.com/)
- Media Metrix (www.jmm.com)
- The Conference Board Consumer Research Center (www.crc-conquest.org)

Selected online sources for researching business segments and behavior:

- American City Business Journals (www.bizjournals.com)
- Brint.com (www.brint.com/interest.html)
- CEO Express (www.ceoexpress.com)
- *Fortune* 500 (www.fortune.com)

- *Inc.* magazine (www.inc.com)
- International Trade Administration of U.S. Department of Commerce (www.ita.doc.gov)
- U.S. Census Bureau NAICS classification (www.census.gov/epcd/www/naics.html)

Selected online sources for researching high-tech markets and buyer behavior:

- Forrester Research (www.forrester.com)
- Gartner Group (www.gartnergroup.com)
- Giga Information Group (www.gigaweb.com)
- IDC (www.idc.com)
- Jupiter Media Metrix (www.jmm.com)
- NUA (www.nua.ie/surveys)
- ZDNet Research Center (researchcenter.zdnet.com/index.html)
- New product ideas and technologies (www.yet2com.com)

Selected online sources to support planning of marketing strategies and tactics:

- *Advertising Age* advertising coverage (www.adage.com)
- American Marketing Association (www.marketingpower.com)
- Business Marketing Association (www.marketing.org)
- Customer Relationship Daily.com news (www.crmdaily.com)
- E-business basics and links (www.ebusiness.com)
- E-Commerce Times news site (www.ecommercetimes.com)
- eMarketer online marketing news (www.emarketer.com)
- Internet Advertising Bureau (www.iab.net)
- Marketing Click (marketingclick.com)
- Online media site guidelines (www.nngroup.com)
- Outdoor Advertising Association of America (www.oaaa.org)
- Public Relations Society of America (www.prsa.org)
- Truste.com e-commerce security (www.truste.com)
- U.S. Census Bureau Industrial Products Data (www.census.gov/)
- U.S. Patent and Trademark Office (www.uspto.gov)

Selected online resources for entrepreneurs:

- Entrepreneurial links and tutorials (www.entreworld.com)
- Small business basics (www.abcsmallbiz.com)
- CCH Business Owner's Toolkit (www.toolkit.cch.com)
- *Entrepreneur* magazine (www.entrepreneur.com)
- Small business resources and tips (www.businessownersideacafe.com)

SAMPLE MARKETING PLAN: SONIC PERSONAL DIGITAL ASSISTANT

Sonic, a hypothetical start-up company, is about to introduce a new multifunction personal digital assistant (PDA), also known as a handheld computer. Sonic's product is entering a marketplace crowded with offerings from Palm, Handspring, and other rivals. The following sample marketing plan shows how Sonic is preparing to market its first PDA.

Executive Summary

Sonic is preparing to launch a new PDA product in a very competitive but fast-growing market. Despite intense competition from Palm, which leads the market, and from Handspring, which holds the second largest share of this market, we can compete effectively because our offering combines innovative features at a value-added price. We are targeting specific segments in the consumer and business markets, taking advantage of opportunities indicated by forecasts of significant growth in demand for wireless-enabled PDAs during the next 4 years.

Given Sonic's highly efficient product development and assembly procedures, we have minimized variable costs to establish a reasonable wholesale price, achieve market-share objectives, and reach break-even volume early in the product's second year. Competitively, we will create differentiation by emphasizing our product's unique voice recognition system and communicating the value of our total product offering.

Situation Analysis

Sonic, founded 18 months ago by two entrepreneurs with extensive experience in the PC market, is about to enter the highly competitive $3.7 billion PDA market. This market is currently dominated by Palm, which pioneered the PDA product by selling 13 million units in its first 5 years. Industry-wide sales are expected to accelerate for at least the next 5 years, with multi-function devices attracting an ever-increasing share of the overall market. Analysts predict 4 million in total PDA sales for next year and 5 million for the following year.

Sonic's personal digital assistant is designed to meet the communication and information needs of consumers and business users. Our PDA meets these needs by delivering the following benefits: the ability to stay in touch while away from the home or office; the ability to record information while away from the home or office; and the ability to perform multiple communication functions without carrying multiple devices. The product meets an additional personal need, that of being able to communicate while expressing the user's individuality, by providing a case wardrobe of different colors and patterns.

Despite intense competition from Palm and other rivals, Sonic can rely on numerous strengths. First, our PDA includes a voice recognition system licensed from Cellport Systems, a unique feature that simplifies usage and allows hands-free operation. Second, we bundle valuable features found only on higher priced rival products. Third, our PDA can accept any Palm-compatible peripheral, which adds to its versatility. And fourth, ours comes standard with many features found only as options on other models, yet it is priced lower than competing models. However, our weaknesses include lack of brand awareness and image; lack of color display screen; and slightly heavier weight than most competing models (see SWOT analysis section for further details).

The following sections provide further detail about the market, market demographics, market needs, market trends, target market growth, SWOT analysis, competitive analysis, product offering, keys to success, critical issues, and the macroenvironment and microenvironment.

Market Summary

Sonic's market consists of consumers and business users who need to communicate and exchange information when they're away from the home or office. Particular segments being targeted include professionals, college and graduate students, corporations, and entrepreneurs. An additional segment being considered for late-year entry is medical users, including doctors and nurses who want to reduce paperwork and quickly update or access patients' medical records.

MARKET DEMOGRAPHICS

Sonic is focusing on both the consumer and business markets.

Consumer Market

Within the consumer market, the primary target is middle- to upper-income professionals who need one portable device to coordinate their busy schedules and communicate with family and colleagues. These consumers prefer lower priced PDAs with expandable memory and functionality. Demographically, this segment is defined according to professional occupation and annual income above $75,000. A secondary target is college and graduate students who need a multifunction device to organize their school, work, and personal schedules, to store needed documents and information for access anywhere, and to communicate with family and friends. This segment can be described demographically by age (18–30) and education status (entering or in college or graduate school).

Business Market

Within the business market, the primary target is mid- to large-sized corporations that want to help their managers and employees stay in touch and input or access critical data on the go. These buyers want durable, powerful, easy-to-use PDAs that can operate customized business applications. Demographically, this segment consists of companies with more than $25 million in annual sales and more than 100 employees. A secondary target is entrepreneurs and small business owners who need to stay in touch and organize their busy schedules at all times.

Toward the end of the year, we may enter a specialized segment of the business market. This segment consists of medical users, doctors and nurses who want to reduce paperwork and quickly update or access patients' medical records. Research shows that this segment's usage of PDAs nearly doubled in the past year, with similar increases expected in the future.

According to market forecasts, the U.S. PDA market will continue to grow for the next 5 years, with 4 million units forecast to be sold next year and 5 million forecast for the year after. As multifunction and wireless PDAs become more popular, market volume is expected to increase to 10 million units or more sold annually within 4 years, when roughly one-third of the units will allow wireless communication.

MARKET NEEDS

Communication and information are the two general needs of consumers and business users of PDAs. Exhibit A2.1 shows how the Sonic PDA addresses the specific needs of targeted segments within the consumer and business markets.

Our licensing arrangement with Cellport Systems allows us to provide the unique feature of voice recognition for hands-off operation. This adds to the convenience and ease of use that customers enjoy with Sonic PDAs and gives us a strong point of differ-

EXHIBIT A2.1 Needs, Features, and Benefits for Sonic PDA

Targeted Segment	*Need*	*Feature*	*Benefit*
Business travelers (professionals in the consumer market)	Stay in touch while away from the office	Wireless e-mail	Conveniently send and receive messages from anywhere
Business travelers (professionals in the consumer market)	Record information while away from the office	Voice recognition	Simple, no-hands operation to record information
College and graduate students (consumer market)	Communicate using a device that expresses their individuality	Case wardrobe of different colors and patterns	Change the case to make a fashion statement
College and graduate students (consumer market)	Perform multiple functions without carrying multiple gadgets	Works with Palm-compatible cameras, software, and other peripherals	Convenient, cost-effective way to do more
Corporate users (business market)	Communicate by inputting and accessing critical data on the go	Works with Palm-compatible custom applications	Convenience of using a portable device with readily-available programs
Entrepreneurs (business market)	Organize and access contacts and schedule information	Hands-off access to calendar and address book features	Quickly check appointments and locate contacts

entiation for competitive advantage in satisfying market needs. Ongoing research will help us identify additional benefits and associated features that we can offer to maintain our differentiation.

MARKET TRENDS

PDA purchasers have to decide between models based on two different operating systems. Sonic uses the market-dominant Palm system, developed by Palm and also licensed by Handspring and Sony, among others. Thousands of software applications and hardware peripherals are currently available for devices that use Palm's operating system, including the Sonic PDA. As a result, customers have numerous choices for selecting add-ons that will provide the functionality and features they require. The Pocket PC system, a variation of Microsoft's Windows software, has been gaining in popularity due to its use in more powerful PDAs made by Hewlett-Packard, Casio, NEC, and others. Models that run on the Pocket PC system also offer higher standard memory than Palm-compatible models and can more easily handle multimedia applications.

Product proliferation and increased competition have resulted in lower prices and lower profit margins. Lower prices are helping to expand sales of PDAs, especially in the lower end of the consumer market, but gross margins continue to be under pressure. Formerly, Handspring enjoyed gross margins in the 30 percent range; such margins are rare today and may be unattainable for the foreseeable future as pricing continues to be a key competitive strategy. At the same time, customers with first-generation PDAs are starting to reenter the market by buying newer, high-end multi-function units with desirable features such as wireless access. Given this trend, customers who are already familiar with the Palm operating system are a good target for trading up to Sonic PDAs.

Other market trends relate to demand for technological advances such as the integration of cell phone functionality and other capabilities; sharper and larger screen displays; speedier processing of information; memory expansion; applications for specific consumer and business purposes; and more fashion-oriented accessories for PDAs.

TARGET MARKET GROWTH

Overall growth continues strong in the consumer and business markets for PDAs. However, wireless functionality is driving sales of higher-end and replacement models. As shown in Exhibit A2.2, estimated growth in wireless PDA sales is projected to outpace growth in nonwireless PDA sales for the next 4 years.

As more applications become available for voice-activated PDAs, our product will be able to address additional market needs for current and future segments. Although some competitors will likely be able to develop or license similar voice recognition systems within 6 to 12 months, our head start should enable us to create strong brand recognition and build sales and brand loyalty among targeted market segments.

EXHIBIT A2.2 Target Market Growth

	2002	*2003*	*2004*	*2005*
Wireless	500,000	800,000	1,200,000	3,100,000
Nonwireless	3,500,000	4,200,000	5,800,000	6,900,000

SWOT Analysis

In taking advantage of growth opportunities in the wireless segment of the U.S. PDA market, Sonic has several powerful strengths on which to build. The most important is voice recognition capability, a feature unmatched by competitors at this time. We also see the product's value-added features offered at a low price as a second major strength.

However, we face the threat of ever-higher competition and downward pressure on pricing. In addition, our major weakness is the lack of brand awareness and image. Exhibit A2.3 summarizes the strengths, weaknesses, opportunities, and threats facing the Sonic PDA.

STRENGTHS

Sonic can build on three important strengths:

- *Unique product offering.* We offer the unmatched feature of voice recognition capability plus features such as built-in wireless Web access and built-in MP3 capabilities. Research shows that these three aspects of our offering are in demand by our targeted market segments.
- *Compatibility.* Our PDA also can work with the hundreds of Palm-compatible peripherals and applications currently available, making it more versatile and easily customized to each user's needs and circumstances.
- *Pricing.* Our product is priced lower than competing models—all of which lack voice recognition. Thus, our PDA is perceived as delivering more value, which is especially important in our increasingly price-sensitive market segments.

WEAKNESSES

Among Sonic's weaknesses are:

- *Lack of brand awareness.* As a start-up, Sonic has not yet established our brand and image in the target market. Because Palm and Handspring both have strong

EXHIBIT A2.3   SWOT Analysis for Sonic PDA

Strengths (internal capabilities that can support the firm in achieving its goals)	Weaknesses (internal factors that can prevent the firm from achieving its goals)
Voice recognition capabilities	Lack of brand awareness and image
Built-in wireless Web access	Monochrome display
Built-in MP3 capabilities	Heavier than most competing models
Can use Palm-compatible peripherals	
Priced lower than competing models	
Opportunities (external circumstances that may be exploited for higher performance)	**Threats (external circumstances that may potentially hurt performance)**
Increasing demand	Increasing competition
Availability of diverse add-on peripherals	Downward pressure on pricing
Availability of diverse applications for home and business use	Growing popularity of multifunction cell phones

brand recognition, we need to call attention to our brand and our product's strengths.

- *Monochrome display.* Many competitors are offering color displays; Sonic's PDA has a monochrome display geared for easy text reading, which allows us to price this model relatively low.

- *Heavier weight.* To accommodate the multifunction features, Sonic's PDA is slightly heavier than most competing models—a disadvantage for a product being marketed on the basis of convenient portability. As a result, we will put more emphasis on our model's unmatched set of multifunction features and its value-added pricing, two important competitive strengths.

OPPORTUNITIES

Sonic can take advantage of three major market opportunities:

- *Increasing demand.* The market for wireless Web-enabled PDAs is projected to grow much faster than the market for nonwireless models. As market penetration increases, more prospects are seeing PDAs in use in work and education settings, which in turn is boosting demand for entry-level models. Also, demand for more sophisticated, higher-end replacement models is expanding as customers who bought entry-level models are trading up to gain new features and functionality.
- *Add-on peripherals.* More peripherals such as cameras, global positioning systems, and cell telephones are available for PDAs that use the Palm operating system. Consumers and business users who are interested in any of these peripherals will see the Sonic PDA as a value-priced device able to be conveniently and quickly expanded for multiple functions.
- *Diverse applications.* The wide range of Palm-compatible software applications available for home and business use makes the Sonic PDA a convenient multi-function device for satisfying communication and information needs.

THREATS

Three main threats face Sonic at the introduction of the first PDA model:

- *Increased competition.* More companies are entering the U.S. PDA market with models that offer some but not all of the features and benefits provided by Sonic's PDA. Competing Pocket PC models are becoming more popular as well. This increased competition adds to the noise and confusion in the marketplace, making it more important that the Sonic marketing communication strategy stress our clear differentiation and value-added pricing.
- *Downward pressure on pricing.* Increased competition and market-share strategies are pushing PDA prices down. This can be a significant threat to Sonic's long-term financial stability if we don't maintain tight cost controls and take advantage of economies of scale as volumes increase. Our objective of seeking a 10% profit on second-year sales of the original model is realistic, given the lower margins in the PDA market.
- *Multifunction cell phones.* Kyocera and other manufacturers are introducing multifunction cell phones with some PDA features, such as organizers and wireless Web access. Because cell phones have much higher market penetration, this trend can potentially slow growth in the PDA market. To guard against this threat, we will emphasize the size, convenience, and multifunction features of our PDA.

Competition

In the short term, Sonic is facing two main competitors in the PDA market. Palm dominates the market with PDAs for consumers and businesses; its growing product line ranges from a low-end, non–Web-enabled, monochrome model to a slimmer, high-end model with color display that is equipped for Web access and e-mail notification. Handspring, the aggressive number 2 company in the market, attracted an estimated 21 percent share in its first year and helped drive Palm's dominance to below a 70 percent market share. Handspring also licenses the Palm operating system for its PDAs, which are lower-priced and generally more versatile than Palm's PDAs. Handspring's most recent models are slimmer and lighter than previous models despite the added functionality of use as a cell phone, as a Web access device, and for e-mail communication.

Most other competing PDA models are based on the Pocket PC operating system, a variation of Microsoft's Windows system. Compaq, Hewlett-Packard, and Casio all produce PDAs that use the Pocket PC system. Combined, these PDA models account for about 10 percent of the market, but analysts expect their share to continue growing. The Pocket PC PDAs generally use more powerful processors and come with more standard memory than Palm-compatible PDAs.

Sonic will have to take share away from Palm and Handspring—the two market leaders—to achieve our aggressive first-year objective of attaining 6 percent share of the U.S. PDA market. This objective is achievable because of Sonic's superior features and value-added retail pricing of about $350. Our model is therefore highly attractive to first-time PDA buyers in our targeted segments as well as to PDA owners in those segments who want the convenience of voice recognition commands. The following table shows the current estimated market share of major competitors in the PDA market (Exhibit A2.4).

EXHIBIT A2.4 Estimated Market Share Analysis	
Competitor	*Current Share (Estimated By Revenue)*
Palm	64%
Handspring	21%
Casio	5%
All others	10%

Product Offering

Our first product is the Sonic PDA, with the following standard features:

- Voice recognition for hands-free commands and communication
- Built-in wireless Web access and e-mail capabilities
- Built-in MP3 music downloading and play capabilities
- Full range of organization and communication functions, including calendar, address book, memo pad, world clock, Web browser, e-mail program, and expense organizer
- Connectors to accommodate all Palm-compatible peripherals
- Functionality to run any Palm-compatible application
- Monochrome sharp-text display
- Cradle for synchronizing data with PC
- Interchangeable case wardrobe of different colors and patterns

First-year sales revenues are projected to be $60 million, based on sales of 240,000 units at a wholesale price of $250 each. Our financial target is to hold first-year losses at $10 million or less, including product development and production expenses as well as communication and channel costs to support the initial product introduction.

Sonic plans a second product for introduction during the following year. This second model will be a higher-end product, wholesale priced at $350 per unit, with these additional standard features:

- Color display
- Cell phone functionality (requires subscription to service provider partner)
- Global positioning system locator function

Our second-year objective is to achieve a 10 percent share based on sales of two models in the product. This second model will help expand our reach in the business market and attract a larger share of PDA users who want to trade up to a more sophisticated multifunction model.

Keys to Success

A major key to success in the U.S. PDA market is the establishment of a well-regarded brand name linked to a meaningful positioning. Palm is the best-known brand in the PDA market at this time, and although Handspring is younger, it has quickly achieved widespread brand recognition as well. Compaq and Casio, among other competitors, can leverage their existing brands and images built during decades of experience in marketing other electronic products. Therefore, to be competitive in this market, Sonic will have to create a memorable and distinctive brand image projecting innovation, quality, and value.

A second key to success is the proper promotion of the voice-recognition system that Sonic has licensed from Cellport Systems. Users may be skeptical that a PDA can accurately recognize and act on their verbal commands. For its part, Cellport is already implementing a marketing campaign in support of a separate contract it has negotiated with Ford to supply voice-activated cell phone systems as an option for installation in Ford Taurus, Mercury Sable, Ford Windstar, and Lincoln Town Car vehicles. Building on this existing publicity and awareness of the value of voice activation, we will launch a campaign featuring celebrities voicing a variety of commands as the Sonic PDA responds. We will also develop a competitive comparison ad showing how much faster Sonic PDA users can accomplish tasks using voice recognition, compared with traditional PDA models. Finally, we will provide Sonic PDAs to selected opinion leaders as a way of stimulating positive word-of-mouth communication in the targeted consumer and business market segments.

Critical Issues

Sonic faces several critical issues:

- Increased competition from multifunction cell phone combinations offered by Kyocera and others could slow acceptance of our model, even though the Sonic PDA can use the Palm-compatible cell-phone attachment. We plan to conduct in-depth marketing research to determine which segments are especially open to this type of competition.

- Competitive advances in new product innovation will challenge our ability to differentiate the Sonic PDA in a way that is meaningful to the marketplace. Currently, no other model operates on a voice recognition system; within a year, however, competitors will be able to match this valuable feature. Sonic must continue to identify points of differentiation that are valued by the targeted segments and incorporate them into new models at attractive yet profitable price points.
- The downward pricing pressure caused by the proliferation of PDA and hybrid products requires us to tightly control product and marketing costs to avoid unacceptable loss levels. However, as a start-up, we must invest heavily in a marketing activities to establish our brand and positioning. Therefore, we need to carefully measure awareness and response to our marketing activities so we can make any needed adjustments in a timely and cost-effective manner.
- Other issues that Sonic will need to resolve in the coming months include: (1) Should Sonic develop a proprietary operating system, switch to the competing Pocket PC system, or continue to pay licensing fees for the Palm system? (2) Should Sonic offer to develop customized applications for business users? (3) Should we expand our consumer market by creating a game-playing peripheral to make our PDA compatible with Sony's PlayStation 2? (4) Should we use mass media or concentrate on creating buzz from favorable expert reviews?

Macroenvironment and Microenvironment

Sonic is influenced by factors in both the macroenvironment and the microenvironment:

- *Macroenvironmental factors* that are likely to affect Sonic's performance include demographics (especially the huge echo boomer segment of 72 million U.S. consumers); economic issues (particularly the purchasing power of echo boomers and business buyers); technology (mainly investment in and faster development of new advances for voice recognition and other PDA-related technologies); laws and regulations governing wireless communications; and social issues (including the perceived social status of PDA users).
- *Microenvironmental factors* that are likely to affect Sonic include suppliers (especially the continued willingness of Palm and Cellport to license their systems at reasonable fees); marketing intermediaries (particularly our ability to distribute PDAs through key channels such as computer retail chains and office supply superstores); competitors (especially new product innovations introduced by Palm and Handspring); and customers (particularly, the operating system preferences of PDA users).
- *Competitive strategy*. Sonic plans to compete with Palm and Handspring through a product feature strategy of specializing in voice recognition technology. No other PDA currently offers this technology, which gives us an opportunity to establish the Sonic brand and image in the targeted customer segments. However, we anticipate that competitors will quickly follow suit with proprietary versions of voice recognition systems within 6 months of our first model's introduction. To counter such competitive moves, we must maintain our planned schedule of introducing a second higher-end model with additional features within 1 year. This will allow us to maintain our innovative image, improve profit margins, and focus on additional segments within the consumer and business markets. We also can attract current PDA owners who are familiar with the Palm operating system, because there are fewer switching costs and less inconvenience in trading up to Sonic's PDA, which uses the same operating system.

Marketing Strategy

Our marketing strategy is designed to support our successful entrance into the competitive PDA market. We plan to build brand awareness and image while emphasizing our competitive superiority based on innovation quality, and value. Using all elements of the marketing mix, as well as service and internal marketing, we will educate our targeted segments about the features and benefits of our new PDA and motivate purchases by first-time users as well as PDA owners seeking to trade up. Although television advertising is not affordable under start-up budget constraints, we will use radio, online, and other media to reach our targeted segments in creative and effective ways.

The following sections examine our mission, marketing and financial objectives, target markets, positioning, strategy, marketing-mix elements, service and internal marketing, and marketing research plans.

MISSION

Sonic's mission is to produce and market high-quality, value-priced PDA products that enable U.S. consumers and business users to use voice recognition to organize data and stay in touch whenever and wherever they choose. As this mission indicates, we have chosen to operate in the U.S. market for handheld computing devices. Our core competence is producing quality electronics with innovative features, notably the incorporation of unique voice recognition technology for hands-free operation.

We define our vertical scope as manufacturing Sonic-branded products for distribution through a network of select online and computer retailers and office supply superstores in the top 50 U.S. markets. Geographically, our scope initially covers the 50 states; in later years, we will consider expanding to the Canadian market and, if demand is strong, beyond.

MARKETING OBJECTIVES

Our primary marketing objectives are to:

- Achieve first-year unit sales volume of 240,000, which represents a projected market share of 6 percent with one model in product line.
- Increase second-year share to 10 percent, based on sales of two models in product line.
- Generate 40 percent brand awareness within the consumer target market and 50 percent brand awareness within the business target market by the end of next year.
- Arrange for distribution through Amazon.com and through the leading computer and office-supply retailers in the top 50 U.S. markets within 3 months, followed by distribution coverage in the remaining major metropolitan areas within 6 months.

FINANCIAL OBJECTIVES

Sonic's primary financial objectives are to:

- Restrict first-year losses to less than $10 million and seek a 10 percent profit on second-year sales of the original product.
- Achieve first-year total sales revenue of $60 million, based on an average wholesale price of $250 per unit.
- Earn an annual rate of return on investment of 15 percent after taxes within the first 4 years.

TARGET MARKETS

On the consumer side, the primary target market is middle- to upper-income professionals who need one portable device to coordinate their busy schedules and communicate with family and colleagues. These consumers prefer lower-priced PDAs with expandable memory and functionality. The secondary consumer target is college students and graduate students who want to organize their school, work, and personal schedules, input and access information at any time from any location, and stay in touch with family and friends.

On the business side, the target market is mid- to large-sized corporations that want to help their workforce stay in touch and input or access critical data on the go. These buyers want durable, powerful, easy-to-use PDAs that can operate customized business applications. The secondary business target consists of entrepreneurs and small business owners who need to stay in touch and organize their busy schedules at all times. A possible tertiary business target is medical users, doctors and nurses who want to reduce paperwork and quickly update or access patients' medical records.

POSITIONING

Using product differentiation, we are positioning the Sonic PDA as the most versatile, convenient, value-added model for personal and professional use. We are focusing on the voice recognition system as the main feature differentiating the Sonic PDA from all other competing models, because it provides versatility and convenience.

STRATEGY

Because of the intensely competitive nature of the market, our most important strategy relates to the need for clear differentiation to position Sonic as the most versatile, convenient, value-added model for personal and professional use. Supporting that positioning, key points to be emphasized include:

- versatility (the ability to use any Palm-compatible peripheral or software application; the incorporation of MP3 music functionality; case wardrobe as a standard feature)
- convenience (voice recognition software for hands-off operation; wireless e-mail and Web functionality; size and portability)
- value-added (retail price of about $350; standard features that are only available on competing high-end models or as user-installed options)

Marketing Mix

We will move toward our marketing and financial objectives using a variety of product, pricing, promotion, and distribution programs. The following sections are a sample of our marketing-mix programs to support the PDA introduction.

PRODUCT

Our basic PDA model, to be introduced at $250 wholesale/$350 estimated retail price per unit, incorporates voice recognition system for hands-free operation; wireless Web access; MP3 capabilities; use with Palm-compatible peripherals for expanded functionality; use with Palm-compatible software applications; slots for additional memory; black/white sharp text display screen; full range of organization and communication functions, including calendar, address book, memo pad, world clock, Web browser, e-mail program, and expense organizer; cradle for synchronizing data with PC; and interchangeable case wardrobe of different colors and patterns. The product will be sold with a full 1-year warranty; repairs will be provided on a contract basis by a nationwide service organization.

We will focus our research and development efforts on creating a more compact, powerful high-end model for introduction the following year. This second model, to be priced at $350 wholesale per unit, will have even more standard features that are currently available only as options on competing models, including color display, cell phone functionality, and GPS locator functionality. This product will be accompanied by a special subscription offer of cell phone service (arranged through partnerships with regional service providers).

The Sonic brand is an integral part of our product strategy. The brand and logo (Sonic's distinctive yellow thunderbolt) will be displayed on the product and its packaging, and reinforced by its prominence in the introductory marketing campaign. The packaging will protect the product from damage in transit and incorporate security features so the boxes can be displayed store shelves as well as in store showcases. It will also include a competitive comparison chart emphasizing the product's unique features and value-added benefits.

PRICING

Our introductory PDA model will carry a first-year average retail price of $350, which is in the mid-range of the market yet offers unusually high value for so many standard features that are optional on competing models. We expect to lower the price of this first model when we expand the product line by launching a higher-end model in the second year. According to our first-year financial objectives, we plan to limit our losses to $10 million or less. Our pricing objective is to support the sale of 240,000 units in the first year and achieve our market-share objective of capturing 6 percent of the U.S. PDA market.

Exhibit A2.5 shows the features and approximate price levels (which can vary from retailer to retailer) of selected mid-level and high-end PDA models being marketed by Palm and Handspring; none of these currently include voice recognition capa-

EXHIBIT A2.5 Pricing

Competitor	Model and Features	Approximate Price
Palm	Palm m500 (monochrome screen, expansion slot for memory cards, organizer features, cradle for data exchange)	$399
Palm	Palm m505 (color screen, expansion slot for memory cards, organizer features, cradle for data exchange)	$449
Palm	Palm vX (monochrome screen, no expansion slot, organizer features, leather cover)	$299
Handspring	Treo 180 (keyboard, cell phone, monochrome screen, Web-browsing and e-mail, organizer features)	$399
Handspring	Treo 270 (keyboard, cell phone, color screen, Web-browsing and e-mail, organization features)	$599
Handspring	Visor Prism (color screen, cradle for data exchange, organizer features, expansion slot, e-mail function, speaker and microphone)	$299

bilities. As a result, such competitive comparisons support our strategy of value-added pricing.

To encourage retailers to stock our PDAs in larger quantities, Sonic will extend payment terms for an additional 30 days for volume orders. We will also support cooperative advertising by channel partners that agree to specially feature the Sonic product in their display ads, catalogs, and Web sites.

PROMOTION

One set of marketing objectives to be supported by promotion activities is to generate 40 percent brand awareness within the consumer target market and 50 percent brand awareness within the business target market by the end of next year. To achieve these objectives, we will create a multimedia advertising campaign to build brand awareness and differentiate the product from competitors. We also will emphasize trade sales promotion to support our distribution strategy and develop a high-profile product launch strategy to generate publicity and media coverage.

Highlights of our initial 6 month promotion activities:

- *January.* We will initiate a $500,000 trade sales promotion campaign to educate dealers and generate excitement for the product launch in February. As part of this trade push, we will exhibit at the major consumer electronics trade show and invite head-to-head comparisons with leading PDA competitors to showcase the speed and convenience of our product's voice recognition capabilities. We will also provide Sonic PDAs to selected product reviewers, opinion leaders, and celebrities as part of our public relations strategy to generate prelaunch buzz. In addition, our training staff will work with sales personnel at major retail chains to explain Sonic's features, benefits, and competitive advantages. Finally, we will work with key channel partners to initiate sales activities targeting the corporate PDA market.
- *February.* We will start an integrated print/radio/Internet campaign targeting professionals and consumers. The centerpiece of this campaign will be a competitive comparison ad for print and online media showing how much faster Sonic PDA users can accomplish tasks using voice recognition, compared with traditional PDA models. This multimedia campaign will be supported by point-of-sale signage and demonstrations as well as online-only specials.
- *March.* As the multimedia advertising campaign continues, we will add consumer sales promotion tactics such as discounting selected accessories to encourage purchases during a period when sales are traditionally lower. We will also distribute new point-of-purchase displays to generate retail excitement and continue supporting the corporate sales activities of our channel partners.
- *April.* Our main focus this month will be on a trade sales contest offering prizes for the salesperson and chain that sells the most Sonic PDAs during the 4-week period. To support this contest, we will launch a new trade ad campaign emphasizing Sonic's unique features and value-added pricing.
- *May.* We plan to roll out a new national campaign this month. The radio ads will feature celebrity voices using the voice recognition system to operate their Sonic PDAs. The print ads will show these celebrities holding their Sonic PDAs. Coordinated point-of-purchase displays will carry through the theme and graphics of the national campaign.
- *June.* Our radio campaign will add a voice-over tag line promoting Sonic PDAs as a graduation gift. We will also exhibit at the semiannual electronics trade show

and provide channel partners with new competitive comparison handouts as a sales aid. In addition, we will tally and analyze the results of our first customer satisfaction survey for possible use in future promotions and to provide feedback for product and marketing activities. Finally, we will work with the top retail chains to plan holiday season promotions and new corporate sales drives.

CHANNELS

Our channel strategy is to use selective distribution to have Sonic PDAs sold through the best-known computer stores and online retailers, starting with the top 50 U.S. markets. During the first year, we will add channel partners until we have coverage in all major U.S. markets and the product is included in all major electronics catalogs.

This phase-in approach will allow our training staff to familiarize retail sales personnel with our PDA's unique features and benefits. We will put special emphasis on key points of competitive differentiation, including our unique voice recognition system. In support of our channel partners, Sonic will provide demonstration products, detailed specification handouts, and full-color photos and displays featuring the product. We will also arrange special trade terms for retailers that place volume orders.

Channel partners will be able to access Sonic's Web-based system to place orders, check on inventory and shipments, and receive information about trade promotions and other details. Sonic will ship all orders via air or fastest available method to ensure minimal stock-out situations. We also will work with channel partners to plan optimal order quantities and ensure adequate stock levels for peak sales periods.

SERVICE AND INTERNAL MARKETING

Sonic plans a multifaceted service strategy. Buyers will receive a 1-year warranty on parts and labor, with repairs handled by a nationwide service provider on a contract basis. The service provider will be trained by Sonic engineers and will provide Sonic with weekly reports on service issues so we can quickly identify any problems and address them through manufacturing or design adjustments. To ensure that customers are receiving the expected level of warranty service, we will conduct quarterly customer satisfaction surveys.

Sonic will provide comprehensive training and point-of-sale service for retail partners. Customers and retailers will be able to contact service support 24 hours a day, 7 days a week, on the Web or by calling a toll-free hotline. Sonic will also survey a sample of customers monthly and annually to track service satisfaction and pinpoint areas for improvement. Our director of service quality, who reports to the CEO, is responsible for establishing appropriately high service quality standards and ensuring that the company consistently meets those standards, backing up our brand image.

To build internal support for the product launch and improve internal knowledge of our target markets and their needs, we will use internal marketing as follows:

- Conduct monthly staff meetings to update the entire company on current plans and achievements.
- Issue a weekly bulletin via e-mail to communicate each week's activities and any changes that are being made.
- Invite staff members to beta-test pre-production models and offer feedback.
- Coordinate joint planning of marketing and production schedules.
- Provide recognition and rewards for exceeding planned sales levels.

Marketing Research

Sonic is using marketing research to support marketing planning in a number of ways:

- *Product development.* Through concept testing, surveys, focus groups, and market tests, we have identified and incorporated the most highly valued features and benefits of a PDA product. As we plan for our second PDA model, we are collecting additional data on usability, quality and value perceptions, and new features needed by consumer and business users. We are continuing to measure and analyze customers' attitudes toward the Sonic brand compared with those of Palm, Handspring, and other competitive brands.
- *Marketing communication.* We plan to measure brand awareness before, during, and after our major national marketing campaign begins. In particular, we want to determine the effectiveness of each medium in reaching the targeted audience and stimulating response. We also want to analyze how customers receive and interpret each message so we can refine our communications for more impact.
- *Customer satisfaction.* Customer satisfaction is critical to creating a buzz through positive word-of-mouth communication. Therefore, we are planning comprehensive studies to gauge customer satisfaction with the initial Sonic PDA model and with warranty services; this will help us quickly identify any product or warranty service issues that require immediate attention.
- *Pricing.* To support the pricing process for our second Sonic model, we will conduct marketing research to test different offerings at different price levels and to examine the role of pricing in helping Sonic compete with specific rival models.

Financials

Total first-year sales revenue for the Sonic PDA is projected at $60 million, with an average wholesale price of $250 per unit and variable cost per unit of $150 on unit sales volume of 240,000. On a quarterly basis, we project sales of $8 million, $12 million, $11 million, and $29 million, based on cumulatively higher business sales and a spike in year-end consumer PDA sales.

Heavy investments in product development, promotion, and channel support are expected to contribute to a first-year loss of up to $10 million on the initial PDA model. However, longer term projections call for achieving a 10% profit on second-year sales of the original PDA model, a realistic profit level given the lower margins in the PDA market. Break-even calculations indicate that Sonic will begin to profit from the sale of the initial PDA product once sales volume exceeds 267,500, early in the product's second year. At that time, we plan to lower the wholesale price of the first model—in line with standard industry practice—to lower the retail price and increase sales volume.

(Each individual action program will carry its own financial assumptions, managerial assignments, and scheduling, not shown in this sample plan. The full marketing plan also would include a detailed profit and loss analysis for each product. All these financial projections lay the foundation for planning in the manufacturing, human resources, research and development, and finance and accounting departments.)

BREAK-EVEN ANALYSIS

Our break-even analysis of Sonic's first PDA product assumes:

- per-unit wholesale revenue of $250 per unit

- variable cost of $150 per unit
- estimated first-year fixed costs of $26,750,000 (including investments in product development and design, manufacturing setup and overhead, marketing, and other fixed costs)

Based on these assumptions, the break-even calculation is:

$$\frac{26,750,000}{250 - 150} = 267,5000 \text{ units}$$

Projections call for selling 240,000 units in the introductory year; therefore, we will reach the break-even point early in the second year of sales, just when we will be lowering the wholesale price as we launch the higher-end second product in our line.

SALES FORECAST

For our initial PDA model, we project sales to each targeted segment in the first year of product availability as shown in Exhibit A2.6.

In line with these sales projections, we are putting more marketing emphasis on the consumer market while working through channel partners to reach the corporate and entrepreneur market. *(Full month-by-month sales forecasts—per channel and per segment—would be provided in an actual marketing plan.)*

EXHIBIT A2.6   Sales Forecast

	Unit sales
Consumer market	
Professionals	84,000
College/graduate students	48,000
Business market	
Corporations	74,000
Entrepreneurs	34,000
Total	240,000

MARKETING EXPENSE BUDGET

We are budgeting for first-year marketing expenses relating to advertising, sales collateral, point-of-purchase displays, consumer sales promotion, trade sales promotion, public relations, online marketing, channel allowances, travel, marketing research, new product development, sales training and support, shipping, and customer service support. *(In an actual marketing plan, this section would include detailed monthly budgets for each of those activities.)*

Controls

Because Sonic's PDA is a new product, we are planning special control activities to monitor quality and customer service satisfaction. This will enable us to react very quickly in correcting any problems that may occur. We are also monitoring customer service communications to detect any early signs of customer concern or confusion. Other early warning signals that will be monitored for signs of deviation from the plan include monthly sales (by segment and channel) and monthly expenses. In addition, we are tightly controlling marketing schedules to assure timely implementation of planned programs. A contingency plan also has been developed for immediate implementation in the case of severe downward pricing pressure on PDA products.

(The full marketing plan would include a detailed schedule and managerial assignment for every action program and activity, not shown in this sample. For control purposes, an actual plan would also allow for month-by-month comparison of actual versus projected sales and expenses.)

IMPLEMENTATION

To guide implementation, our complete marketing plan will include detailed week-by-week schedules for each marketing activity and program, including budget and managerial responsibility *(not shown in this sample)*. This will enable us to coordinate and track our resource commitments as planned.

MARKETING ORGANIZATION

Sonic was founded 18 months ago by CEO Minoru Yamagishi and President Sandra E. Blaine, two former executives of Compaq. The executive team consists of Frederic Somers, chief financial officer; Jane Melody, chief marketing officer; Phillip Goodman, vice president of production; Marc E. Holley, director of human resources; and Dianne Cheskey, vice president of technology.

As chief marketing officer, Jane Melody holds overall responsibility for marketing strategy and direction; she also directs channel sales and all marketing communication and promotion activities. Reporting to Jane Melody in the marketing organization are:

- Tony Calella, sales manager, responsible for channel sales, sales training for retail partners, and sales collateral
- Caitlin Howard, advertising manager, responsible for supervising both message development and media selection by the advertising agency
- Rob Barnet, marketing coordinator, responsible for trade and consumer sales promotion campaigns

Sonic has hired Worldwide Marketing to handle mass and online media advertising. The agency also will prepare trade and consumer sales promotion materials to support our product introduction campaign. Media buying will be reviewed by Media Specialists, Inc. to ensure the best balance of efficiency with effective reach and frequency levels.

CONTINGENCY PLANNING

Sonic has prepared a contingency plan to implement if the PDA market begins to experience severe downward pricing pressure. This may occur if a major competitor initiates a price war or develops a lower cost technology. It also may occur if cell phone combinations (such as the product made by Kyocera) become much more popular than PDA products. Our contingency plan *(not included with this sample plan)* calls for introducing a significant but short-term price promotion such as a rebate to remain competitive while gauging the price sensitivity of different targeted segments. Based on the results of this short-term promotion, we will be able to take longer term steps to defend market share while retaining a minimally acceptable level of profitability.

DOCUMENTING A MARKETING PLAN WITH *MARKETING PLAN PRO* SOFTWARE

Introduction to *Marketing Plan Pro* Software

The *Marketing Plan Pro* software provided with this handbook is a useful tool for documenting a marketing plan. It guides users through each step of the process and provides tools for creating tables and charts to illustrate the plan, with Web-based resources for support and assistance. *Marketing Plan Pro* helps users conveniently graph growth projections for a new product, for example, or break down costs and sales for a particular sales territory. Users also can customize a cover page, choose fonts and type sizes, and print the entire marketing plan when completed.

In addition, *Marketing Plan Pro* includes sample marketing plans showing how real-world businesses and nonprofit organizations approach the wide variety of issues and choices they face. Although these sample plans cover various types of organizations, products, and customer segments, they all follow the same format, so plans can easily be compared and contrasted. Each of the sample plans contains instructions for entering data in all sections, an example of text information for the sample company, and a full set of tables and charts to supplement the text.

This appendix shows how to use the software for studying sample marketing plans, setting up a new marketing plan, and entering data during each part of the marketing planning process. This first part introduces the basic features of *Marketing Plan Pro* software; later parts provide instructions keyed to the planning steps covered in each chapter of this book.

Be aware that the *Marketing Plan Pro* software tailors the contents of your marketing plan to the organization for which you are creating the plan. As you set up a new plan, you will be asked whether you are planning for a manufacturing business, a nonprofit organization, or another type of organization. Based on your response, the software will prepare the appropriate sections to be documented for your marketing plan. As a result, the sections and numbering you see on your screen may be *slightly different* from those shown in this appendix.

For additional information and technical support, see the special *Marketing Plan Pro* Web site at <u>www.paloalto.com/prenticehall/</u>.

EXPLORING SAMPLE MARKETING PLANS

Marketing Plan Pro contains a variety of sample marketing plans from for-profit and nonprofit organizations offering goods and services to consumers and businesses, as shown in Exhibit A3.1.

To explore a sample marketing plan using the "Plan Outline" function:

1. Launch *Marketing Plan Pro*, look at the four choices on the welcome screen, and click "Open a Sample Plan."
2. You will see a dialogue box containing the names of all the sample plans. Highlight the one you want to open, then click "Open" (Exhibit A3.2).
3. Once you have opened the sample plan, you can explore it by clicking on "Your Plan Outline" in either of two places: in the center of the "Plan Manager" screen that appears over the sample plan text or at the bottom of the main screen.
4. The "Plan Outline" function brings up a formatted outline of the topics included in the sample plan, as shown in Exhibit A3.3. Text sections are identified by a document icon featuring a capital T. Tables are identified by an icon that looks like the grid of a spreadsheet, while charts have a pie chart icon.
5. Double-click on any topic in the outline to go directly to that part of the plan. This method lets you browse topics in the order in which they are to appear in the final printed marketing plan.

EXHIBIT A3.1   Sample Plans Included in *Marketing Plan Pro*

Name of Firm	Type of Firm	Description
Franklin & Moore	Service firm targeting consumers	An established CPA firm seeking to expand its client base
Willamette Furniture	Company marketing tangible products to consumers	A furniture retail company specializing in high-quality products
Acme Consulting	Service firm targeting businesses	A consulting firm providing specialized services to business customers
AMT	Company marketing tangible products to businesses	A computer company specializing in computers for business customers
All4Sports	Nonprofit organization benefiting youth	A nonprofit sports program providing athletic experiences for youth
Adventure Travel	Service firm targeting consumers	Start-up travel agency specializing in international travel
Boulder Stop	Specialty store/café targeting consumers	Combination store and café selling rock-climbing equipment and branded coffee
JavaNet	Service firm targeting consumers	Start-up café offering coffee and Internet access
Interior Views	Specialty store targeting consumers	Retail store selling decorator fabrics and home accessories
The Players	Nonprofit cultural organization	Start-up nonprofit community theater organization

EXHIBIT A3.2 Opening a Sample Plan in *Marketing Plan Pro*

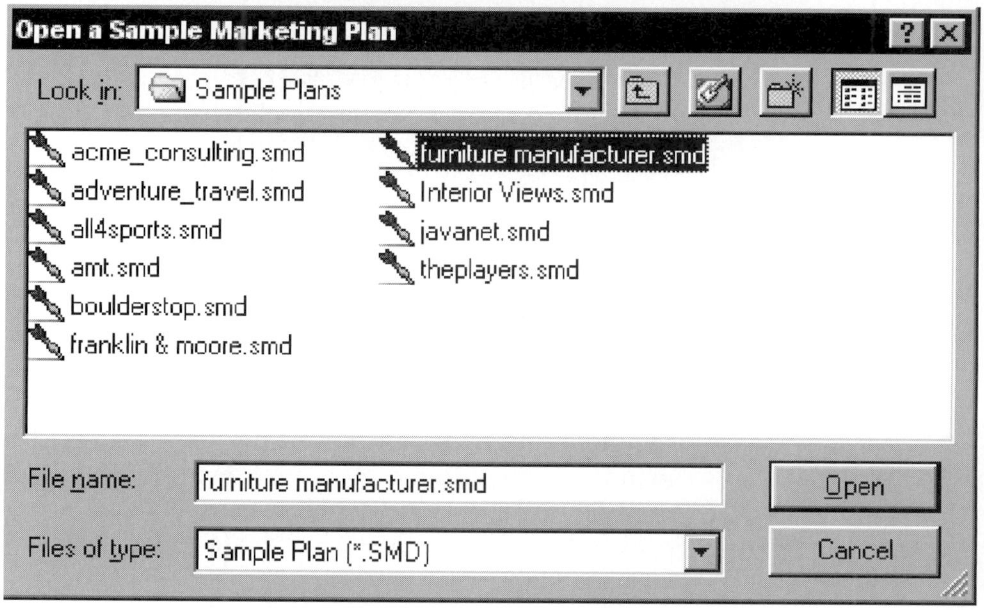

EXHIBIT A3.3 Plan Outline Screen in *Marketing Plan Pro*

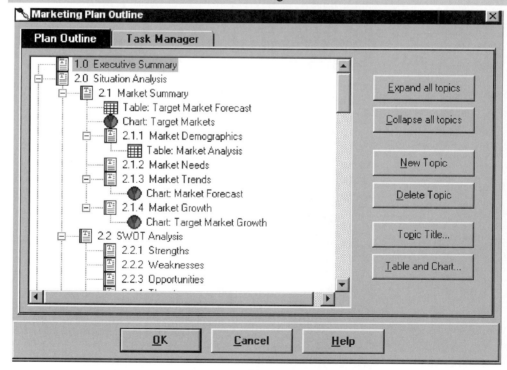

6. Use the "Previous" and "Next" buttons at the bottom of the screen to move between adjacent topics in the outline, or click on "Plan Outline" to bring up the full outline and locate another topic.

Another way to explore a sample marketing plan is to use the "Task Manager" function:

1. Go to the "Plan Outline" screen and click on the "Task Manager" tab to bring up a listing of tasks and the text, charts, and tables related to each task (see Exhibit A3.4). These are listed in the usual order for developing a new marketing plan. For example, you can't complete the steps to summarize your plan (tasks that are at the bottom of the "Task Manager" listing) until you've developed the rest of your plan.
2. Highlight any of the tasks under the "Task Manager" heading (for example, "Your Company" or "SWOT Analysis") to see a brief description of that topic.
3. Click "OK" to see the topic you have highlighted in the sample plan. Use the "Previous Task" and "Next Task" buttons on the bottom right of the screen to move through the tasks in order.
4. To explore further, click on the "Plan Outline" button at the bottom of the screen and look for more tasks listed under the "Task Manager" tab.

Once you have opened a sample plan, you also can use the icons for text, tables, and charts—located near the top center of your screen—to explore. Text sections are identified by a document icon featuring a capital T. Tables are

EXHIBIT A3.4   Using the Task Manager in *Marketing Plan Pro*

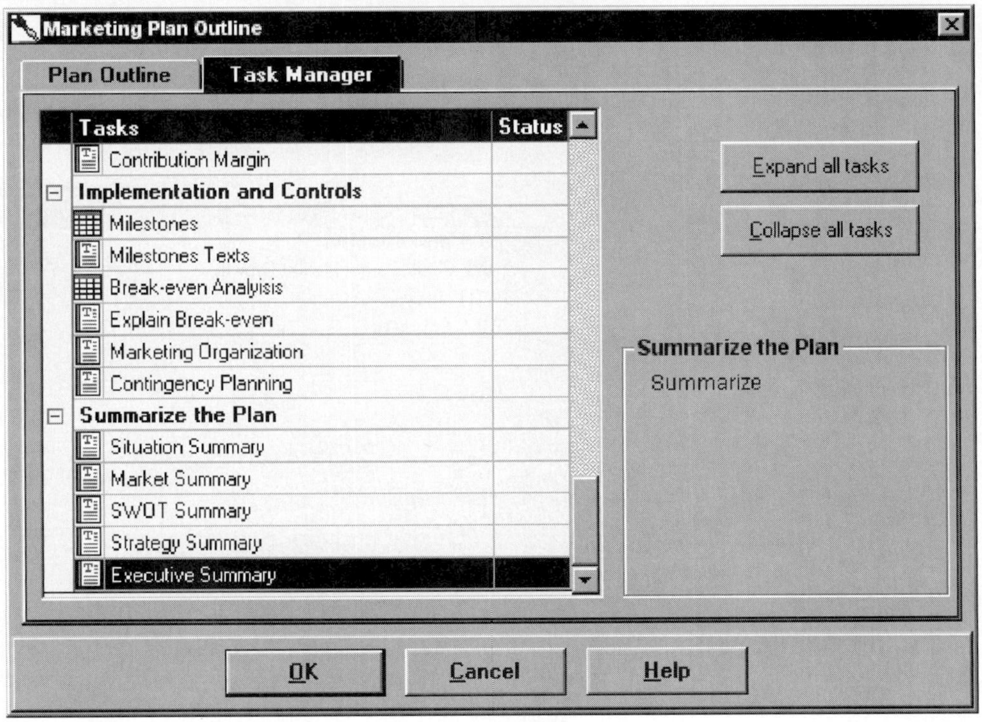

identified by an icon that looks like a gridded spreadsheet, while charts are identified by a pie chart icon.

Every sample plan is based on a set of assumptions about the firm and the marketing plan. To see the assumptions for any sample plan, select "Plan Wizard" from the main "Plan Manager" screen (which comes up whenever you initially open a sample plan). Or you can click on "Plan Manager" at the bottom center of your screen and then select "Plan Wizard" while you have a sample plan open.

For help with the software, select "Help" from the menu at the top of your screen to bring up a listing of help topics, see FAQs (frequently-asked questions), read tips, browse the glossary, or find out how to get other assistance. You can also press F1 to get to the help topics listing. Online, you can get technical support from www.paloalto.com/prenticehall/.

DEVELOPING A NEW MARKETING PLAN

An easy way to develop a new marketing plan with *Marketing Plan Pro* is to use the "Plan Wizard" to organize the proper screens, tables, and charts for a particular business and planning period. It is advisable to set up your marketing plan before continuing with Chapter 2, where you will be entering data based on directions in that chapter.

To print your plan, use the "Plan Options" menu (at bottom left on the "Plan Manager" main screen). This allows you to set up headers, footers, fonts, the table of contents, and other options.

EXHIBIT A3.5   Using the Plan Wizard in *Marketing Plan Pro*

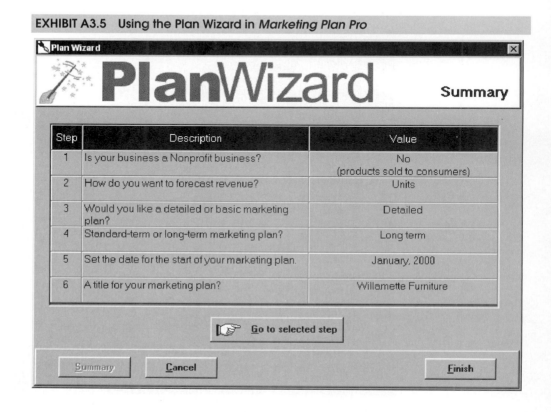

EXHIBIT A3.6   The Welcome Screen in *Marketing Plan Pro*

1. Launch *Marketing Plan Pro*, look at the four choices on the welcome screen (as in Exhibit A3.6), and click "Start a Plan."
2. Click the "Start" button on the bottom of the "Plan Wizard" welcome screen to begin. You will be presented with a series of questions. Select your answer to each question and then click the "Next" button to continue. After you enter the answer to the final question (the title of your marketing plan), click the "Finish" button.
3. The next screen prompts you to save your marketing plan using an appropriate file name. Once you save your file under the name you've chosen, *Marketing Plan Pro* will take a moment to customize the screens you will use to prepare your marketing plan, based on your answers to the "Plan Wizard" questions. Later, when you are adding to your marketing plan, you will simply use the "Open a Plan" option to locate your saved plan or use "Continue Your Last Plan" to work on the plan. After you save your

plan, you will be asked whether you want to use LivePlan.com, an optional feature that enables you to collaborate or share plans with others.

4. Now you will see the "Plan Manager" function on your screen. Highlight "Your Plan Outline" to see a dialogue box with two tabs. The "Plan Outline" tab brings up a formatted outline of the topics included in the sample plan, in the order in which they would appear in a typical plan. As in the sample plans, text sections in a new marketing plan are identified by a document icon featuring a capital T; tables are identified by a gridded spreadsheet icon; and charts have a pie chart icon. This function is useful for working on selected sections of a plan in progress. When starting a new plan, you will often find working through the "Task Manager" more convenient. This method is described in the next step and shown in Exhibit A3.7.

5. Click on the "Task Manager" tab to bring up a listing of tasks and the text, charts, and tables related to each task. These tasks are listed in the usual order for developing a new marketing plan. As you work on a section, you can show its status at the right. This will help you keep track of which sections are complete, which are in progress, which haven't been started, and which should be skipped.

6. You can move through the tasks in the marketing plan by clicking the "Previous Task" and "Next Task" buttons on the bottom right of the screen. Another way to navigate through the tasks is to click on the "Plan Outline" at the bottom of the screen and bring up the "Task Manager" again, where you can select your next topic. Some plans may not include all topics or tasks, depending on the nature of the business or nonprofit organization.

7. As you work through the tasks in your marketing plan, you may decide to change some of the assumptions—which changes the tasks shown under the "Task Manager" heading. To change your assumptions, simply click on "Plan Manager" on the bottom of the screen, then select "Plan Wizard" to bring up the questions as well as the answers you provided. Highlight any answers you want to revise and then click on "Go to selected step."

OVERVIEW OF MARKETING PLAN TASKS

Once you've answered the "Plan Wizard's" questions and moved to the "Task Manager," you can use the *Marketing Plan Pro* software to tackle the basic groups of tasks involved in developing a marketing plan. Although you may choose to prepare your marketing plan in a different order, many marketers follow the general sequence suggested by the order in which topics are listed in the "Task Manager." Note that the "Task Manager" will only present the tasks appropriate for your particular business, as determined by the answers you gave to the "Plan Wizard's" questions.

Here's a brief overview of the tasks in each "Task Manager" group.

- *Your Company.* In this part of the marketing plan, you lay out your organization's ultimate purpose and mission, define what you sell, analyze the competition, identify specific keys to success, and examine critical environmental elements that can affect your organization's performance.

- *Market Analysis.* These tasks take you through the process of getting to know your market and targeted segments, including market demographics, market size forecasts, needs, trends, and growth patterns.
- *SWOT Analysis.* Here, you evaluate the internal strengths and weaknesses and external opportunities and threats of your organization and your major competitors.
- *Channels and History.* These tasks summarize your channel situation, analysis, and forecast for future distribution growth per channel. You'll also summarize your historical results as background for the plans and forecasts in this new marketing plan.
- *Strategies.* This is the part of the plan in which you establish marketing and financial objectives to check your progress, describe your target markets and your positioning, check the link between strategies and tactics, and note the need for additional marketing research to support your strategies.
- *Marketing Mix.* Here you will summarize your marketing-mix strategies for product, price, place, and promotion. You will also describe your chosen service strategy.
- *Sales Forecast.* In this section, you forecast sales for the upcoming year (or the period covered by your marketing plan). Use the tables to show details about month-by-month sales. Explain your forecast, assumptions, sales strategy, and sales tactics in the text that accompanies these detailed tables.
- *Budgets Analysis.* This section of the marketing plan shows the cost side of the marketing equation as well as the planned profitability related to the sales forecasts in the previous section.
- *Implementation and Controls.* Here you lay out the timing and responsibilities for your marketing activities, calculate your break-even point, describe the roles and functions within your marketing organization, and explain your contingency plans for coping with unexpected challenges and opportunities. These tasks help you plan for managing and adjusting your activities to get closer to your objectives.
- *Summarize the Plan.* This set of tasks is completed last, after the entire marketing plan has been drafted. Here, you summarize your overall situation, the key points of your market and SWOT analysis, and the highlights of your strategy. The executive summary is generally the final section you will write—even though it is the first thing readers see when they open your marketing plan.

If you have questions about developing a marketing plan, *Marketing Plan Pro* software allows you to use e-mail to "ask the experts" and "ask the authors" (see "Plan Manager" screen or use the "Resources" menu). Technical support is also available on the Web site if you don't find the answer to your question in the "Help" menu.

Be aware that the *Marketing Plan Pro* software tailors the contents of your marketing plan to the organizaiton for which you are creating the plan. As you set up a new plan, you will be asked whether you are planning for a manufacturing business, a nonprofit organization, or another type of organization. Based on your response, the software will prepare the appropriate sections to be documented for your marketing plan. As a result, the sections and numbering you see on your screen may be slightly different from those shown in this appendix.

For additional information and technical support, see the special *Marketing Plan Pro* Web site at www.paloalto.com/prenticehall/.

Documenting Analysis of the Current Situation (Corresponds to Chapter 2)

This part of the documentation process corresponds to the marketing planning step discussed in Chapter 2, "Analyzing the Current Situation," which includes a competitive analysis. If you haven't already done so, set up and save your new marketing plan in the *Marketing Plan Pro* software. If you previously started a marketing plan, you can open it now by starting the software and clicking on "Continue Your Last Plan" from the "Welcome" menu or by clicking on the "Open a Plan" option to find the plan name.

To enter the data gathered during your environmental scanning and analysis, click on "Plan Outline." Then proceed using one of two options: either the "Task Manager" function or the "Plan Outline" function. The "Task Manager" function is often easier for working on new plans, but either way works.

Note that the exact sections presented in the "Plan Outline" or "Task Manager" function will depend on the "Plan Wizard" questions you answered when setting up the new plan. Some plans, for example, will not show a "Channels and History" section, just a "History" section.

ENTERING CURRENT SITUATION DATA USING THE TASK MANAGER

If you choose to enter data using the "Task Manager," click on "Plan Outline," then choose the "Task Manager" tab to bring up a listing of tasks (Exhibit A3.7). Select "Expand all tasks" to show all sections in the listing. Then enter your data in the following sections, adding tables and graphs as needed to explain and illustrate:

- *Your Company.* Complete the sections "Mission," "Product Offering," "Competition," "Keys to Success," "Critical Issues" (the screen immediately following "Keys to Success"), "Marketing Research," and "Macroenvironment." In addition to explaining your findings, include your conclusions about how all this affects your marketing.
- *Market Analysis.* Include information on market trends and other details gathered during the external environmental analysis. Hold off on writing the overall "Market Summary" until you have worked through the analyses described in Chapter 3, "Understanding Markets and Customers."
- *Marketing Research (under "Strategies").* Indicate any competitive intelligence data or other research needed to further assess competitive

EXHIBIT A3.7   Entering Current Situation Data Using the Task Manager

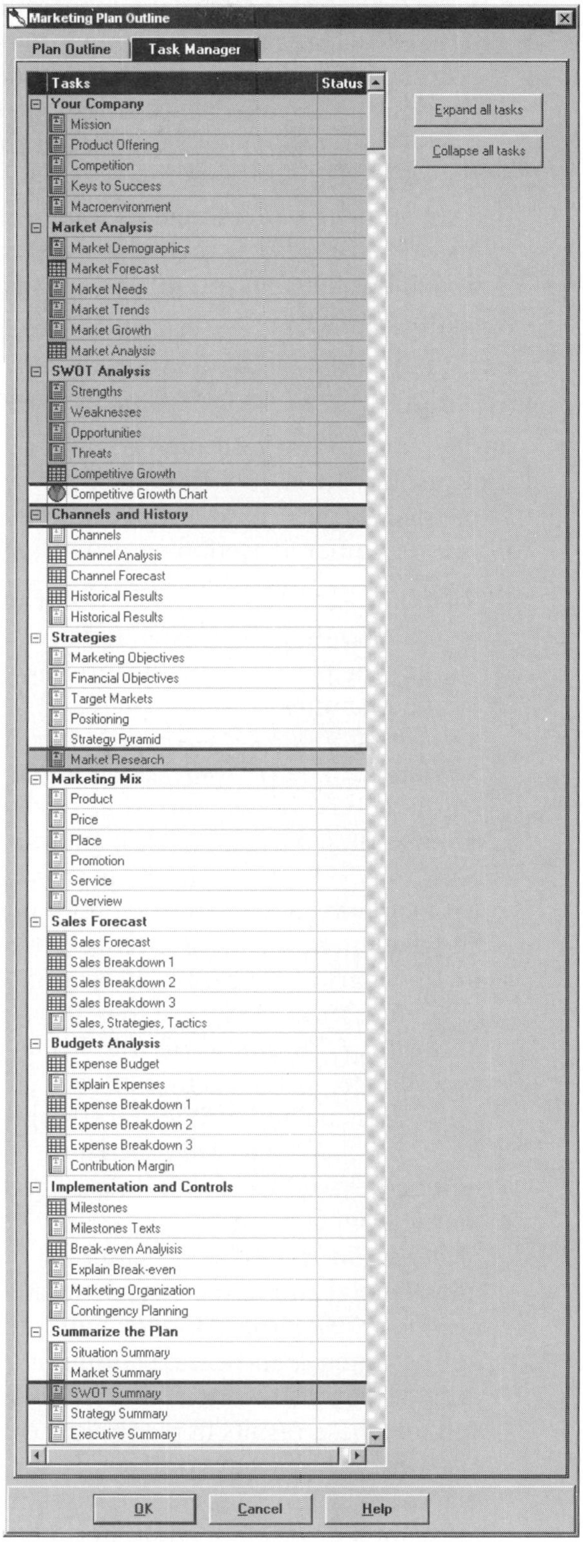

strengths and weaknesses. Also mention studies you will need to monitor customers' perceptions of competitors on an ongoing basis.

- *SWOT Analysis.* Enter data about "Strengths," "Weaknesses," "Opportunities," "Threats," and "Competitive Growth." Again, be sure to interpret the information and indicate what it means for your company and your marketing efforts. After moving through all the screens in this section, write a "SWOT Analysis" summary to briefly outline the high points.
- *Channels and History.* Enter data about your current relationships with distributors, retailers, dealers, and other channel partners. Also include the historical results of previous marketing plans, trends in customer acquisition and retention, and related details—showing what this information means to your marketing efforts.

ENTERING CURRENT SITUATION DATA USING THE PLAN OUTLINE

Another way to work through your marketing plan is using the "Plan Outline" function. If you prefer this method, select the "Plan Outline" tab. Select "Expand all topics" to show all sections in the listing. Next, enter data in the following numbered sections of your plan (see Exhibit A3.8):

Section 2.1.3 Market Trends. Enter information about how the environmental trends you investigated are affecting (or are likely to affect) the market for your products. Note how this knowledge will be used in marketing planning.

Section 2.1.4 Market Growth. Enter your findings about market growth.

Section 2.2 SWOT Analysis. On separate screens, summarize what you've learned about the organization's strengths, weaknesses, opportunities, and threats. Then write an overall analysis on the first screen of this section.

Section 2.3 Competition. Enter a summary of your competitor analysis, with supporting details to identify major rivals, outline important trends, and explain how competition will affect marketing planning. Also indicate in the marketing research section any competitive intelligence data needed to further assess competitive strengths and weaknesses.

Section 2.4 Product Offering. Enter detailed information on the goods and services you currently offer. Comment on how these offerings relate to the mission and to internal strengths and weaknesses.

Section 2.5 Keys to Success. Enter your ideas about the organization's unique keys to success and describe how these will be incorporated into marketing planning.

Section 2.6 Critical Issues. Enter the warning signs you have identified and how these relate to the keys to success and to your SWOT analysis.

Section 2.7 Historical Results. Enter the historical results of previous marketing plans, trends in customer acquisition and retention, and related data gathered from the internal environmental scan. Indicate how you will use these results in planning the coming year's marketing activities.

Section 2.8 Macroenvironment. Enter your overall findings about relevant macroenvironmental trends, highlighting how these trends are likely to affect your marketing planning and activities.

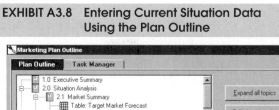

**EXHIBIT A3.8   Entering Current Situation Data
Using the Plan Outline**

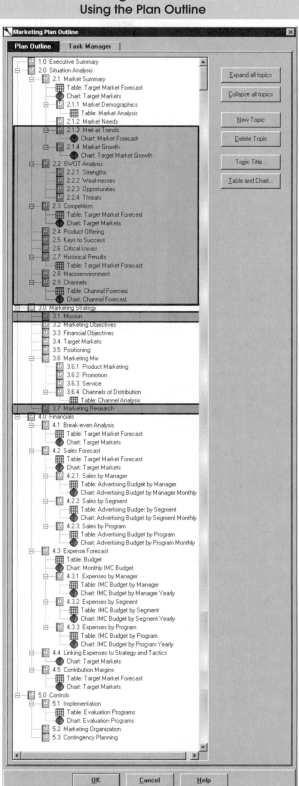

Section 2.9 Channels. Enter data about your current relationships with distributors, retailers, dealers, and other channel partners. Also include your findings about other business relationships and indicate any environmental issues that could affect your supply-chain relationships.

Section 3.1 Mission. Write out the organization's mission statement and discuss how it will guide the marketing planning process.

Section 3.8 Marketing Research. Discuss any competitive intelligence data or other research you will need to more thoroughly analyze competitive strengths and weaknesses or monitor customers' perceptions of competitors.

Documenting Markets and Customers (Corresponds to Chapter 3)

To document the results of your market and customer analysis, open the *Marketing Plan Pro* software. Then click on "Continue Your Last Plan" from the "Welcome" menu or click on the "Open a Plan" option to find your saved plan. Next, click on "Plan Outline," then proceed using either the "Task Manager" function or the "Plan Outline" function. Remember that you will be reviewing some of your entries during later stages of the planning process, which may mean changing or adding to what you've written. Now, for example, you'll want to reread the results of your environmental scanning and analysis before you enter new data on markets and customers.

ENTERING MARKET AND CUSTOMER DATA USING THE TASK MANAGER

If you want to use the "Task Manager," click on "Plan Outline," then choose the "Task Manager" tab to bring up a listing of tasks (Exhibit A3.9). Enter your data in the following sections, adding tables and graphs as needed to explain and illustrate:

Market Analysis. Enter data on market demographics, needs, trends, growth, and other details gathered during the market analysis, adding to what you entered after your environmental analysis in the previous chapter.

Marketing Research (under "Strategies"). Input descriptions of the marketing research you need to put the marketing plan in motion. Also include descriptions of ongoing marketing research needed to guide implementation and evaluation of the plan.

Situation Analysis (under "Summarize the Plan"). Draft a brief summary of the company's overall current situation, based on your market and customer analysis combined with your environmental analysis.

Market Summary (under "Summarize the Plan"). Review data entered from the environmental analysis in Chapter 3, reread your market analysis data, and draft an overall market summary.

ENTERING MARKET AND CUSTOMER DATA USING THE PLAN OUTLINE

If you use the Plan Outline function to enter data about markets and customers, select the "Plan Outline" tab and complete the following numbered sections of your plan (Exhibit A3.10):

EXHIBIT A3.9   Entering Market and Customer Data Using the Task Manager

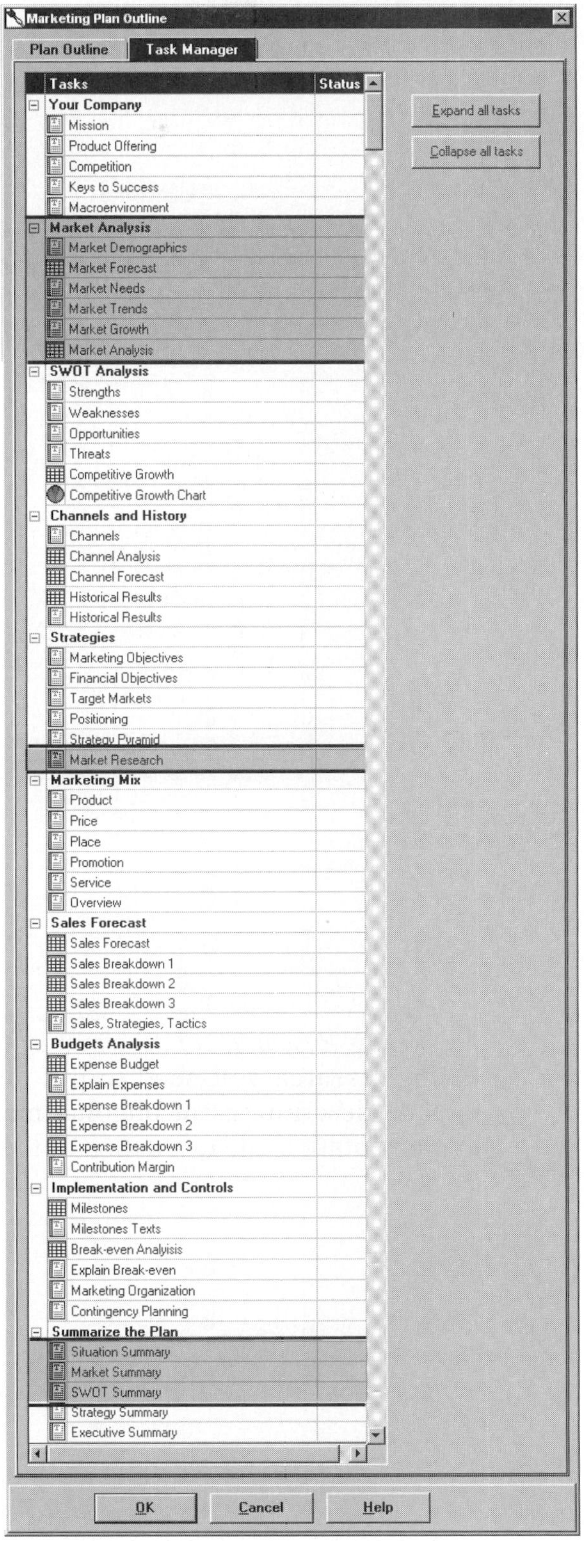

Marketing Plan Outline

| Plan Outline | Task Manager |

Tasks	Status
Your Company	
Mission	
Product Offering	
Competition	
Keys to Success	
Macroenvironment	
Market Analysis	
Market Demographics	
Market Forecast	
Market Needs	
Market Trends	
Market Growth	
Market Analysis	
SWOT Analysis	
Strengths	
Weaknesses	
Opportunities	
Threats	
Competitive Growth	
Competitive Growth Chart	
Channels and History	
Channels	
Channel Analysis	
Channel Forecast	
Historical Results	
Historical Results	
Strategies	
Marketing Objectives	
Financial Objectives	
Target Markets	
Positioning	
Strategy Pyramid	
Market Research	
Marketing Mix	
Product	
Price	
Place	
Promotion	
Service	
Overview	
Sales Forecast	
Sales Forecast	
Sales Breakdown 1	
Sales Breakdown 2	
Sales Breakdown 3	
Sales, Strategies, Tactics	
Budgets Analysis	
Expense Budget	
Explain Expenses	
Expense Breakdown 1	
Expense Breakdown 2	
Expense Breakdown 3	
Contribution Margin	
Implementation and Controls	
Milestones	
Milestones Texts	
Break-even Analysis	
Explain Break-even	
Marketing Organization	
Contingency Planning	
Summarize the Plan	
Situation Summary	
Market Summary	
SWOT Summary	
Strategy Summary	
Executive Summary	

Expand all tasks

Collapse all tasks

OK   Cancel   Help

EXHIBIT A3.10 Entering Market and Customer Data Using the Plan Outline

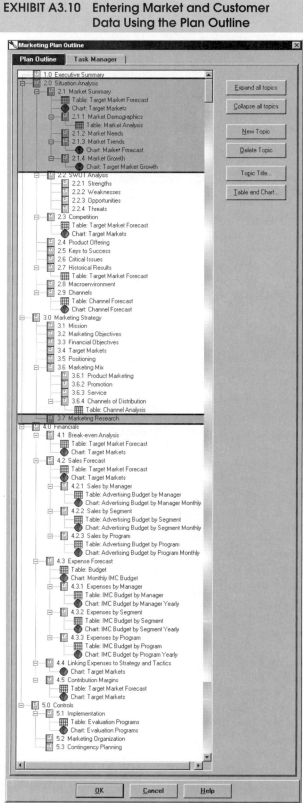

Sections 2.1.1, 2.1.2, 2.1.3, 2.1.4, Market Demographics, Needs, Trends, Growth. In these subcategories of the Market Summary section, enter your findings about the market and its needs, trends, and growth. Also interpret how these findings are likely to influence your marketing plan. *Section 3.8 Marketing Research.* Describe the marketing research you will need to develop and implement this marketing plan. Also indicate the ongoing marketing research you will need to conduct once the marketing plan is put into operation.

Finally, summarize what you've learned by entering data in these two sections of the marketing plan outline:

Section 2.1 Market Summary. Based on data entered from the environmental analysis in Chapter 3 and your market and customer analysis, write an overall "Market Summary," briefly outlining the most relevant information about the market. Be prepared to revise this summary as you gather new data or make decisions later in the planning process.
Section 2.0 Situation Analysis. Write a concise summary of the company's overall current situation, based on the big picture formed by the data gathered during your environmental analysis and your market analysis.

Documenting Segmentation, Targeting, and Positioning (Corresponds to Chapter 4)

To document your segmentation, targeting, and positioning decisions, open the *Marketing Plan Pro* software. Then click on "Continue Your Last Plan" from the "Welcome" menu or click on the "Open a Plan" option to locate your marketing plan. Next, click on "Plan Outline," then proceed using either the "Task Manager" function or the "Plan Outline" function.

ENTERING SEGMENTATION, TARGETING, AND POSITIONING DATA USING THE TASK MANAGER

If you use the "Task Manager" to enter data, click on "Plan Outline," then choose the "Task Manager" tab to bring up a listing of tasks (Exhibit A3.11). Reread what you've already entered under "Market Analysis." Now you're ready to input information into the following sections, adding tables and graphs as needed to explain and illustrate:

Market Analysis. Input the information gathered during the segmentation process on the appropriate pages in this section, supplementing the data you entered during the market analysis phase.
Target Markets (under "Strategies"). Enter data on your segmentation process, choice of segments, evaluation criteria and results, and the coverage strategy you will use.
Positioning (under "Strategies"). Describe the positioning for each brand, product, or target segment. Explain how the differentiation is meaningful and contributes to competitive advantage.

EXHIBIT A3.11 Entering Segmentation, Targeting, and Positioning Data Using the Task Manager

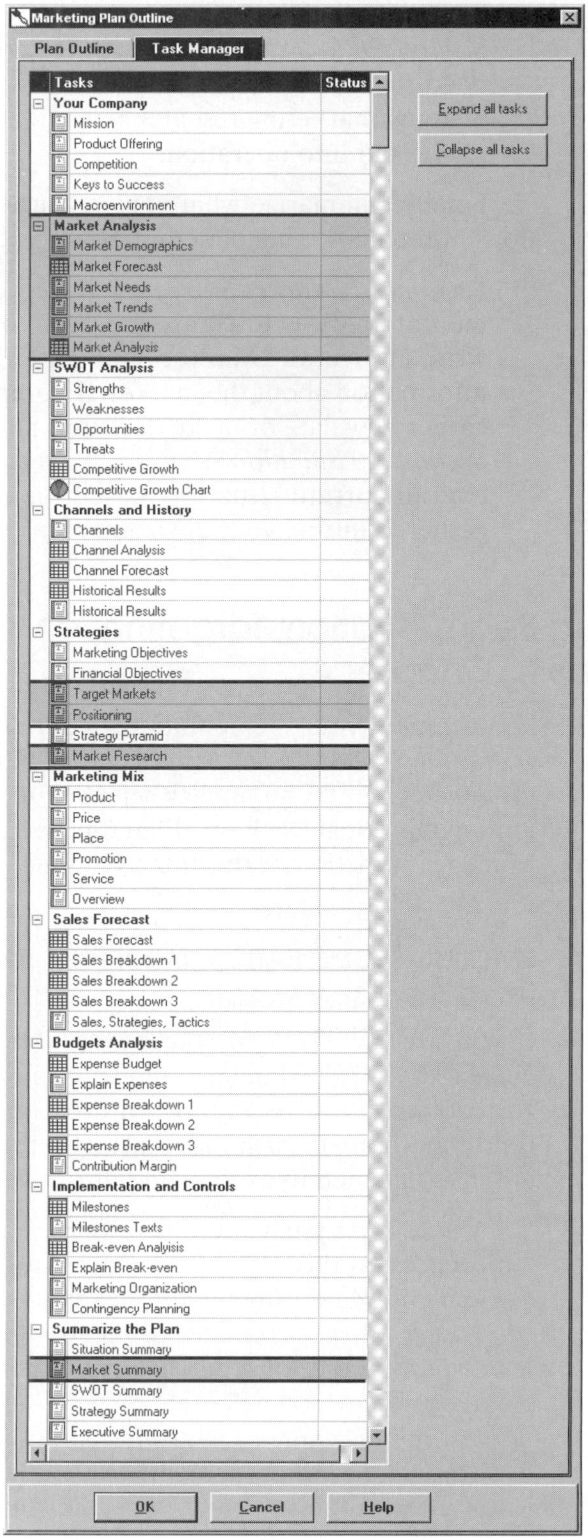

Marketing Research (under "Strategies"). Explain any studies you conducted or need to conduct to support your segmentation, targeting, and positioning decisions.

Market Summary (under "Summarize the Plan"). Amend your previous text, tables, and charts, as needed, to reflect additional information and findings on market segments.

ENTERING SEGMENTATION, TARGETING, AND POSITIONING DATA USING THE PLAN OUTLINE

If you prefer to enter data using the "Plan Outline" method, select the "Plan Outline" tab. Reread what you've already entered in the sections under "Market Summary." Next, enter your latest findings in the following numbered sections of your plan (see Exhibit A3.12):

Sections 2.1.1, 2.1.2, 2.1.3, 2.1.4, Market Demographics, Needs, Trends, Growth, Forecast. In these subcategories of the "Market Summary" section, input any additional segment data and update tables and charts. Also show how target market data will affect the marketing plan.

Section 3.4 Target Markets. Discuss your segmentation process, choice of segments, evaluation criteria and results, and the coverage strategy you will use.

Section 3.5 Positioning. Enter the positioning for each brand, product, or target segment and indicate how the differentiation is meaningful and how it contributes to competitive advantage.

Section 3.8 Marketing Research. Describe the marketing research you will need to develop and implement this marketing plan. Also indicate the ongoing marketing research you will need to conduct once the marketing plan is put into operation.

Finally, use segmentation data to enhance your comments in this summary section of the marketing plan outline:

Section 2.1 Market Summary. Modify your existing text, tables, and charts, as needed, to reflect additional information and findings on market segments.

EXHIBIT A3.12 Entering Segmentation, Targeting, and Positioning Data Using the Plan Outline

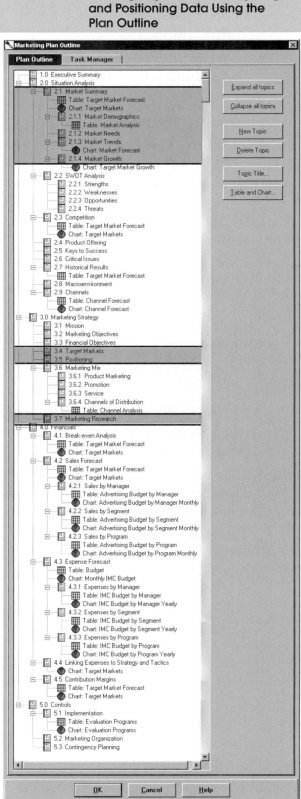

Documenting Objectives and Strategic Direction (Corresponds to Chapter 5)

To document the objectives and strategic direction for your marketing plan, open the *Marketing Plan Pro* software. Then click on "Continue Your Last Plan" or "Open a Plan" on the "Welcome" menu to locate the plan you've been developing. Next, click on "Plan Outline," then proceed using either the "Task Manager" function or the "Plan Outline" function.

ENTERING DATA ON OBJECTIVES AND DIRECTION USING THE TASK MANAGER

If you want to use the "Task Manager," click on "Plan Outline," then choose the "Task Manager" tab to bring up a listing of tasks (Exhibit A3.13). Select "Expand all tasks" to see all the sections in the plan. Review the "Mission" shown under "Your Company" to be sure your latest decisions are consistent with this overall purpose. Now enter your data in the following sections, adding tables and graphs as needed to explain and illustrate:

Strategies. Input your marketing and financial objectives in the "Marketing Objectives" and "Financial Objectives" screens, along with any commentary explaining how they relate to the strategic direction and mission. Then write about your strategic direction in the opening "Strategies" section and indicate how this direction relates to the way you will create and deliver customer value through marketing.

Strategic Pyramid. If desired, use the strategic pyramid to show how tactics and programs will be support key higher-level strategies.

ENTERING DATA ON OBJECTIVES AND DIRECTION USING THE PLAN OUTLINE

Another way to work through your marketing plan is using the "Plan Outline" function. If you prefer this method, select the "Plan Outline" tab. Review the "Mission" shown under section 3.0 "Marketing Strategy" to be sure your latest decisions are consistent with this overall purpose. Now enter data in the following numbered sections of your plan (Exhibit A3.14):

Sections 3.2 and 3.3, Marketing Objectives and Financial Objectives. In these subcategories of the "Marketing Strategy" section, enter the objectives you have developed, along with any commentary explaining how they relate to the strategic direction and mission.

Section 3.0 Marketing Strategies. Input your strategic direction here, and explain how it relates to the customer value you will create through marketing and to the objectives you entered above.

EXHIBIT A3.13 Entering Data on Objectives and Direction Using the Task Manager

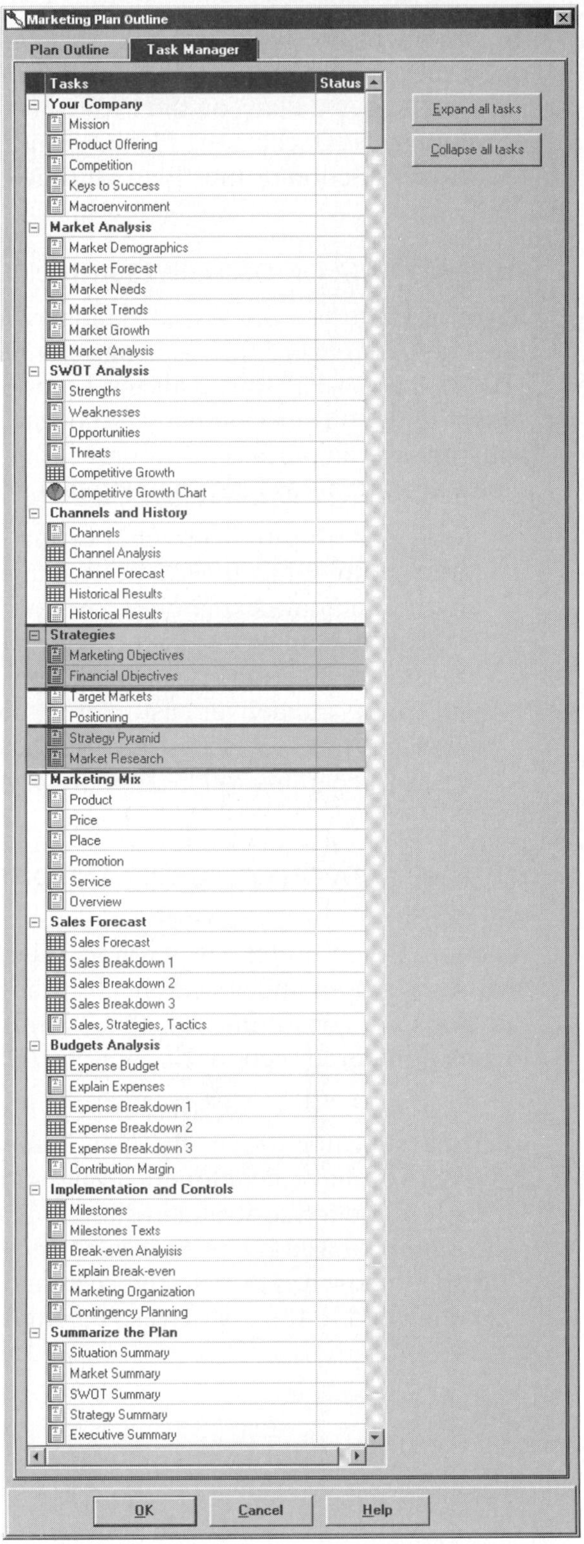

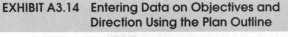

EXHIBIT A3.14   Entering Data on Objectives and Direction Using the Plan Outline

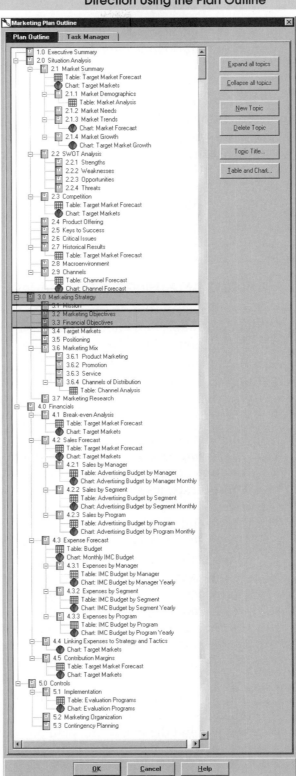

Documenting Marketing Strategies and Programs (Corresponds to Chapter 6)

To document the marketing strategies and programs in your marketing plan, open the *Marketing Plan Pro* software. Now choose either "Continue Your Last Plan" or "Open a Plan" on the "Welcome" menu to locate the plan you've been developing. Click on "Plan Outline" and then proceed using either the "Task Manager" function or the "Plan Outline" function. Note that your plan may not include every section mentioned below, depending on your type of business and your original answers to "Plan Wizard" questions.

If you need to add a new section to the plan, go to "Plan Outline" and then click on "New Topic" at right to create a new section and indicate where it should be positioned within the marketing plan document. You can change the title of existing sections using the "Topic Title" button, also on the right of the "Plan Outline" screen. If there are sections you will not need, use the "Delete Topic" to remove them from your plan.

ENTERING DATA USING THE TASK MANAGER

If you like using the "Task Manager" to input your plan decisions, click on "Plan Outline," then choose the "Task Manager" tab to bring up a listing of tasks (Exhibit A3.15). Select "Expand all tasks" to see all the sections in the plan and then enter your data in the following sections, adding tables and graphs as needed to explain and illustrate:

Marketing Research (under "Strategies"). Enter information about the marketing research you need to support your marketing mix strategies, including research pretesting advertising messages and other studies.

Marketing Mix. Input details about your product, price, channel, and promotion strategies, as well as your customer service strategy. Discuss how these strategies support the strategic direction and marketing plan objectives. Then summarize the strategies on the Marketing Mix summary page at the end of this section.

Break-Even Analysis (under "Implementation and Controls"). Enter details about costs, pricing, and projected sales volumes to calculate the break-even point. Use the related table and chart to show assumptions about costs, revenues, and sales.

Marketing Organization (under "Implementation and Controls"). Input information about your marketing organization, internal communication, and other aspects of your internal marketing program.

Contingency Planning (under "Implementation and Controls"). Summarize environmental changes that could force you to change one or more marketing mix strategies and programs, such as competitive pricing changes. Briefly state how the organization might react in each case, bearing in mind the marketing plan objectives and strategic direction.

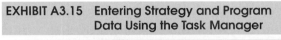

EXHIBIT A3.15 Entering Strategy and Program
Data Using the Task Manager

Marketing Plan Outline

Plan Outline | Task Manager

Tasks	Status
Your Company	
Mission	
Product Offering	
Competition	
Keys to Success	
Macroenvironment	
Market Analysis	
Market Demographics	
Market Forecast	
Market Needs	
Market Trends	
Market Growth	
Market Analysis	
SWOT Analysis	
Strengths	
Weaknesses	
Opportunities	
Threats	
Competitive Growth	
Competitive Growth Chart	
Channels and History	
Channels	
Channel Analysis	
Channel Forecast	
Historical Results	
Historical Results	
Strategies	
Marketing Objectives	
Financial Objectives	
Target Markets	
Positioning	
Strategy Pyramid	
Market Research	
Marketing Mix	
Product	
Price	
Place	
Promotion	
Service	
Overview	
Sales Forecast	
Sales Forecast	
Sales Breakdown 1	
Sales Breakdown 2	
Sales Breakdown 3	
Sales, Strategies, Tactics	
Budgets Analysis	
Expense Budget	
Explain Expenses	
Expense Breakdown 1	
Expense Breakdown 2	
Expense Breakdown 3	
Contribution Margin	
Implementation and Controls	
Milestones	
Milestones Texts	
Break-even Analysis	
Explain Break-even	
Marketing Organization	
Contingency Planning	
Summarize the Plan	
Situation Summary	
Market Summary	
SWOT Summary	
Strategy Summary	
Executive Summary	

Expand all tasks

Collapse all tasks

OK   Cancel   Help

ENTERING DATA USING THE PLAN OUTLINE

If you want to use the "Plan Outline" function, select the "Plan Outline" tab and click to "Expand all topics" in the outline listing. If necessary, click on the "+" sign at the left of any topics that need to be expanded to show subtopics. Now you're ready to enter data in these numbered sections of your plan (Exhibit A3.16):

Sections 3.7, Marketing Mix. Start by discussing your product, price, promotion, and channel strategies, including how these relate to the marketing plan objectives and strategic direction. Also enter data about your customer service strategy. Then summarize the strategies and include your internal marketing strategy on the Marketing Mix summary page.

Section 3.8 (under "Marketing Strategy"). Enter information about the marketing research you need to support your marketing mix strategies, including research about advertising effectiveness and other evaluative research.

Section 4.1 Break-even Analysis. Enter details about costs, pricing, and projected sales volumes to calculate the break-even point. Use the related table and chart to show assumptions about costs, revenues, and sales.

Section 5.2 Marketing Organization. Input information about your marketing organization, internal communication, and other aspects of your internal marketing program.

Section 5.3 Contingency Planning. Summarize environmental changes that could force you to change one or more marketing mix strategies and programs, such as competitive pricing changes. Briefly state how the organization might react in each case, bearing in mind the marketing plan objectives and strategic direction.

Documenting Budgets, Forecasts, and Progress Measurements (Corresponds to Chapter 7)

To document the way you will measure progress toward marketing plan objectives, open the *Marketing Plan Pro* software. Now choose either "Continue Your Last Plan" or "Open a Plan" on the "Welcome" menu to locate the plan you've been developing. Click on "Plan Outline" and then proceed using either the "Task Manager" function or the "Plan Outline" function. Remember that your plan may not include every section mentioned below, depending on your type of business and your original answers to "Plan Wizard" questions.

If you need to add a new section to the plan, go to "Plan Outline" and then click on "New Topic" at right to create a new section and indicate where it should be positioned within the marketing plan document. You can change the title of existing sections using the "Topic Title" button, also on the right of the "Plan Outline" screen. If there are sections you don't need, just use the "Delete Topic" to remove them from your plan.

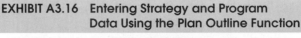

EXHIBIT A3.16   Entering Strategy and Program Data Using the Plan Outline Function

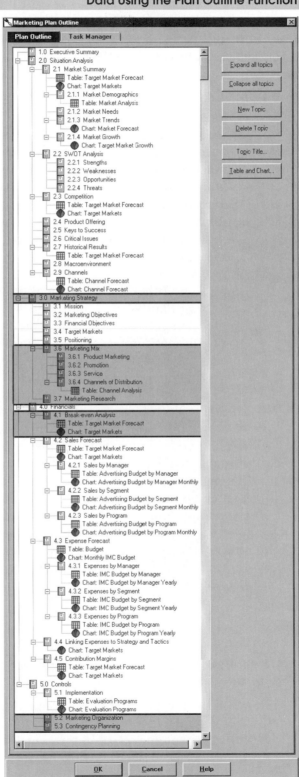

ENTERING BUDGET, FORECAST, AND PROGRESS DATA USING THE TASK MANAGER

If you like using the "Task Manager" to input your plan decisions, click on "Plan Outline," then choose the "Task Manager" tab to bring up a listing of tasks (Exhibit A3.17). Select "Expand all tasks" to see all the sections in the plan and then enter your data in the following sections, adding tables and graphs as needed to explain and illustrate:

Market Forecast (under "Marketing Analysis"). Input your forecasts for overall sales in each segment of the market. Note that the totals and the compound annual growth rate are automatically calculated, based on the values you enter, to help you analyze forecast trends.

Channel Forecast (under "Channels and History"). If you forecast sales by channel or by intermediary, input your data into this table, editing the row labels as needed. As with the market forecast, the totals and the compound annual growth rate are automatically calculated, based on the values you enter.

Sales Forecast. Enter your sales and cost forecasts by product, segment, or using some other organizational method. The choices you made when answering Plan Wizard questions will dictate the structure of the tables you see, but you can easily edit or add tables as needed. Note that the program automatically calculates certain values. Be sure to summarize your forecasts and explain any assumptions on the text pages of this section.

Budgets Analysis. Enter your budget data by program, segment, region, manager, or other organizational method. Note the program automatically ties some figures in these budgets to other spreadsheets; it also calculates totals and averages for you. Then summarize key budget data and explain your assumptions on the text pages of this section. Also discuss how the budgets for programs or activities are expected to support marketing strategies and performance, and identify any environmental issues that could interfere with expense control or allocation of funds.

Milestones (under "Implementation and Controls"). List the specific activities or programs and then enter start and end dates, budgets (if desired), and manager and department. You may want to create new milestone tables and charts, depending on the level of detail you want.

Market Summary (under "Summarize the Plan"). Modify the summary you previously drafted, if necessary, to reflect the market forecast you've formulated.

ENTERING DATA USING THE PLAN OUTLINE

If you prefer to use the "Plan Outline" function, select the "Plan Outline" tab and click to "Expand all topics" in the outline listing. If necessary, also click on the "+" sign at the left of any topics to expand and show all subtopics. Now you're ready to enter data in these numbered sections of your plan (Exhibit A3.18):

EXHIBIT A3.17   Entering Budget, Forecast, and Progress Data Using the Task Manager

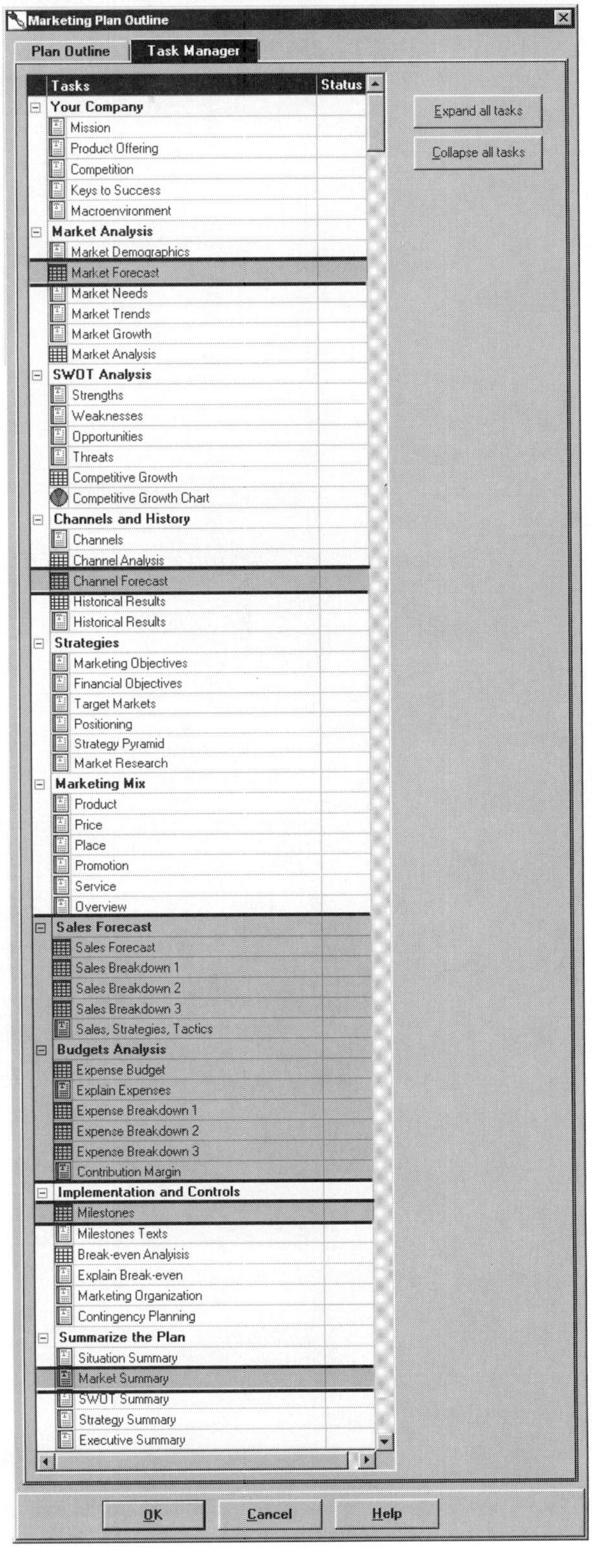

Marketing Plan Outline

Plan Outline | **Task Manager**

Tasks	Status
Your Company	
Mission	
Product Offering	
Competition	
Keys to Success	
Macroenvironment	
Market Analysis	
Market Demographics	
Market Forecast	
Market Needs	
Market Trends	
Market Growth	
Market Analysis	
SWOT Analysis	
Strengths	
Weaknesses	
Opportunities	
Threats	
Competitive Growth	
Competitive Growth Chart	
Channels and History	
Channels	
Channel Analysis	
Channel Forecast	
Historical Results	
Historical Results	
Strategies	
Marketing Objectives	
Financial Objectives	
Target Markets	
Positioning	
Strategy Pyramid	
Market Research	
Marketing Mix	
Product	
Price	
Place	
Promotion	
Service	
Overview	
Sales Forecast	
Sales Forecast	
Sales Breakdown 1	
Sales Breakdown 2	
Sales Breakdown 3	
Sales, Strategies, Tactics	
Budgets Analysis	
Expense Budget	
Explain Expenses	
Expense Breakdown 1	
Expense Breakdown 2	
Expense Breakdown 3	
Contribution Margin	
Implementation and Controls	
Milestones	
Milestones Texts	
Break-even Analysis	
Explain Break-even	
Marketing Organization	
Contingency Planning	
Summarize the Plan	
Situation Summary	
Market Summary	
SWOT Summary	
Strategy Summary	
Executive Summary	

Expand all tasks

Collapse all tasks

OK | Cancel | Help

EXHIBIT A3.18 Entering Budget, Forecast, and Progress Data Using the Plan Outline

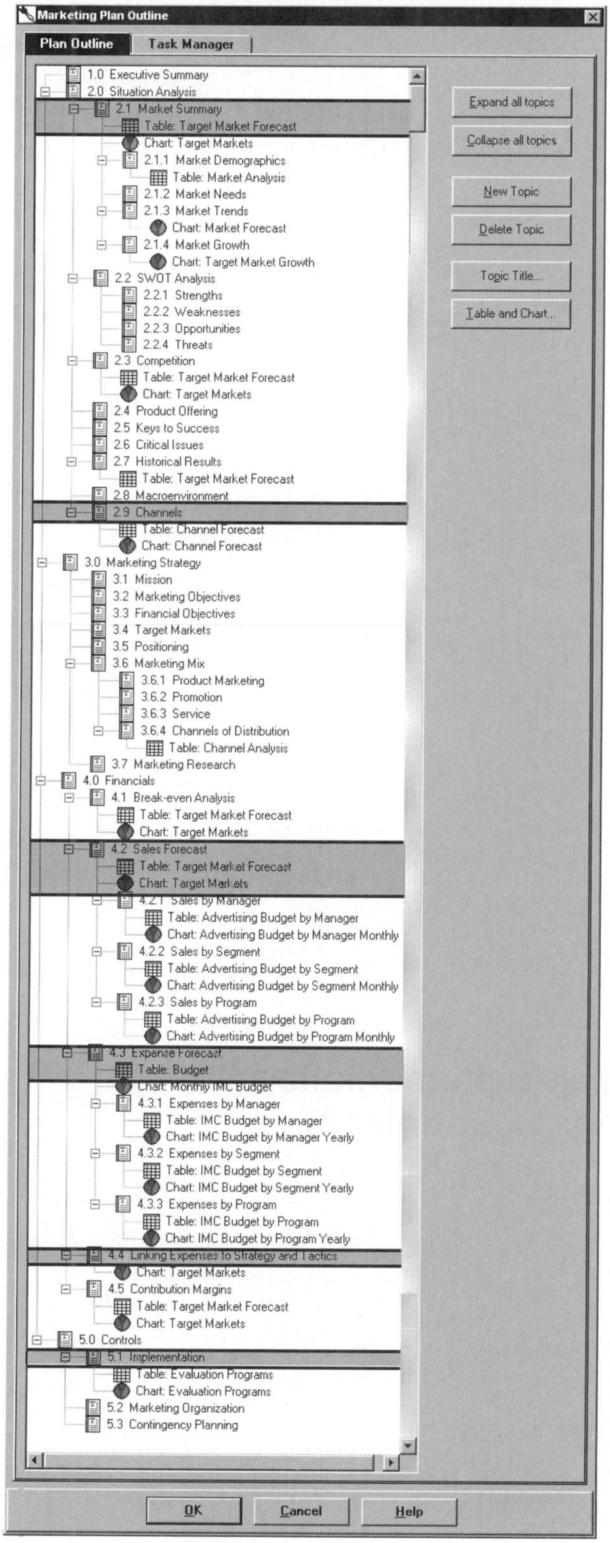

Section 2.1, Target Market Forecast. Enter forecasts for overall sales in each segment of the market. Note that the totals and the compound annual growth rate are automatically calculated, based on the values you enter, to help you analyze forecast trends. Also use the "Market Forecast" chart in section 2.1.4 if desired.

Section 2.9, Channels. If you forecast sales by channel or by intermediary, enter your data in this table (or use the chart), editing labels as needed. As with the market forecast, the totals and the compound annual growth rate in the spreadsheet are automatically calculated, based on the values you enter.

Section 4.2, Sales Forecast. Enter your sales and cost forecasts by product, segment, or using some other organizational method. The choices you made when answering "Plan Wizard" questions will dictate the structure of the tables you see, but you can easily edit or add tables as needed. Note that the program automatically calculates certain values. Be sure to summarize your forecasts and explain any assumptions on the text pages of this section.

Section 4.3, Expense Forecast. Enter your budget data by program, segment, region, manager, or other organizational method. Note that the program automatically ties some figures in these budgets to other spreadsheets; it also automatically calculates totals and averages. Then summarize key expense data and explain your assumptions on the text pages of this section.

Section 4.4, Linking Expenses to Strategy and Tactics. Briefly explain how the budgets for programs or activities are expected to support marketing strategies and performance. Mention any environmental issues that could interfere with expense control or allocation of funds for programs that support strategy.

Section 5.1, Implementation. Use the table to list the specific activities or programs and enter start and end dates, budgets (if desired), and manager and department. You may want to create new milestone tables and charts, depending on the level of detail you want.

Documenting Implementation Control (Corresponds to Chapter 8)

To document the way you will measure progress toward marketing plan objectives, open the *Marketing Plan Pro* software. Now choose either "Continue Your Last Plan" or "Open a Plan" on the "Welcome" menu to locate the plan you've been developing. Click on "Plan Outline" and then proceed using either the "Task Manager" function or the "Plan Outline" function. Remember that your plan may not include every section mentioned below, depending on your type of business and your original answers to "Plan Wizard" questions.

If there are sections you don't need, just use the "Delete Topic" (when in the "Plan Outline" mode) to remove them from your plan. You can change the title of existing sections using the "Topic Title" button, also on the right of the "Plan Outline" screen. If you need to add a new section to the plan, go to "Plan

Outline" and then click on "New Topic" at right to create a new section and indicate where it should be positioned within the marketing plan document.

ENTERING CONTROL DATA USING THE TASK MANAGER

If you use the "Task Manager" to input your plan information, click on "Plan Outline," then choose the "Task Manager" tab to bring up a listing of tasks (Exhibit A3.19). Select "Expand all tasks" to see all the sections in the plan and then enter your data in the following sections, adding tables and graphs as needed to explain and illustrate:

> *Implementation (under "Implementation and Controls").* Enter information about the marketing plan controls you will implement; also summarize what standards and measurement timing you plan to use during the control cycle. Also enter deadlines, tasks, and responsibilities under the "Milestone" heading. Also enter deadlines, tasks, and responsibilities under the "Milestones" heading.
>
> *Contingency Planning (under "Implementation and Controls").* Input an overview of the contingency plans you have prepared. Explain the nature of each emergency, the potential impact on the organization and its performance, and the major steps to be taken to address the emergency if it occurs.
>
> *Executive Summary (under "Summarize the Plan").* Now that the marketing plan is complete, use the executive summary to highlight the main points.

ENTERING CONTROL DATA USING THE PLAN OUTLINE

If you prefer to use the "Plan Outline" function, select the "Plan Outline" tab and click to "Expand all topics" in the outline listing. If necessary, also click on the "+" sign at the left of any topics to expand and show all subtopics. Now you're ready to enter data in these numbered sections of your plan (Exhibit A3.20):

> *Section 1.0, Executive Summary.* Now that the marketing plan is complete, write an executive summary to highlight the main points.
>
> *Section 5.1, Implementation.* Enter information about the marketing plan controls you will implement; also summarize what standards and measurement timing you plan to use during the control cycle.
>
> *Section 5.3, Contingency Planning.* Input an overview of the contingency plans you have prepared. Explain the nature of each emergency, the potential impact on the organization and its performance, and the major steps to be taken to address the emergency if it occurs.

EXHIBIT A3.19   Entering Control Data Using the Task Manager

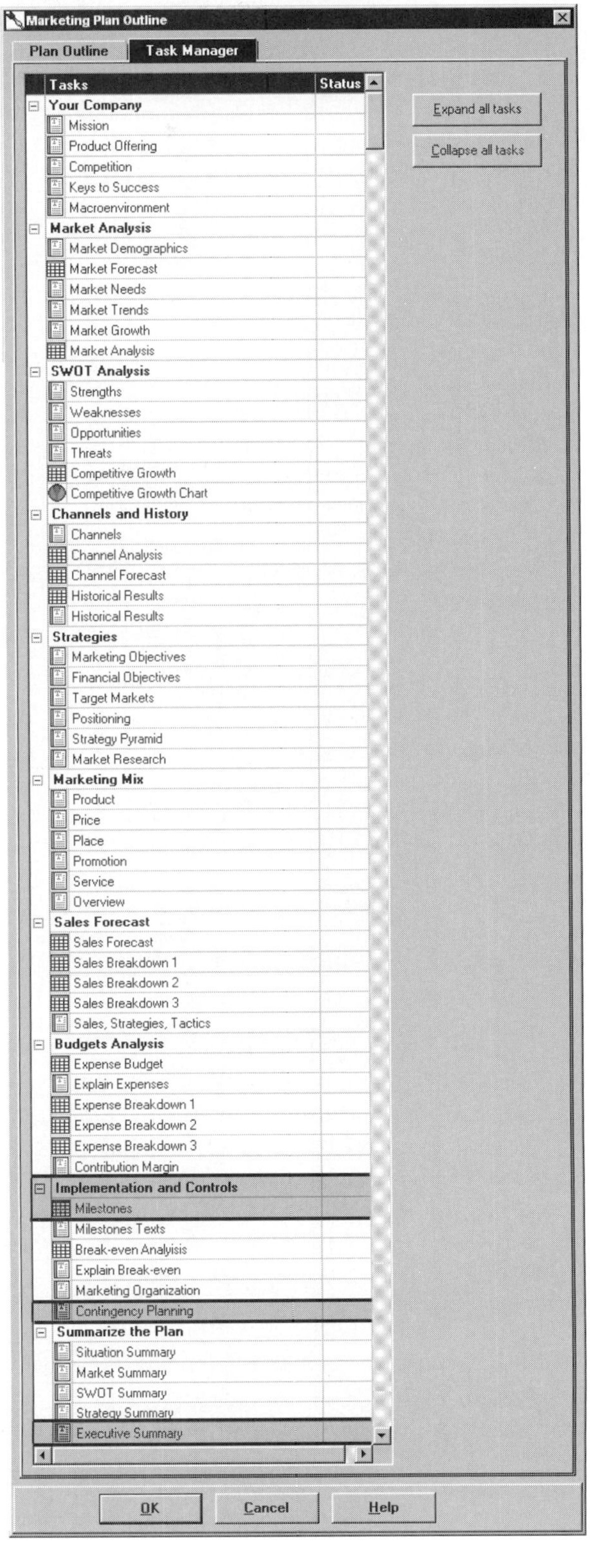

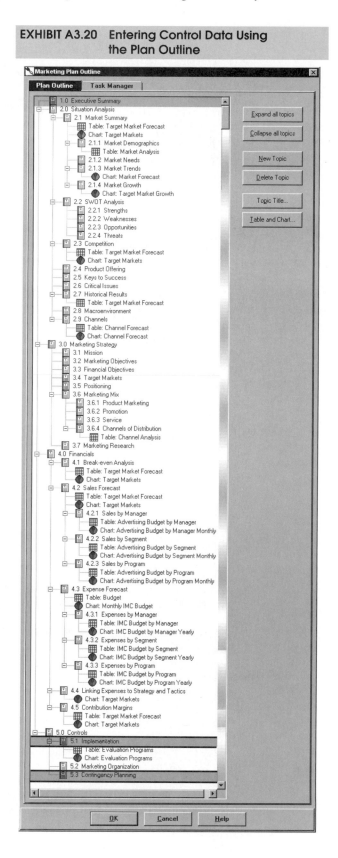

EXHIBIT A3.20   Entering Control Data Using the Plan Outline

References

Chapter 1

1. Personal communication, February 2001.
2. Paul A. Greenberg, "E-Tailers Benefit When Customers Run the Show," *E-Commerce Times,* May 4, 2001, ecommercetimes.com/perl/story/?id=9477; Alison Stein Wellner, "Beauty in Distress," *American Demographics,* January 2001, 62–64; Paul A. Greenberg, "Online Beauty Sites Face Uncertain Future," *E-Commerce Times,* March 30, 2000, www.ecommercetimes.com/news/articles2000/000330-5.shtml; Amanda Beeler and Jack Neff, "P&G Cosmetics Startup Sets Out to Be Different," *Advertising Age,* October 1999, www.adage.com.
3. Lee Clifford, "Breaking Away: A Man With a Plan," *Smart Money,* June 2000, 170, 172.
4. Sir George Bull, "What Does the Term Marketing Really Stand for?" *Marketing,* November 30, 2000, 30.
5. Tam Harbert, "A Tale of Two Mobile Telephone Makers," *Electronic Business,* May 2000, 88+; Justin Fox, "Nokia's Secret Code," *Fortune,* May 1, 2000, 160+; "Nokia Boss Marks 10 Years," *CNN.com,* January 16, 2002, www.cnn.com/2002/BUSINESS/01/16/nokiaboss/index.html.
6. Alexandra Kirkman, "Zoom! Zoom!" *Forbes,* May 14, 2001, 205.
7. Johanne Torres, "IBM's Content-Driven Marketing Plan," *Econtent,* July 2001, 60.
8. Mike Musgrove, "Dreamcast Exits Competitive Field," *Washington Post,* February 1, 2001, E03, www.washingtonpost.com/wp-dyn/articles/A10866-2001Jan31.html; Chris Morris, "Sony's PlayStation 2 Shortage," *CNNfn.com,* September 27, 2000, cnnfn.com/2000/09/27/technology/sony/; "Sony Stung By PlayStation 2 Delays," *CNN.com,* January 23, 2001, www.cnn.com/2001/world/asiapcf/east/01/23/sony.playstation/.
9. Satoko Suzuki, "PlayStation 2 with Bonus 'Flaw' Sells Millions in Japan," *CNN.com,* October 26, 2000, www.cnn.com/2000/technologycomputing/10/26/japan.playstation/index.html.
10. John Chartier, "Rescue-Hero Toy Sales Surge," October 8, 2001, www.money.cnn.com/2001/10/08/companies/toys.
11. Stephanie Balzer, "Suns Search for Fan Rebound," *Phoenix Business Journal,* May 4, 2001, 3.
12. Bill Breen, "Forced to Face the Web," *Fast Company,* February 2001, 162+.
13. George Anders, "Why Real-Time Business Takes Real Time," *Fast Company,* July 2001, 158–161.
14. Kevin J. Clancy and Peter C. Krieg, *Counterintuitive Marketing* (New York: Free Press, 2000), 199–201.
15. Vera Gibbons, "How Does Your Garden Grow?" *SmartMoney,* November 2000, 214–216.
16. Kohl's Web site, www.kohlscorporation.com.
17. Susan Chandler, "Designers Find Their Target," *News-Times (Danbury, CT),* September 4, 2001, C8.
18. See Philip Kotler, *Marketing Management, 10th edition* (Upper Saddle River, NJ: Prentice Hall, 2000), 74–75.

19. Ben Elgin, "Will Business Yahoo! Too?" *Business Week,* February 5, 2001, 52.
20. Katrina Brooker, "A Game of Inches," *Fortune,* February 5, 2001, 98–100.
21. Robert D. Hof, "Amazon's Go-Go Growth? Gone," *Business Week,* February 12, 2001, 39.
22. Hof, "Amazon's Go-Go Growth? Gone," 39.
23. Holly Vanscoy, "Life After Living.com," *Smart Business,* February 2001, 68–70.
24. U.S. Census Bureau, "State and County QuickFacts," quickfacts.census.gov/cgi-bin/usa.
25. Susan Stellin, "This Web Site Rocks! (It's Turning a Profit.)," *New York Times,* December 3, 2000, sec. 3, 4.
26. William Echikson, "The Mark of Zara," *Business Week,* May 29, 2000, 98–100.
27. Clare Saliba, "Walmart.com Harvests Garden.com Assets," *E-Commerce Times,* January 18, 2001, www.ecommercetimes.com/perl/story/?id=6818.
28. Christopher Caggiano, "Cruising for Profits," *Inc. Tech 2000,* no. 4, November 15, 2000, 45–60.
29. Duncan Hughes, "Slowing Global Economy to Affect Harley-Davidson's Earnings," *Sunday Business,* July 8, 2001, www.sundaybusiness.co.uk; Katie Muldoon, "Direct From Muldoon: Keeping the Growth Curve Growing," *Direct,* December 2000, 53+.
30. Flora Tartakovsky, "Top 10 Digital Workplaces," *Time Digital,* October 2000, 32–36.
31. Adam Lashinksy, "Valley Keiretsu: Beware 'Alliances,'" *Fortune,* November 13, 2000, 448–450.
32. Bob Donath, "Irritations Lead Users to Innovations," *Marketing News,* October 9, 2000, 16; Michael Arndt, "3M: A Lab for Growth?" *Business Week,* January 21, 2002, pp. 50–51.
33. Karen Talaski, "Shoppers Answer Surveys with Lure of Prizes," *The Journal News* (Rockland, New York), November 11, 2000, 2D.
34. Michael Mahoney, "Special Report: Look Who's Making Money Online, Part I," *E-Commerce Times,* March 27, 2001, ecommercetimes.com/perl/story/?id=8233; Ken Yamada, "Shop Talk: Doppelgangers Live to Shop," *Redherring.com,* December 12, 2000, www. red herring.com/industries/2000/1212/ind-shoptalk121200.html.
35. Diane Brady, "Why Service Stinks," *Business Week,* October 23, 2000, 118–128.

Chapter 2

1. Personal communication with Dr. Joseph Blackburn, June 2001.
2. Jennifer Lee, "Gateway Awaits the Next Bounce," *New York Times,* September 2, 2001, sec. 3, 6; Katrina Brooker, "I Built This Company, I Can Save It," *Fortune,* April 30, 2001, 94–102; "Gateway's Credit Rating Cut," *CNN.com,* January 8, 2002, www.cnn.com/2002/business/01/08gateway.junk.
3. Personal communication with Dr. Kevin Lane Keller, author of *Strategic Brand Management: Building, Measuring, and Managing Brand Equity,* May 2001.
4. James C. Collins and Jerry I. Porras, *Built to Last* (New York: HarperBusiness, 1994), 220–221.
5. IBM 2000 Annual Report, 48.
6. Morgan Stanley Dean Witter 2000 Annual Report, 1.
7. "Merchants Cut Market Costs," *CNNfn.com,* November 28, 2000, cnnfn.com/2000/11/28/electronic/online.
8. Calmetta Coleman, "Pruning Costs," *Wall Street Journal,* February 12, 2001, R30.
9. Kate Murphy, "Food Brokers Are Bigger, So Shelves Look Smaller," *New York Times,* September 2, 2001, sec. 3, 4.
10. J.B. Houck, "Connected Travelers 'Go Stay' at Wireless-Wise Hotels," *CRM Daily.com,* May 8, 2001, www.crmdaily.com/perl/story/9549.html.
11. Daniel F. DeLong, "Lights Out for Yahoo! in Power Outage," *E-Commerce Times,* May 8, 2001, ecommercetimes.com/perl/story/9557.html.
12. Thea Singer, "Can Business Still Save the World?" *Inc.,* April 2001, 58–72.
13. Lori Enos, "Price-Fixing Worries Aired at U.S. B2B Seminar," *E-Commerce Times,* May 8, 2001, ecommercetimes.com/perl/story/?id=9550.
14. Andrew Hill, "GE Likely to Challenge EU Veto of Honeywell Deal," *Financial Times,* August 1, 2001, www.ft.com.

15. Sofia Javed, "Ethnic E-Tailer Builds Expertise in Untapped Market," *Marketing News,* October 9, 2000, 24.
16. Kristin Harmel, "Who Eats Beef? Consumption Depends on Age, Education, UF Study Shows," *ScienceDaily,* September 28, 2000, www.sciencedaily.com/releases/2000/000914104820.htm.
17. Discussion is based on Michael Porter, *Competitive Advantage* (New York: Free Press, 1985), 11–26.

Chapter 3

1. Personal communication with Dr. Kevin Clancy of Copernicus Marketing and Consulting, May 2001.
2. Based on Gary L. Lilien and Arvind Rangaswamy, *Marketing Engineering* (Reading, MA: Addison-Wesley, 1998), 129.
3. Ken Belson, "Using the Web to Trap Car Thieves," *Business Week,* June 18, 2001, 77.
4. Thea Singer, "Curricular Extras," *Inc.,* May 1, 2001, 55–56; Thea Singer, "Comeback Markets," *Inc.,* May 1, 2001, 53–54.
5. Elizabeth Blakey, "Exclusive Interview: Sun Microsystems," *E-Commerce Times,* October 3, 2000, ecommercetimes.com/perl/story/?id=4450.
6. Daniel Kadlec, "Handheld Computers: Growing Pains," *On Magazine,* May 2001, 66; Kim Girard, "The Palm Phenom," *Business 2.0,* April 3, 2001, 74–80; Ian Fried and Richard Shim, "Handheld Industry Sees Hope in Wireless," *CNET News.com,* January 16, 2002, news.com.com/2100-1040-814416.html.
7. Girard, "The Palm Phenom," 74–80.
8. Ronna Abramson, "Newspapers Caught in Web Squeeze," *Thestandard.com,* March 23, 2001, www.thestandard.com/article/display/0,1151,23085,00.html; Stefanie Olsen, "Encouraging Signs for Online Ad Market," *CNET News.com,* December 11, 2001, news.com.com/2100-1023-276841.html.
9. Edmund Sanders, "AOL Cookies, Web Bugs to Track Advertising," *Los Angeles Times,* October 5, 2001, www.latimes.com/technology/la-000079627oct05.story.
10. Pete Engardio, "Smart Globalization," *Business Week,* August 27, 2001, 132–136.
11. Philip Kotler, *Marketing Management* (Upper Saddle River, NJ: Prentice Hall, 2000), 21.
12. Tony Smith, "Resurrected Harp-Maker Plays to Win," *Marketing News,* February 26, 2001, 47.
13. "In Living Color," *Washington Post,* May 2, 2001, C15.
14. "The Perfect Models: Celebrities Smack Down the Nerd Image," *Business 2.0,* April 3, 2001, 78.
15. Elizabeth Blakey, "Success Story: JCPenney.com," *E-Commerce Times,* August 3, 2000, www.ecommercetimes.com/perl/story/?id=3941.
16. D. M. Osborne, "Upstarts: Photo Opportunities," *Inc.,* December 2000, 25+.
17. Marty Jerome, "Instant E-Business," *Smart Business,* December 2000, 130–140.
18. John Gaffney, "How Do You Feel About a $44 Tooth-Bleaching Kit?" *Business 2.0,* September 2001, 126–127.

Chapter 4

1. Personal communication with Dr. Mohan Sawhney, May 2001.
2. Michael Pollan, "Naturally: How Organic Became a Marketing Niche and a Multibillion-Dollar Industry," *New York Times Magazine,* May 13, 2001, 30–37, 57–58, 63–64.
3. Jack Neff, "General Mills to Customize Cereal on the Web," *Advertising Age,* November 20, 2000, 40; Evantheia Schibsted, "The Sizzle," *Business 2.0,* March 20, 2001, 80.
4. Henri Cauvin, "Braving War and Graft, Coke Goes Back to Angola," *New York Times,* April 22, 2001, sec. 3, 1, 13.
5. Devin Leonard, "Madison Ave. Fights Back," *Fortune,* February 5, 2001, 150–154; Kimberly-Clark site (www.kimberly-clark.com)
6. Robert Sharoff, "Diversity in the Mainstream," *Marketing News,* May 21, 2001, 1, 13, 14.

7. Hassan Fattah, "The Rising Tide," *American Demographics,* April 2001, www.american demographics.com.

8. "Taste the Differences," *Grocer,* January 20, 2001, S10+.

9. "Taste the Differences," S10+.

10. Dale Buss, "The New Company Car," *Business 2.0,* March 6, 2001, 80–81; "Rental Cars Find Their Way Home," *Reuters,* January 17, 2002, news.com.com/2100-1033-817433.html.

11. Ken Belson, "Net Shopping" Why Japan Won't Take the Plunge," *Business Week,* July 31, 2000, 64; "Hit the Net, Then the Met," *Business Week,* January 29, 2001, 8.

12. "Volvo Cars Launches Interactive TV Promotion," Volvo news release, March 16, 2001, www.marketingclick.com; "Volvo Hitches Ride on MSN," *Reuters,* December 3, 2001, news.com.com/2110-1023-276497.html.

13. Keith Regan and Nora Macaluso, "Netscape Unveils Small Biz Service," *E-Commerce Times,* September 13, 2000, ecommercetimes.com/perl/story/?id=4273.

14. Desiree De Myer, "Get Smart," *Smart Business,* February 2001, 92–99; "ERoom Technology Receives the CIO Web Business 50 Award for Its Hosted Service Offering ERoom.net," *CNet News.com,* January 7, 2002, investor.cnet.com/investor/news/newsitem/0-9900-1028-8391643-0.html.

15. Robert Conlin and Larry Seben, "Avaya Puts Quintus Assets to Work," *CRM Daily.com,* May 15, 2001, www.crmdaily.com/perl/story/9740.html; "Russo Returns to Lucent as CEO," *Reuters,* January 7, 2002, news.com.com/2100-1033-802322.html.

16. Dana James, "Play It Straight," *Marketing News,* May 21, 2001, 15.

17. Lauren Gibbons Paul, "When Bad Economies Happen to Good Companies," *Inc.,* October 30, 2001, 128–131.

Chapter 5

1. Personal communication with Dr. Judy Strauss, August 2001.

2. H. Igor Ansoff, "Strategies for Diversification," *Harvard Business Review,* September–October 1957, 113–124; Philip Kotler, *Kotler on Marketing* (New York: The Free Press, 1999), 46–48.

3. Alynda Wheat, "Fortune 500 Retail Champs: J.C. Penney, No. 43," *Fortune,* April 16, 2001, 198–199.

4. Stephanie Mehta, "Don't Call Me Baby," *Fortune,* April 16, 2001, 162–170; "Verizon Seeks Long-Distance in Vermont," *Reuters,* January 17, 2002, news.com.com/2110-1033-817428.html.

5. Jill Hecht Maxwell, "Been There, Grown That: Net Wages," *Inc.,* October 30, 2001, 39.

6. Arlene Weintraub, "Chairman of the Board," *Business Week,* May 28, 2001, 96.

7. Nelson D. Schwartz, "Colgate Cleans Up," *Fortune,* April 16, 2001, 179–180.

8. Stephanie N. Mehta, "Cisco Fractures Its Own Fairy Tale," *Fortune,* May 14, 2001, 104–112; Ben Elgin and Jim Kerstetter, "No Silver Lining for Tech Sales," *Business Week,* October 22, 2001, 16.

9. Roger O. Crockett, "Chris Galvin Shakes Things Up—Again," *Business Week,* May 28, 2001, 38–39; "Motorola Set to Sell Phones in Japan Again," *CNN.com,* January 18, 2002, www.cnn.com/2002/BUSINESS/asia/01/17/motorola.japanmobile.

10. Michael Arndt, "There's Life in the Old Bird Yet," *Business Week,* May 14, 2001, 77–78.

11. General Electric Annual Report, 2000, 8, 18.

12. "Empire Builders: Monica Luechtefeld," *Business Week,* May 14, 2001, EB28–29.

13. Janice Revell, "The Price Is Not Always Right," *Fortune,* May 14, 2001, 240.

Chapter 6

1. Personal communication with Dr. A. Parasuraman, May 2001.

2. Kate Murphy, "A Better Mousetrap? For This Immigrant, It's a Plastic Bag," *New York Times,* May 20, 2001, sec. 3, 7.

3. Martyn Williams, "Sony: New Hue on PlayStation 2," *CNN.com,* October 14, 2001, www.cnn.com/2001/tech/fun.games/10/14/ps2.colors.idg; Chris Morris, "GameCube to Sell

for $199," *Cnnfn.com,* May 21, 2001, cnnfn.cnn.com/2001/05/21/companies/gamecube; "Nintendo GameCube Makes European Debut," *Animation World Network,* January 9, 2002, news.awn.com/index.php3?ltype=top&newsitem_no=6261.

4. Keith Regan, "BabiesRUs.com to Get Amazon Treatment," *E-Commerce Times,* May 22, 2001, www.ecommercetimes.com/perl/story/9918.html.

5. "Take Your Office Anywhere," *Smart Business,* May 2001, 84–85.

6. Lauren R. Hartman, "Ore-Idea's New Recipe for Bagmaking," *Packaging Digest,* January 2001, pp. 38+.

7. Mike Wendland, "Hogan's Mission: the Webification of General Motors," *Detroit Free Press,* March 7, 2001, www.auto.com/industry/mwend7_20010307.htm.

8. Larry Seben, "Schwab Tackles Online Trading's 'Weakest Link,' " *CRMDaily.com,* May 22, 2001, www.crmdaily.com/perl/story/9929.html.

9. Keith Naughton, "Fixing Cadillac," *Newsweek,* May 28, 2001, 36–37; "GM to Offer XM Radio in 23 Vehicle Models," *Reuters,* January 14, 2002, news.com.com/2110-1033-813751.html.

10. "Oreo's Chocolate Cousin," *CNNfn.com,* May 10, 2001, cnnfn.com/2001/05/10/news/oreo; Randy Kennedy, "In Canada, a Clothing Company Tries on an Airline," *New York Times,* March 18, 2001, sec. 9, 6; Joe Ashbrook Nickell, "Radar: The Dot-Com Class of 2000 Grows Up," *Smart Business,* May 2001, 32–34.

11. "General Motors to Bring Oldsmobile Brand to an End," *Knight-Ridder/Tribune Business News,* December 12, 2000, www.chicagotribune.com; Rick Popely, "GM Claims Olds Owners Have Little to Worry About Except Resale Value," *Knight-Ridder/Tribune Business News,* January 21, 2001, www.chicagotribune.com.

12. Brian Garrity, "Grammys OK Downloads," *Billboard,* October 13, 2001, www.billboard.com/billboard/sitesandsounds/index.jsp.

13. "WebSmart: Michael Dell," *Business Week,* May 14, 2001, 52; "Bleak Earnings News Depresses Techs," *Reuters,* January 18, 2002, news.com.com/2100-1017-818387.html.

14. "Online Travel Market Continues Surge," *Cyberatlas.com,* February 4, 2000, www.cyberatlas.com.

15. "Supermarket Banking a Hit with Consumers," *Australian Banking & Finance,* August 31, 2000, 5; "Kiosk Concept Back on the Shelf," *Sydney Morning Herald,* August 2, 2000, www.smh.com.au/news/0008/02/busines/business2.html.

16. Saul Hansell, "Listen Up! It's Time for a Profit," *New York Times,* May 20, 2001, sec. 3, 1, 14.

17. Noah P. Barsky and Alexander E. Ellinger, "Unleashing the Value in the Supply Chain," *Strategic Financing,* January 2001, 33+.

18. Chuck Moozakis, "No-Slack Supply Chain: General Mills Maximizes Truck Loads to Cut Logistics Spending," *InternetWeek,* January 29, 2001, 1+.

19. Elizabeth Blakey, "Success Story: JCPenney.com," *E-Commerce Times,* August 3, 2000, www.ecommercetimes.com/perl/story/?id=3941.

20. Peter Meyer, "Is the Price Right?" *Across the Board,* July 2000, 31+.

21. Keith Reid, "The Science of Pricing," *NPN International,* March 2000, 33+.

22. Wendy Taylor and Marty Jerome, "Body-Bag Capitalism," *Smart Business,* May 2001, 25.

23. Thomas T. Nagle and Reed K. Holden, *The Strategy and Tactics of Pricing,* 2d ed. (Upper Saddle River, NJ: Prentice Hall, 1995), 95–99.

24. Donald V. Potter, "Discovering Hidden Pricing Power," *Business Horizons,* November 2000, 41+.

25. "The Delicate Art of Price Hikes," *Business Week,* November 6, 2000, F12; "VC Watch: Onset Tech Gets $3.5 Million," *CNET News.com,* December 10, 2001, news.com.com/2100-1017-276826.html.

26. Jamie Smith, "Put Out the Word," *Marketing News,* May 7, 2001, 6–8.

27. Michelle Jeffers, "Greenbacks for Greenery," *Business 2.0,* February 20, 2001, 66; Marian Wood, *Prentice Hall's Guide to E-Business for General Business* (Upper Saddle River, NJ: Prentice Hall, 2002), 7.

28. Pamela L. Moore, "An Overdose of Drug Advertising?" *Business Week,* May 22, 2000, 52; Vanessa O'Connell and Rachel Zimmerman, "Drug Pitches Resonate With Edgy Public," *Wall Street Journal,* January 14, 2002, B5.

29. Joseph Pereira, "The 'Big' Idea: Itz-Toys Flipped When 2 Kids Invented a New Game," *Wall Street Journal,* February 12, 2001, A1, A10.

30. Tom Lowry and Ronald Grover, "For the Love of the Game—and Cheap Seats," *Business Week,* May 28, 2001, 46–47.

31. William Lee, "Underachievers Club: Lowe's," *Smart Money,* November 2000, 46.

32. Gary L. Lilien and Arvind Rangaswamy, *Marketing Engineering* (Reading, MA: Addison-Wesley, 1998), 247.

33. Martha Visser, "Forget the Tupperware Party," *Fortune Small Business,* May 18, 2001, www.fsb.com/fortunesb/articles/0,2227,1667,00.html.

34. Jennifer Gilbert, "Running on Empty," *Ad Age,* adage.com/i20/srmain.html.

35. Michelle Jeffers, "Money for Nothing, Hits for Free," *Business 2.0,* June 12, 2001, 40.

36. Maggie Overfelt, "Service on a Shoestring," *Fortune,* June 12, 2000, F264T–F264V.

37. Charles Keenan, "Translating Customer Service to the Front Lines," *American Banker,* May 7, 2001, 18A+.

38. "Dell's Support Services Split Into Four Tiers," *Computer Weekly,* April 12, 2001, 6.

39. Jennifer Gilbert, "A Dotcom That's (Holy Discredited Business Paradigms!) Doing Things Right," *Business 2.0,* August–September 2001, 168–169; Karen Lake, "Battling the Brick-and-Mortars," *StrategyWeek.com,* November 17, 1999, www.strategyweek.com.

40. James R. Peterson, "A Bank Where the Customer Is Always Right," *ABA Banking Journal,* March 2001, p. S16+.

41. Susan Greco, "The Best Little Grocery Store in America," *Inc.,* June 2001, 54–61.

Chapter 7

1. Personal communication with Dr. Arvind Rangaswamy, July 2001.

2. "P&G Sets $5B Clairol Deal," *CNN.com,* May 21, 2001, www.cnn.com/2001/business/05/21/clairol.

3. Stephanie N. Mehta, "Cisco Fractures Its Own Fairy Tale," *Fortune,* May 14, 2001, 104–112.

4. "Downturn in Fast-Forward," *Business Week,* February 19, 2001, 32+.

5. See David B. Whitlark, Michael D. Geurts, and Michael J. Swenson, "New Product Forecasting with a Purchase Intention Survey," *Journal of Business Forecasting* 12, Fall 1993, 18–21.

6. Gary L. Lilien and Arvind Rangaswamy, *Marketing Engineering* (Reading, MA: Addison-Wesley, 1998), 195–200.

7. Andy Hemmer, "Entrepreneurs Clean Up," *Cincinnati Business Courier,* May 28, 2001, cincinnati.bcentral.com/cincinnati/stories/2001/05/28/smallb1.html.

8. Russ Banham, "The Revolution in Planning," *CFO,* August 1999, 47+.

9. John Sawhill and David Williamson, "Measuring What Matters in Nonprofits," *McKinsey Quarterly,* 2001, no. 2, www.mckinseyquarterly.com; Sean Madigan, "War Stories," *Washington Business Journal,* January 11, 2002, washington.bcentral.com/washington/stories/2002/01/14/story2.html.

10. Christopher Ittner and David Larcker, "Non-Financial Performance Measures: What Works and What Doesn't," *Wharton Knowledge,* October 16, 2000, knowledge.wharton.upenn.edu/articles.cfm?catid=1&articleid=279.

11. Ittner and Larcker, "Non-Financial Performance Measures: What Works and What Doesn't."

12. Cliff Edwards, "Intel: Can CEO Craig Barrett Reverse This Slide?" *Business Week,* October 15, 2001, 80–90; Janice Revell, "The Price Is Not Always Right," *Fortune,* May 14, 2001, 240; John G. Spooner, "Intel Preparing New Mobile Chips," *CNET News.com,* January 18, 2002, news.com/2100-1040-818827.html.

13. Kate Maddox, "Marketers Tie Value to Bottom Line," *B to B,* April 2, 2001, 1+; Wylie Wong, "NTT Joins Web Services Directory Effort," *CNET News.com,* January 17, 2002, news.com/2100-1001-817566.html.

14. Maddox, "Marketers Tie Value to Bottom Line," 1+.

15. "Empire Builders: Monica Luechtefeld," *Business Week,* May 14, 2001, EB28–29; Maddox, "Marketers Tie Value to Bottom Line," 1+.

16. Shirley Siluk Gregory, "New DigiMine Tool Digs in to Marketing Analysis," *CRMDaily.com,* February 26, 2001, www.crmdaily.com/perl/story/?id=7744.
17. Ittner and Larcker, "Non-Financial Performance Measures."
18. "Downturn in Fast-Forward," *Business Week,* 32+.
19. Dan Brekke, "The Future Is Now—or Never," *New York Times Magazine,* January 23, 2000, 30–33.

Chapter 8

1. Personal communication with Dr. Gary Lilien, June 2001.
2. Troy Wolverton, "EToys Reopens for Business As KB Unit," *CNET News.com,* October 17, 2001, news.cnet.com/news/0-1007-200-7559577.html; Michael Mahoney and Jon Weisman, "The Last Days of eToys," *E-Commerce Times,* March 7, 2001, www.ecommercetimes.com/perl/printer/7978.
3. Claudia H. Deutsch, ". . . And to Penny-Pinching Wizardry," *New York Times,* May 6, 2001, sec. 3, 1, 14; "Social Responsibility: Leadership, Examples," Business for Social Responsibility (n.d.), www.bsr.org; "Xerox Seeks $500 Million in Note Placement," *Reuters,* January 7, 2002, news.com.com/2110-1001-802170.html.
4. Kevin J. Clancy and Peter C. Krieg, *Counter-Intuitive Marketing* (New York: Free Press, 2000), 298–299.
5. Chris Nelder, "Social Assessment," *Better World 'Zine,* (n.d.), www.betterworld.com/BWZ/9604/cover1-1.htm.
6. "Social Responsibility," Business for Social Responsibility, www.bsr.org.
7. Michael Mahoney, "Net Appliance 'Audrey' Sacked after Five Months," *E-Commerce Times,* March 22, 2001, www.ecommercetimes.com/perl/printer/8362.
8. Keith Regan, "Netcentives, HealthCentral Seek Bankruptcy Protection," *E-Commerce Times,* October 10, 2001, www.ecommercetimes.com/perl/story/?id=14068; Steven Musil, "Buy.com Wins Financial Rescue," *CNet News.com,* August 23, 2001, news.cnet.com/news/0-1007-200-6958495.html; Elizabeth Blakey, "Survivors of the E-Commerce 'Death Watch,' " *E-Commerce Times,* June 4, 2001, www.ecommercetimes.com/perl/story/10212.html; Sergio G. Non, "The Starting Line: Falling Techs Turn to Buyouts," *CNET News.com,* December 5, 2001, news.com.com/2100-12-276588.html.
9. Russ Banham, "The Revolution in Planning," *CFO,* August 1999, 47+.
10. Chris Isidore, "GM May Sales Edge Up," *CNNfn.com,* June 1, 2001, cnnfn.cnn.com/2001/06/01/companies/autosales/index.htm.
11. "Merrill's Profit Slumps 52% on Drop in Equity Trading, Soaring Expenses," *Wall Street Journal,* October 18, 2001, interactive.wsj.com/articles/SB1003409681239405800.htm.
12. "PanAmSat Develops Contingency Plan in Wake of Satellite Problem," *SpaceViews News,* October 2, 2000, www.spaceviews.com/2000/10/02a.html.

Source Notes

Chapter 1

Exhibit 1.3   Growth Strategies Grid
Adapted from Igor Ansoff, "Strategies for Diversification," *Harvard Business Review,* September–October 1957, 114.

Exhibit 1.5   The Marketing Mix
Adapted from Figure 1.5, "The Four P Components of the Marketing Mix," in Philip Kotler, *Marketing Management,* 11th ed. (Upper Saddle River, NJ: Prentice Hall, 2003), Chapter 1.

Chapter 2

Exhibit 2.6   Competitive Forces Affecting Industry Profitability and Attractiveness
Michael E. Porter, *Competitive Advantage.* © 1985 The Free Press, imprint of Simon & Schuster. Reprinted with permission.

Chapter 4

Exhibit 4.4   ERoom Technology
eRoom Technology, Inc. All rights reserved.

Chapter 5

Exhibit 5.3   Office Depot.com
Reprinted with permission.

Exhibit 5.4   Strategy Pyramid
Adapted from Tim Berry and Doug Wilson, *On Target: The Book on Marketing Plans.* (Eugene, OR: Palo Alto Software, 2000), 107.

Chapter 6

Exhibit 6.6   Break-Even Analysis
Tim Berry and Doug Wilson, *On Target: The Book on Marketing Plans* (Eugene, OR: Palo Alto Software, 2000), 163.

Exhibit 6.7   Alternative Reactions to Competitive Price Cuts
Framework of Marketing Management by Kotler, Philip, © 2001. Reprinted by permission of Pearson Education Inc., Upper Saddle River, NJ.

Exhibit 6.9   UPS Ad
Reprinted with permission of UPS.

Chapter 7

Exhibit 7.6   Common Online Marketing Metrics
Adapted from Chris Ryan, "Web Site Metrics," *Direct*, March 2001, D2+; Judy Strauss and Raymond Frost, *E-Marketing* 2d ed. (Upper Saddle River, NJ: Prentice Hall, 2001), 254–255.

Chapter 8

Checklist 8.1   Planning a Marketing Audit
Adapted from Philip Kotler, *Marketing Management,* 10 ed. (Upper Saddle River, NJ: Prentice Hall, 2000) 710–711; Kevin J. Clancy and Peter C. Krieg, *Counter-Intuitive Marketing* (New York: Free Press, 2000), 296–301; Monique Reece Myron, "Marketing Audit Can Put You Back on Track," *Denver Business Journal,* February 25, 2000, 33A+.

Exhibit 8.2   Environmental Affairs at Starbucks
www.starbucks.com

Appendix 2

Background information and market data adapted from: "Handspring Unveils 2 PDAs," *CNNMoney.com,* October 15, 2001, money.cnn.com/2001/10/15/news/wires/handspring ap; "U.S. PDA Owners with Wireless Modems, 2000," *Econtent,* October 2001, 16; Kristen Kenedy, "Pocket PC Enters PDA Arena," *Computer Reseller News,* October 8, 2001, 4; "Nurses, Physicians Increase PDA Usage," *Health Management Technology,* October 2001, 10; "Interactive PDA Users in the U.S., 2000 and 2005," *Econtent,* October 16, 2001; Lisa M. Bouchey, "PDAs, Software, and Accessories," *OfficeSolutions,* September 2001, 41; John Kador, "A Hands-On Business," *Electronic Business,* September 2001, 46+; Mindy Sink, "A New Car Phone (No Strings Attached)," *New York Times,* August 19, 2001, sec. 3, 6; Janet Rae-Dupree, "In PDA Wars, It's Palm vs. the Pocket PC," *U.S. News & World Report,* June 18, 2001, 50; Mike Dano, "PDA Price Wars Pummel Industry," *RCR Wireless News,* June 11, 2001, 1+; Cliff Edwards, "Palm's Market Starts to Melt in Its Hands," *Business Week,* June 4, 2001, 42; "Top Handheld PCs," *Smart Business,* May 2001, 85; John Simons, "Has Palm Lost Its Grip?" *Fortune,* May 28, 2001, 104–108; Kim Girard, "The Palm Phenom," *Business 2.0,* April 3, 2001, 74–81; Ian Fried and Richard Shim, "Handheld Industry Sees Hope in Wireless," *CNET News.com,* January 16, 2002, news.com. com/2100-1040-814416.html.

Glossary

affordability budgeting   Method in which companies budget for marketing based on what they believe they can afford. (Chapter 7)

annual plan control Type of marketing control used to assess the progress and performance of the current year's marketing plan. (Chapter 8)

attitudes   An individual's lasting evaluations of and feelings toward something. (Chapter 3)

benefits   Need-satisfaction outcomes customers desire from the product. (Chapter 6)

brand (category) extension   Putting an established brand on a new product in a different category, aimed at a new customer segment. (Chapter 6)

branding   Using words, designs, or symbols to give a product a distinct identity and differentiate it from competing products. (Chapter 6)

budget   Time-defined allocation of financial outlays for a specific function or program. (Chapter 7)

cannibalization   Allowing a new product to cut into sales of one or more existing products. (Chapter 6)

competitive-parity budgeting   Method in which company creates a budget by matching what competitors spend, as a percentage of sales or a specific dollar amount. (Chapter 7)

concentrated marketing   Focusing one marketing strategy on one attractive market segment. (Chapter 4)

core competencies   The set of skills, technologies, and processes that allow a company to effectively and efficiently satisfy its customers. (Chapter 1)

cost leadership strategy   Generic competitive strategy in which the company seeks to become the lowest-cost producer in its industry. (Chapter 2)

customer lifetime value   Total amount a customer spends with a company over the course of a long-term relationship. (Chapter 6)

differentiated marketing   Creating a separate marketing strategy for each targeted segment. (Chapter 4)

differentiation strategy   Generic competitive strategy in which the company creates a unique differentiation for itself or its product based on some factor prized by the target market. (Chapter 2)

diversification   Growth strategy of offering new products to new markets through internal product development capabilities or by starting (or buying) a business for diversification purposes. (Chapter 5)

dynamic pricing   A strategy in which prices are varied from customer to customer or situation to situation. (Chapter 6)

emotional appeal   Message strategy that relies on feelings rather than facts to motivate audience response. (Chapter 6)

features   Specific attributes that enable the product to perform its function. (Chapter 6)

financial objectives   Targets for performance in managing specific financial results. (Chapter 5)

fixed pricing   A strategy in which prices do not vary from customer to customer or situation to situation. (Chapter 6)

focus strategy   Generic competitive strategy in which the company narrows its competitive scope to achieve a competitive advantage in its chosen segments. (Chapter 2)

forecast   Future projection of what sales and costs are likely to look like in the period covered by the plan. (Chapter 7)

frequency   How many times, on average, the target audience is exposed to the message during a given period. (Chapter 6)

goals   Longer-term performance targets for the organization or a particular unit. (Chapter 1)

integrated marketing communication   Coordinating the content and delivery so all marketing messages are consistent and support the positioning and strategic direction outlined in the marketing plan. (Chapter 6)

internal marketing   Marketing that targets managers and employees inside the organization. (Chapter 6)

lifestyle   The pattern of living that an individual exhibits through activities and interests. (Chapter 3)

line extension   Putting an established brand on a new product added to the existing product line. (Chapter 6)

logistics   Managing the movement of goods, services, and related information from the point of origin to the point of sale or consumption. (Chapter 6)

macroenvironment   Largely uncontrollable elements outside the organization that can potentially influence its ability to reach set goals: demographic, economic, ecological, technological, political-legal, and social-cultural forces. (Chapter 2)

market   All the potential buyers for a particular product. (Chapter 3)

market development   Growth strategy in which the company identifies and taps new segments or markets for existing products. (Chapter 5)

market penetration   Growth strategy in which the company sells more of its existing products to customers in existing markets or segments. (Chapter 5)

market segmentation   Grouping customers within a market according to similar needs, habits or attitudes that can be addressed through marketing. (Chapter 4)

market share   The percentage of sales in a given market held by a particular company, brand, or product; can be calculated in dollars or units. (Chapter 3)

marketing audit   A detailed, systematic analysis of an organization's marketing capabilities and performance. (Chapter 8)

marketing control   The process of setting goals and standards, measuring and diagnosing results, and taking corrective action when needed to keep marketing plan performance on track. (Chapter 1)

marketing objectives   Targets for performance in managing specific marketing relationships and activities. (Chapter 5)

marketing plan   A document that summarizes marketplace knowledge and the marketing strategies and specific plans to be used in achieving marketing goals and objectives. (Chapter 1)

marketing planning   The process of researching and analyzing the market and situation and developing marketing objectives, goals, strategies, and plans that are appropriate for the organization's resources, competencies, mission, and objectives. (Chapter 1)

metrics   Numerical measures of specific performance-related activities and outcomes. (Chapter 7)

microenvironment   Groups that have a more direct effect on the organization's ability to reach its goals: customers, competitors, channel members, partners, suppliers, and employees. (Chapter 2)

mission   Statement of the company's fundamental purpose, its focus, and how it will add value for customers and other stakeholders. (Chapter 2)

motivation   What drives the consumer to satisfy needs and wants. (Chapter 3)

niche   Smaller segment within a market that exhibits distinct needs or benefit requirements. (Chapter 4)

objective-and-task budgeting   Method in which budget is determined by totaling the cost of completing all marketing tasks needed to achieve the marketing mix objectives and marketing plan objectives. (Chapter 7)

objectives   Shorter-term performance targets that support the achievement of an organization's or unit's goals. (Chapter 1)

percentage-of-sales budgeting   Method in which company allocates a certain percentage of sales revenues to fund marketing programs. (Chapter 7)

positioning   Using marketing to create a distinctive place or image for a brand or product in the mind of customers. (Chapter 1)

primary research   Research conducted specifically to address a certain situation or answer a particular question. (Chapter 3)

product development   Growth strategy in which the company sells new products to customers in existing markets or segments. (Chapter 5)

product life cycle   The stages of introduction, growth, maturity, and decline through which a product moves in the marketplace. (Chapter 6)

productivity control   Type of marketing control used to assess the organization's performance and progress in managing the efficiency of key marketing areas. (Chapter 8)

profitability control   Type of marketing control used to assess the organization's progress and performance based on profitability measures. (Chapter 8)

psychographic characteristics   Variables used to analyze consumer lifestyle patterns. (Chapter 3)

quality   How well the product satisfies customer needs. (Chapter 6)

rational appeal   Message strategy that relies on facts or logic to motivate audience response. (Chapter 6)

reach   How many people in the target audience are exposed to the message during a particular period. (Chapter 6)

schedule   Time-defined plan for completing work that relates to a specific purpose or program. (Chapter 7)

secondary research   Research data already gathered for another purpose. (Chapter 3)

segments   Groups within a market having distinct needs or characteristics that can be effectively addressed by specific marketing offers and programs. (Chapter 1)

spam   Unsolicited e-mail messages from marketers, often transmitted in bulk. (Chapter 6)

stakeholders   People and organizations that are influenced by or that can influence an organization's performance. (Chapter 1)

strategic control   Type of marketing control used to assess the organization's performance and progress in the strategic areas of marketing effectiveness, customer relationship management, and social responsibility and ethics. (Chapter 8)

subcultures Distinct groups within a larger culture that exhibit and preserve distinct cultural identities through a common religion, nationality, ethnic background, or lifestyle. (Chapter 3)

SWOT analysis Summary of an organization's strengths, weaknesses, opportunities, and threats. (Chapter 2)

target costing Using research to determine what customers want in a product, the price they will pay, then finding ways of producing the product at a cost that will accommodate that price and return a profit. (Chapter 6)

target market Segment of the overall market that a company chooses to pursue. (Chapter 4)

targeting Decisions about which market segments to enter and in what order, and how to use marketing in each. (Chapter 1)

undifferentiated marketing Targeting all market segments with the same marketing strategy. (Chapter 4)

value The difference between total benefits and total costs, as perceived by customers. (Chapter 1)

viral marketing Use of promotional e-mail messages that encourage recipients to send the message to others. (Chapter 6)

Index